ALSO BY
HUGH BYAS

THE JAPANESE ENEMY
His Power and His Vulnerability

*" What we most need just now is to be reminded of the strength
of Japan and just what elements compose it. Byas does that and
has given me a better idea of what makes the place run than has
anybody else."* — ELMER DAVIS

PUBLISHED BY
ALFRED A. KNOPF

Government by Assassination

GOVERNMENT BY ASSASSINATION

BY

HUGH BYAS

1942

ALFRED A KNOPF · *NEW YORK*

To My Wife

THE CONSTANT COMPANION

OF THOSE YEARS

PREFACE

The rise of Japan has been one of the major events of our age. Without Japan the present war would wear a very different aspect. With Japan's entry into it the Pacific has become the theatre of sea-air warfare on a scale of speed and space never before known. The lines of communication are global; the battlefields are countries and oceans.

Even before Japan doubled the task of the United Nations her achievement had been remarkable. In 1868 the newspapers of the West reported the overthrow of the " Tycoon " of Japan and the restoration of a hitherto unsuspected Emperor. Fifty-one years later, in 1919, they were announcing that Japan was one of the six powers included in the original Council of the League of Nations. In half a century, no more, an Asiatic feudal state, self-secluded and hardly known, had modernized itself with astonishing adaptiveness and taken its seat among the somewhat surprised great powers.

On their introduction to the world, the Japanese subdued their martial proclivities and appeared in the role of student. Never has any government sent a nation to school, and accompanied it there, with greater efficiency. Foreign experts were imported by the hundred. They were in general well chosen with the assistance of the friendly governments of the United States and European countries. They were the technicians who created new Japan. Englishmen organized the navy. Americans created a modern educational system. A Frenchman codified Japanese law. Germans directed the whole of the higher medical education. An Englishman reformed the mint and gave Japan a uniform currency. Posts, telegraphs, the army, the land survey, sanitary reform, prison reform, cotton and paper mills, improved mining methods, harbor works, modern shipping and navigation — all were the creation of foreign advisers. The Japanese retained executive power in the hands of nominal Japanese chiefs, but they never disdained advice. For half a century they were the most successful learners in Asia.

Emerging from their seclusion late in the humane nineteenth century, the Japanese escaped the rough edge of Europe's early expansion, but they were shrewd enough to represent their militarism as a response to Europe's imperialism. How often have I listened while American " goodwill missions " were told that Japan had built up a great army and fleet because only thus could she defend her independence against European rapacity! No European nation coveted a yard of Japanese territory; none asked anything of Japan except facilities for trade. Foreign trade, foreign machinery, foreign industry were the making of modern Japan. In fifty years it had doubled its population and far more than doubled its wealth and power.

The appearance of a new nation is certainly an event of importance. And what has the new nation made of itself?

Twenty years after acquiring a seat on the League Council, Japan conceived herself strong enough to make war on the United States and the British Empire. The outcome of that challenge will change Japan's future in ways we cannot now foresee. It may be that the ironic time spirit is repeating on a fantastic scale the allegory of the frog who wanted to become a bull. It may be that the energy and teachableness that carried Japan so far in so short a time will overcome the errors of her military rulers and enable her to attain by happier ways the high position to which her ambitious people aspire.

The political history of ancient Japan is a record of clan strife as dreary as the battles of the kites and the crows. The history of modern Japan is still to be written. The histories that have hitherto appeared are records of adolescence. They were written while Japan faced the West with the respectful amiability of the eager student. Japan had not then displayed her ambition to found by force a greater empire than has yet existed, an empire in which the Japanese state would be over-lord of 600,000,000 human beings and one fourth of the earth. Failure may doom Japan to a minor position, domi-nated by the gigantic bulk of awakened China, or it may leave her still a mighty force in Asia. In any case we should know our Japanese. We cannot again afford to regard them as quaint performers, sometimes charming and sometimes re-pulsive, on an exotic stage remote from our affairs.

This book is only a chapter in the recent history of Japan. It is an attempt to describe some aspects of the Japanese mind which, to the Occidental, are difficult to understand — in-deed, difficult to believe in, and impossible to explain by the standards he is accustomed to use. Parts of the record will recall the feuds and crimes of the bands of gangsters which arose in American cities and grew like mushrooms during and after the prohibition experiment. The ideas of the Japa-nese movement resemble those that have been proclaimed from so many megaphones in Germany and Italy. Yet there are sinister differences. The Japanese gangsters were not aliens without standards nor followers of demagogues thrown up from the depths of society in the convulsions that followed a terrible war. The Japanese assassins were officers, and in Japan, as elsewhere, an officer is presumed to be also a gen-tleman. And while the sentiments and passions that consti-tute the so-called ideology of the Japanese movement re-semble those by which Nazis and Fascists have rationalized their lust for domination, the Japanese brewed their hell broth from ancient native stock.

I was a householder in Tokyo when the events I describe occurred and for many years before. The sources used were chiefly my own files, which I fortunately got out by a ruse and the help of some friends shortly before the outbreak of war. These files included not only my own day-by-day records but a mass of contemporary evidence from Japanese news-papers, magazines, and official sources. In the ordinary course of my duty I was in continuous contact with Japanese government departments, and in twenty-three years I had come to know most of the men who, as Prime Ministers, Foreign Ministers, and Ministers of War and the Navy directed the destinies of the country. I have also been greatly indebted for such knowledge of the people as I may have gained to many Japanese friends, women as well as men, whom my wife and I got to know intimately in the long pleasant years of peace.

The young officers, the preposterous patriots, the incredible state- and emperor-worshippers of Japan have for the most part psychoanalyzed themselves in my narrative. They have spoken in word and action. The stirring gossip of the Imperial Hotel lobby and the deathless legends of the liner smoking-rooms have never been my authorities. I believe that all statements in the book — except those of opinion — are capable of proof; but as it is not a formal history I have eschewed footnotes and exercised economy in the use of Japanese names and terms which, because of their unfamiliarity, are more of a stumbling-block than a help to American readers.

The section headed "Post-war" was written with some misgiving. The field is one in which I do not see my way clearly or very far ahead. The kind of peace we get will depend on the kind of victory we win. The completeness of our victory will be the measure of the Japanese war lords' failure and it will be more important than anything we write into a peace treaty. The suggestions for "geographical disarmament" may seem tame, but they go to the root of the matter. All that I have written under the heading "Post-war," however, is simply a contribution to a common pool of ideas that still needs to be enriched by much study.

HUGH BYAS

Center Conway, New Hampshire
September 30, 1942

CONTENTS

Contents

Government by Assassination

INTRODUCTION: BACKGROUND

This section can be skipped by readers acquainted with the high lights of Japanese history.

Although the book is not a history of Japan, or even of the last ten years, in which its action takes place, some knowledge of the background is needed if the often fantastic ideas and events recorded are to be rationally comprehended.

Japan is the only nation which in this century combines modern military and industrial power with religious and political ideas inherited from the primitive ages of mankind. From the beginning of their national existence the Japanese have displayed some characteristics peculiarly their own. Those peculiarities have not been modified by contact with the general stream of human progress. Geographical and cultural isolation has kept them artificially alive until they have given Japan a distorted conception of her national mission and her place in the world.

The following pages are intended to provide a selective background in which those deformative influences are emphasized.

Who are the Japanese? There has been great discussion and not much agreement among scholars as to the origin of the Japanese people. Modern Japanese historians, supported by the best foreign scholarship, believe that the Japanese race is a mixture of Asiatic and Polynesian stocks, descended from invader immigrants of prehistoric times. The two strains are visible in the faces of the people today. The Asiatic type is

3

the handsomer; it is the type a Japanese actor assumes when he is playing the part of a nobleman. Its physical marks are thin features, slanting eyes, a faintly aquiline nose, a slightly receding chin, a small mouth, delicate hands, and small feet. Princes Chichibu and Takamatsu of the Imperial family, and some members of the " first " families, such as Prince Konoye and Count Makino, are good examples. The South Sea breed is coarser, with a pudding face, flat nose, the large mouth and teeth which caricaturists exaggerate, high cheeks, and thick bones.

Japanese history as taught in schools and standard works states that the first human Emperor was Jimmu Tenno, great-grandson of the grandson of Amaterasu, the Sun Goddess. The date assigned to Jimmu Tenno is 660 B.C. It is clearly fabulous. Written records were not kept in Japan till more than a thousand years later because the Japanese had no written language. The earliest histories are the *Kojiki* (Record of Ancient Matters) A.D. 712, and the *Nihongi* (Record of Japan) A.D. 720. They were a compilation of primitive legends of creation and genealogies constructed to support the theory that the Emperor was a descendant of the gods. The fictional element is revealed by the claim that seventeen of the first twenty Emperors lived for an average of 96 years and that one reigned for 99 years.

It is not uncommon to meet Japanese who will smile cautiously (if no other Japanese are around) at the legends of the Sun Goddess, but who regard Jimmu Tenno as a historical person. The evidence for Jimmu is exactly the same as that for the Sun Goddess, yet they belong to different categories of existence and historians accept Jimmu Tenno as a real person. He was in all probability the leader of the invading band who conquered the earlier inhabitants of Japan.

Introduction: Background

Those legends belong to the same class as the story of Romulus and Remus, but the student of modern Japan must take notice of them because they are used today to furnish an ethical justification of armed expansion. The mythical maxims of Jimmu Tenno are repeated by Japanese generals; the slogan *" Hakko Ichiu "* (eight corners under one roof) with which he is supposed to have brought Japan under his rule, is invoked to throw an air of morality and order over the conquest of China; the latest of the patriotic gangs which incarnate Japanese chauvinism calls itself the Jimmu Society.

The religion of Jimmu Tenno and his followers was a simple pantheistic creed which saw spiritual life in all nature. Every grove and mountain and waterfall had its resident deity; and many aristocratic families claimed to be descended from a god, like their chief. This religion feared ghosts and dreaded the corruption of death, and its rites required the observance of strict cleanliness.

The name Shinto came later and was simply a Japanese copy of Chinese ideographs meaning the Way of the Gods. Shinto absorbed Chinese ancestor-worship and it is as ancestor-worship that the ordinary Japanese is familiar with Shinto. Japanese children in well-regulated households begin their day by standing before the family shrine, usually a small cabinet of white wood, and bowing with clasped hands and closed eyes to the memory of those of the family who have gone before — it may be a sister or a soldier brother or a grandfather or grandmother. By a natural development, as the child grows older and is instructed at school, this worship is extended to include all the progenitors of the family and finally of the nation and the Emperor. In the life of the individual Shinto is ancestor-worship; in the life of the community it is Empire-worship.

5

Introduction: Background

The Japanese did not develop a written language of their own until they came in contact with the civilization of China in the fourth and fifth centuries of our era. They then took over Chinese ideographs, and as these had been evolved by an entirely different type of language, the ensuing confusion haunted the Japanese for centuries and haunts them today. Japanese newspapers have to assist their readers by printing alongside the more difficult Chinese ideographs a few letters from the Japanese alphabet indicating the tenses of the verbs and the character of the adjectives and adverbs and giving the correct pronunciation. The Japanese language today is probably the clumsiest instrument used by any great nation. Scholars have agitated for adoption of the Roman alphabet, but in vain. Innate conservatism, racial conceit, and a passion for secrecy combine to maintain the Japanese language as one of the most difficult and complicated in the world. It has helped to perpetuate a habit of loose statement and a tendency to think in clichés, and it is proving a serious handicap to empire-builders.

Very early in their history the Japanese developed a system of indirect rule or figurehead government, and it has remained with them to this day. In the seventh century executive power passed from the hands of the titular emperors into those of their hereditary ministers, the aristocratic Fujiwara family. For three centuries (A.D. 670 till 1050) this family ruled Japan, and the emperors (who had copied that title from the emperors of China) were their puppets, removable at will.

The rule of this family came to an end when stronger forces arose and Japan became a feudal state, composed of some three hundred separate clans and governed despotically by a shogun, or generalissimo, in the name of the figurehead emperor. As Rome remained a republic in theory during the reigns of the Cæsars, Japan remained an empire in name though the power had passed to military rulers.

For seven hundred years (1155 to 1868) shogun succeeded shogun. Wars were frequent and four military dynasties successively held the supremacy. They did not aspire to the title of emperor, which had become an empty honor, and the family of Jimmu Tenno lived meagerly in ancient moldy palaces discharging its antique priestly functions. It seems to have been preserved by its peculiar circumstances. It was too weak to challenge the feudal lords and their vassal armies and it was still the head of the old national cult. Except for its poverty and its pretensions to divinity, the position of the Imperial family during those centuries was not greatly different from that of the Hohenzollerns in Germany today.

In the political aspects of this record there is nothing uncommon. Japan was going through the stages which have marked the growth of other nations. But there was a major difference which has no parallel elsewhere. In Europe religion was the affair of the church. There could be no royal deities where the people worshipped an unseen and universal spirit. In Japan church and state were one. Jimmu and his chiefs had established a primitive theocracy; the ruler was the god as well as the king of the tribe. The theory survived though actual rulership passed to other hands, and it is still the official dogma of the Japanese state. Only five years ago a Prime Minister, General Senjuro Hayashi, proclaimed that his platform was the unity of religion and politics. Only by understanding the origin of this concept can readers accustomed to an atmosphere where thought is free realize what a world of make-believe the Japanese have built themselves into.

Introduction: Background

The feudal age culminated in one of the most extraordinary episodes recorded in human history. Japan closed her doors on the world and went into seclusion. From 1636 to 1855 Japan was a sealed country; no ships of over 150 tons might be built; all larger vessels were destroyed; Japanese mariners were ordered to confine themselves to coastwise traffic under pain of death; no Japanese might leave Japan, no foreigner might enter. Christianity was extirpated by wholesale slaughter; of scores and perhaps hundreds of thousands of converts, not one was left alive. In the so-called island of Deshima at Nagaski, a place 200 yards long by 80 yards wide, a few Dutch merchants were isolated and allowed to remain for trade. The islet was surrounded by a fence so high that the Dutchmen could only see the tops of the hills. Those prisoners of commerce were allowed to receive and dispatch one or two ships yearly. Mummies from Egypt were among the queer cargoes imported; the spices in which dead Pharaohs had been embalmed commanded a high price in the Far East as medicine. This isolation was not broken until in 1855 Commodore Matthew Calbraith Perry of the United States navy compelled the Shogun's government to admit foreign trade and foreign representatives.

What needs explanation is not the edict of a despotic government, but the submission of the Japanese nation to two hundred years of self-imprisonment. The government which passed sentence was a new military dictatorship, and seclusion was a measure to preserve its authority. It was completely successful. The Tokugawa shogunate became the most stable and the most civilized regime Japan had known. Security brought no relaxation. The law continued to be jealously enforced. The Japanese nation, like the wise monkeys of Nikko, was deaf, dumb, and blind to the movement of the world. Rulers elsewhere have sometimes tried to arrest the march of time and fix an order of things in which they were supreme, but there is no other instance of a whole nation submitting to perpetual imprisonment.

What Japan lost is beyond computation. When she closed her shell, the great navigators were opening new worlds and the wealth they gained was laying the foundations of a new and richer economy. The intellectual loss was even heavier than the material. It was the age of Leonardo da Vinci and Copernicus; of Newton and Bacon. A new intellectual life had begun; modern science was born. When the Japanese at last unwillingly opened their doors the modern world had taken shape. The Americas had been colonized. The thirteen states had extended their dominion to the Pacific. Australia and New Zealand had been settled. Russia had advanced to the Sea of Japan. The British and Americans had built up a vast trade with China and the East.

The Japanese might have shared in this mighty movement of thought and action. They shut themselves up and elaborated their own sterile culture, the original elements of which they had borrowed from China. In his *Cultural History of Japan,* a work in which scholarly equipment and the scientific temper are highly combined, Sir George Sansom notes that before they closed their doors the Japanese had shown themselves unable or unwilling to receive the intellectual treasures of post-Renaissance Europe. He suggests an explanation of the contrast between Europe's expansive receptivity and Japan's failure to hear a single note of the grand symphony of the Renaissance. European culture, he points out, was not borrowed as Japanese culture had been borrowed from China, but was inherited in direct succession from the ancient world, and though there had been interruptions in

9

the Dark Ages, the intellectual movement was continuous. Japan was so situated that she could only borrow from the static culture of China.

Some of the charming apostles of the half-truth who have explained Japan to Western peoples have claimed that this voluntary seclusion in an age of wars testified to a Japanese love of peace. Possibly there might have been more blood shed in the seventeenth and eighteenth centuries if Japan had not retired to her cave. What is the gain if the Pacific is deluged with blood in an age when mechanized war is the elephantiasis of social diseases?

What meaning can we extract from Japan's great seclusion? What was its motive? Why does a man seclude himself from the world? Because he fears the world or the world irks him. The Japanese fear the free air of science and untrammeled thought which would transform their stunted native culture. They insist on the uniqueness of their civilization because if they measure themselves by world standards the result is humiliating to the inordinate national pride they have cultivated. They make themselves believe that their Imperial family is divine and has been preserved to an unparalleled age because they know that the truth about its origin and history would destroy their pretensions to have something no other nation possesses. They want a sphere abounding in everything they desire, one which they think they can hold against all comers and in which they can shut themselves up with their fabulous cosmogony and their psychopathic pride. What is the Greater East Asia Co-prosperity sphere but an enlarged feudal Japan in which the new war lords dream of a grander seclusion where they may live with the dwarf-tree civilization they love?

Modern Japan began in 1868 with the revolution commonly called the Restoration. Popular discontent with the 265-year-old Tokugawa shogunate crystallized into a movement for the return of Imperial rule. Two powerful clans, Satsuma and Choshu, took the field and ousted the shogunate. The descendant of Jimmu Tenno, a youth of sixteen called Mutsuhito, was enthroned as Emperor with the name of Meiji (Enlightened Rule). The Meiji era (1868–1912) was the golden age of modern Japan.

The revolution was more than the substitution of one ruling group for another. The victorious clans produced a remarkable group of young statesmen. They decided that the country must be modernized. They brought in hundreds of foreign experts — lawyers, diplomats, educators, doctors, engineers. Seclusion was forgotten like a dream of the night. The keynote of the new regime was the " charter oath " by which the young Emperor undertook to bring knowledge from all the world and to govern by public opinion. A Constitution was granted and parliament established. New Japan piled up a record of progress that no nation of the time surpassed. In thirty years the population had doubled (30,000,-000 to 60,000,000) and achieved a higher standard of life. Factories, ironworks, shipyards came into existence. Wealth increased by leaps and bounds. Careers were opened to talent all over the country. There was a school in every village; the government boasted of a population 97 per cent literate. Japan had awakened at a happy moment and her leaders responded to the liberating impulse of the nineteenth century. Many, perhaps most, of the leading Japanese statesmen of the Meiji era were sincere in their ambition to build a progressive state. And so long as the consciousness of inferiority to the West in armed strength remained, all Japanese were liberals in their way.

Introduction: Background

The revolution was incomplete. It was not a new building that the revolting clans created but only a new façade. The new government, aiming at setting up a centralized authority in place of clan separatism, revived popular belief in the divinity of the emperors. Shinto was made a state religion. The divinity of the ruler was taught in schools. The children sang that the Emperor was " even as God." They were taught that whereas other countries had man-made rulers, the Sun Goddess had chosen Japan for her domain and had sent her descendants to rule it. The Emperor granted the Constitution and he alone could amend it. Thus were Emperor-worship and Empire-worship inculcated. The people existed for the state. It occurred to no one to ask if the nose existed for the handkerchief or the handkerchief for the nose. None dared to see that the Emperor was still a figurehead and the state a group of men in control of the machinery of government.

A desire to dominate neighboring countries soon revealed itself. A striking and little-known episode of the new era was the Satsuma rebellion of 1877. Its leader was a clansman known to every Japanese as the Great Saigo. He was one of the most forceful of the revolutionary leaders. He opposed the abolition of the privileged military class, or samurai, and he demanded an invasion of Korea to divert the public from political agitation and to re-establish the warrior caste. He assembled an army of 30,000 samurai. With raw conscript forces of farmers and artisans, formerly excluded from the fighting forces, the government had a hard fight to defeat Saigo and his war party, but it succeeded. Saigo committed hara-kiri.

The affair is glossed over by Japanese historians. They evidently shrink from reconciling rebellion with the loyalty expected of a Japanese warrior. The people have no such difficulty. They believe that Saigo was a great patriot because he wanted to conquer Korea thirty years before the government annexed it. In the presence of this shining example of *Yamato damashii* (the Japanese spirit) rebellion becomes a peccadillo. Saigo's statue in Tokyo is an object of popular reverence, manifested in a peculiar but orthodox manner by chewing pieces of paper into a gluey pulp and throwing them at the statue so that they stick.

Ancient forces were living behind the modern façade. While labor unions, political parties, manhood suffrage, and the parliamentary battles between the ins and outs filled the front of the stage, a new warrior caste was growing in the background on the nation-wide basis of conscription. The fighting forces were gradually becoming strong enough to take the place the old ruling clans had held.

On his accession in 1926 Emperor Hirohito chose for the name of his reign the characters Sho-wa, meaning Enlightened Peace. The Showa Restoration movement is the name given to the agitation of the young officers which in the last ten years has proved itself to be the strongest force in Japan. It asserts that the restoration of 1868 has been thwarted by the politicians and the capitalists who have climbed in between the Emperor and his people and it demands a restoration of direct Imperial rule. But direct Imperial rule has not existed for a thousand years and the agitation simply masks a plan for the abolition of representative government and the setting up of a new military system based on national socialism.

The movement has been entirely successful, if success is the word for a policy which has encircled Japan with powerful and implacable enemies from whom she cannot escape — China, Russia, the United States, and the British Commonwealth.

Introduction: Background

The Three Modern Eras and Emperors:

Meiji (Enlightened Rule), the reign-name of the first restored Emperor, Mutsuhito, born 1852, died 1912; reigned 1867–1912. The Meiji era is the period from 1868 to 1912.

Taisho (Great Righteousness), reign-name of the Emperor Yoshihito, only son of the Emperor Meiji. His mother was a court lady, Madam Aiko Yanagiwara. He was born in 1879, died 1926, reigned 1912–26. The Taisho era is the period from 1912 to 1926.

Showa (Enlightened Peace), the name chosen for his reign by the present Emperor Hirohito (pronounced Hirosh'-toh), born 1901, succeeded to the throne 1926. Showa is the name he will be known by after his death.

I. *Oriental Revolution*

Chapter I

MURDER OF A PRIME MINISTER

Nine o'clock on Sunday morning in Tokyo is seven o'clock
on Saturday night in New York and there was plenty of time
to get through to the foreign-news desk in the *New York
Times* office. On Sunday mornings there was usually nothing
to do except go through the Japanese papers. Ofusa-san, my
assistant, had already combed them. I went over them again
with him. There was nothing, not an item, not a hint. All
quiet on the Tokyo front.

My wife came into the room that we called the office. It was
a big room with three tall windows that rattled like the devil.
In winter they were pasted up to keep the wind out. On this
Sunday morning in May they were wide open. You could see
half Tokyo and, on the horizon, a long, saw-tooth ridge of
mountains.

" There's nothing in the papers," I said, " not a damn thing.
I have nothing to do. Let's go off somewhere. We haven't been
out of Tokyo for a couple of years."

I thought we had struck a blind spot in the news, one of
those spells when for days at a time nothing happens that is
worth cable tolls. At first the correspondent enjoys it. Then,
if it lasts more than forty-eight hours, he gets a marooned feeling and begins to think the office will forget him.

But on that Sunday morning a quiet patch was indicated. Many troubles had come to a head and burst in the past six months. In Japan, which has five hundred earthquakes each year, when the dreaded rocking of the house begins, people get the habit of waiting a moment to see if it is a bad one before they run for safety. Ninety-nine times out of every hundred the foundations down below only slip an inch or two and find another base. It seemed as if Japanese affairs had shaken themselves down to a new temporary equilibrium.

To itemize the elements of that entirely erroneous feeling: A " liberal " Cabinet (inverted commas are indispensable; it means liberal relatively to the others) which had timidly opposed the army's policy of grab in Manchuria had fallen and made room for another which accepted the army's program. An administration that knew its place with the army was more likely to have a peaceful existence than one the fighting men disliked. The new government had held an election and received a substantial majority of the popular vote. It had been in for three months and was settling down.

Japan had gone off gold, to the profit, it was said, of some big houses and one powerful politician. Exports were booming and the farmer's burdens had been lightened. The former Finance Minister, Junnosuke Inouye, who had stubbornly stuck to gold, and an American-educated capitalist, Baron Takuma Dan, had been assassinated. The murderers were the usual young morons kept by the patriotic societies for such jobs. The police had caught them and the outburst of political thuggery seemed over for a time.

A bloody miniature war in Shanghai, stupidly provoked by the Japanese navy, had ended without leaving an aftermath. The Japanese sailors were no match for the Chinese 19th Route Army in street fighting and the Japanese army had to send a couple of divisions to extricate them. The fighting was over and the Japanese were withdrawing their troops.

The high spot in the news had been what was called the Manchurian incident, a piece of Japanese understatement which the correspondents adopted, having no word to describe the robbery by violence of a country in time of peace. Japan had a treaty right to maintain troops in Manchuria to protect the South Manchurian Railway, which was Japanese property. This garrison of railway guards, pretending that Chinese soldiers had blown up the tracks (although the night express passed over them without noticing anything), had suddenly attacked the Manchurian army in its barracks at night and seized the whole country.

A diplomatic flurry on the grand scale followed. Japan was a foundation member of the League of Nations and a signatory of the Kellogg Pact renouncing war as an instrument of national policy. The " liberal " Japanese government, subsequently ousted, promised that the Japanese troops would be withdrawn to the railway zone. The army in Manchuria contemptuously and completely ignored the promise. An international commission had come out to patch up peace if possible. Geneva was threatening sanctions. But the fighting was over; the Japanese army had erected its puppet regime and installed Henry Pu Yi as decorative Manchu Emperor and, to observers in Tokyo, Manchuria was already " water over the dam."

The United States, Britain, and most other nations refused to recognize the new state, but there was no reason to suppose that they, or anybody, would go to war about it. Even Chiang Kai-shek did not propose to fight for Manchuria. The cynical but accurate view accepted in Tokyo was that the Japanese government had decided to give the soldiers a field of adventure in Manchuria for the sake of peace at home and that the powers would withhold recognition but fire no cartridges.

That was the immediate background. Looking at it now with ten years' hindsight, it is clear that optimism was based on the illusion that stability could be bought by appeasement, and peace by isolation. We, the democracies, believed in that illusion because it responded to our needs and our wishes. The last great war with its seven million dead was only thirteen years behind us and its economic consequences were still with us. The United States was passing through the terrible winter of 1931–2, when every bank in the country closed, and Britain was staving off communism and starvation with the dole. No democratic government could have led its people into war to prevent Japan from occupying a half-empty country in northern Asia. A successful grab had been pulled off and the only visible victim was the dubious military government of Manchuria, weakly headed by the Young Marshal, son of the old bandit generalissimo who had ruled Manchuria in connivance with the Japanese army for thirty years.

The date was May 15, 1932. It went into Japanese history as the May Fifteenth incident. But at nine a.m. it was just a newless Sunday morning in May and off we went.

Half the fun was the getting out of Tokyo and into Japan. Tokyo is the capital, a great noisy city with eight- and ten-story office buildings that look as if they had been imported from Seattle, a government, a diplomatic corps, and Society with a capital S. Twenty miles out in the country you leave all that behind.

We decided to go up the river Tama and walk part of the way back. From Shinjuku station, swarming like an ant-heap, we took an electric train to the outermost suburbs and then

changed into a little countrified steam train. On such informal trips you see the Japanese as human beings, not as
officers or bureaucrats or politicians or people in Society.
They are for the most part pleasant kindly folks, intent on
their jobs or their simple Sunday amusements. We rode
through miles of suburbs dedicated to the rising incomes of
the white-collar class. They were spreading like a rash over
the dried rice fields. Every new little jerry-built house had
a " foreign " room. It was a cheerful sight to anybody but an
architect. It showed that standards were rising; those sales-
men and bank clerks could afford to swank it a little. They
were all keeping up with the Joneses, hell for leather.

We got out at Mitake and crossed the river by a toy bridge
where buses waited to take picnickers up to the old temple.
We went along the village street to a small restaurant. A
buxom, middle-aged landlady met us with a smile of old ac-
quaintance. She wore a sober dark gray kimono suited to her
years. We took off our shoes and she ushered us up a perpen-
dicular stair and slid back the paper windows of a little room
that contained nothing at all except the glorious view. We
sat on old yellow mats with faded silk edges and looked at
the brawling river and the mountains. The landlady came
back with two bottles of cold beer and we ate our sandwiches
and enjoyed the view and smoked.

We walked downstream for four or five miles past farm-
houses and a sawmill, and then crossed on stepping-stones and
climbed the steep bank to a little inn called Raku Raku En,
which is a poetical way of saying that it is a place where you
can take your pleasure. There we had tea, and so home in
the dusk through those dim raw suburbs where every new
little house had its " foreign " room, bookshelves, radio, and
piano.

There was a light in the office when we got back. Ofusa-san was waiting, an hour ahead of his usual time. " The Prime Minister has been murdered," he said, " the Bank of Japan has been bombed. By army and navy officers." I sat down at the telephone and began.

The story came out in jig-saw fragments, for even in the Metropolitan Police headquarters that day there had only been a doorkeeper on duty at the time of the assassination. It was midnight before I got it pieced together and on the air. I would not say " officers." I could not believe that officers, especially officers of the navy, were getting into political murder. I need not have been so particular. They were officers all right, officers in uniform.

Two days earlier, on Friday, May 13, two young naval officers had made a two-hour train journey from Tokyo to a place with which they were familiar, the drab country town of Tsuchiura, railway station for the inland naval air base and training school called Kasumiga-ura, the Misty Lagoon. An army cadet and a Tokyo student accompanied them. They were met by a teacher of the Native-Land-Loving School, which trained farmer boys in agriculture and patriotism. They all went to a Japanese restaurant where they were as usual given a private room. They did not send for geisha girls though Tsuchiura, a garrison town, has plenty. The inn's rustic slatterns served their food, and after the dishes had been cleared away they sat late talking. On Sunday the same men met some others in various places in Tokyo and their actions became the May Fifteenth incident.

At five o'clock that Sunday evening nine naval and military officers of ages between twenty-four and twenty-eight alighted from two taxicabs at the side entrance of the Yasukuni Shrine in Tokyo. The shrine is dedicated to all members of the fighting services who have died in Japan's wars. There is no holier place in Tokyo. Five white stripes running along its outer wall signify that it is under Imperial protection. It stands — or rather squats, as is the style of Japanese temples — in a small park; all around it are buildings associated with the army — officers' and men's clubs, a military museum, a sports amphitheater. Across a shallow valley filled with humanity the dome of the Russian Cathedral looks down on the main street of Kanda ward, sometimes called the " Boul' Mich' " of Tokyo. Second-hand book shops, an artist's colorman, a few shabby cafés, several universities, and the coming and going of thousands of students give the district an atmosphere, but its resemblance to the Latin Quarter is pathetically remote. The name expresses only the inverted nostalgia of the poor student dreaming of cities he will never see.

If anyone gave a passing glance to the young officers it was only to think that they had probably been ordered to Manchuria, where the Imperial army was then extending the Imperial Way. They worshipped at the shrine, doffing caps, clasping hands, and bowing towards the unseen mirror of the Sun Goddess in homage to the souls of the dead soldiers whose names are inscribed on the books and whose spirits dwell there. One of them bought charms from a priest and gave them to his comrades to protect them from the bullets of the police. They piled into their taxis, five in one, four in the other. In five minutes they had passed the British Embassy with its Sunday Union Jack flying and were entering the front and back gates of the Prime Minister's official residence. The group who dismounted at the front gate carried revolvers and hand grenades, expecting that the police guards would oppose them, but no challenge was offered to officers wearing the Emperor's uniform.

The Prime Minister's official residence is a bastard of the architectural era which followed the building of the Imperial Hotel by Frank Lloyd Wright of Chicago. When George IV built his many-domed pavilion at Brighton, Sydney Smith went to see it and reported: " St. Paul's has been down to Brighton and pupped." It seemed as if the Imperial Hotel had conceived and given birth to a mongrel. The Wright style, motifs, materials, coloring, and general bizarrerie were imitated. The architect had been unable to get away from the hotel idea, and the entrance hall, with its inquiry office, was the Imperial Hotel lobby with its ceiling lifted and the reception desk placed at the right of the entrance instead of the left.

On Sunday the receptionist was absent. One of the officers asked a police sergeant to show them the Prime Minister's private apartments. They pointed revolvers at him but he refused. Lost among passages and staircases, the officers wandered about, not knowing where to go. Some went upstairs and found the cabinet room empty. A " large man " appeared and they asked to be taken to the Prime Minister, saying they had come from the Naval Academy. Before the " large man " had done anything a group of three or four men appeared from somewhere and ran away when a shot was fired in their direction. Then someone heard a key turning in a lock and an officer shouted: " That must be the way to the private apartments." They knocked. A voice called: " Who is there? " A naval lieutenant burst open the flimsy door with his shoulder and they rushed in.

They found the Prime Minister, Mr. Inukai, a diminutive

alert man of seventy-five. His first name was Tsuyoshi but his friends knew him as " Ki." He had been in politics all his life and had at one time led a party of his own called the Kokuminto or Nationalist Party. It did not grow big enough to compete with the major parties, and Inukai finally disbanded it and led his followers into the ranks of the Seiyukai, the more conservative of the two parties which at that time were the alternative ins and outs of Japanese politics. The Seiyukai was looking for a leader; Inukai's age and standing and the " dowry " of voting power that he brought with him got him the post and in due time the Prime Ministership. He was a very small man, quick and fearless. His goatee beard was of a vague gray color which somehow suggested, quite erroneously, that it had once been blond. Late in life he had attained the goal of his ambition and he was intensely proud of being the Emperor's first Minister.

He led the officers into a Japanese room. His daughter-in-law, carrying her baby, was with him, and one of the officers, " knowing what would happen in a few minutes," as he said at the trial, told her to go away, but she stayed. The young men were rather confused and some were impressed by the old man's calm demeanor as he asked them to take off their shoes and sit down and talk it over. He had a cigarette in his hand and he lit it. " As I observed," said one of the officers in his testimony, " our leader was willing to talk with the Prime Minister." The group that had gone to the back door burst in, headed by Lieutenant Masayoshi Yamagishi, a man of action, carrying a dagger.

" No use talking," said Yamagishi. " Fire! " The word was shouted like an order and they all began firing. One shot the Prime Minister in the neck and another, deliberately, in the stomach. The Prime Minister sank on the matted floor and

25

never spoke again. " Believing the whole affair was over," the officers walked out. A policeman armed with a stick challenged them and they shot him. No one else interfered. Their taxi-drivers had been told to wait but had decamped. They walked down the hill and picked up two taxis near the American Embassy and drove off to the Metropolitan Police headquarters, where the " second wave of the attack " was to begin.

Some virtue had gone out of them and the second wave was a fiasco. They thought the police would have been warned by telephone, and with bombs and pistols they intended to put up a fight. Police headquarters were deserted on Sunday afternoon and the first cab-load drove on to the headquarters of the military police, commonly called the gendarmerie, and gave themselves up. The second cab-load entered the police building and found nobody, but at the gendarmerie office they saw a policeman who had arrived from the Prime Minister's house with news of the murder. They fired a shot at him and missed. They drove on to the Bank of Japan, hurled a grenade at the door, and went back to the gendarmerie building, where they surrendered.

A third group of officers had been detailed to destroy the offices of the Seiyukai, the Prime Minister's party. They threw two bombs which did not explode. They went to the Metropolitan Police office and threw three bombs, one of which struck an electric-light pole and shattered a window. Duty done, they proceeded to the gendarmerie headquarters and surrendered. The student who had accompanied the officers to Tsuchiura went to the Mitsubishi Bank and threw a bomb which exploded in the yard. Another conspirator went to the house of Count Makino, Lord Keeper of the Imperial Seals, and flung a grenade at a man who happened to be standing at the front door. It missed him.

26

That evening the official residence of the War Minister was the scene of an incident which was rigidly censored. The War Minister, General Sadao Araki, was out of town. His colleague, General Jinsaburo Mazaki, Vice-Chief of the General Staff, who, like Araki, sympathized with the young officers, hurried to the War Minister's headquarters when he heard of the murder and the attacks on the police headquarters and the Bank of Japan. Many senior officers had already assembled; talk was excited and confused. Some thought the incident merely an escapade by headstrong young men; others saw it as the prelude to revolt.

Several young officers in uniform came from their barracks in Tokyo demanding audience with the War Minister. Mazaki received them. They said they had come to ask the War Minister to rise. " Our comrades are ready all over the country. They expect action. We must rise today."

General Mazaki replied: " The War Minister will not rise. We should not rise. That is General Araki's opinion and mine too."

Mazaki told them to keep cool heads. He reminded them that in the Satsuma revolt of 1877 the nation had been expected to support the rebels, but did not. " Where the great Saigo, the most powerful militarist of his day, failed, how could Araki and Mazaki succeed? "

Mazaki was so afraid of further trouble that he approached the Seiyukai Party (Inukai's) and begged its leaders not to permit speeches or criticisms which, he said, might provoke even the moderate officers to join the extremists. His request was granted. The party of the murdered leader, the government party, fresh from a victorious election, held its breath. Two days later the General Staff informed General Araki that the army would not appoint a war minister to a party cabinet.

The information was conveyed to Prince Saionji, the Elder Statesman, who was then seeking for a new prime minister. A national cabinet was accordingly formed with Admiral Makoto Saito at its head, and party government in Japan was dead.

Messages sent to newspapers abroad that night said the Prime Minister had been shot by " men wearing officers' uniform." The correspondents and the public were unwilling to believe that officers of the army and navy had taken to political murder. The affair looked like a murderous prank by bloody-minded boy scouts carrying pistols and grenades instead of clasp knives and whistles. Its amateurishness seemed to prove that the movement was confined to a few young fanatics. The public soon recovered its confidence in the discipline and loyalty of the army. Actually the army was honeycombed with political agitation. The next intervention of the officers was on a far bigger scale.

The plot was less crude than others that had been proposed. Lieutenant Seishi Koga, naval ringleader of the plot, afterwards told the court martial that the conspirators had discussed a plan to bring about martial law by bombing the House of Representatives. Civilians who could easily get passes were to throw bombs from the public gallery while young officers waited at the doors to kill the members as they rushed out. Another plan which might be too grotesque for credence if it had not been told in court proposed the killing of Charles Chaplin, then visiting Japan. The Prime Minister invited Mr. Chaplin to a tea and the young officers considered a scheme for raiding the official residence while the party was in progress.

JUDGE: " What was the significance of killing Chaplin? "

KOGA: " Chaplin is a popular figure in the United States

and the darling of the capitalist class. We believed that killing him would cause a war with America, and thus we could kill two birds with a single stone."

JUDGE: " Why then did you give up your splendid plan? "

KOGA: " Because the newspapers later reported that the projected reception was still uncertain."

JUDGE: " What was the motive of planning to attack the official residence of the Prime Minister? "

KOGA: " It was to overthrow the Premier, who was also the president of a political party; in other words to overthrow the very center of government."

JUDGE: " Did you intend to kill the Premier? "

KOGA: " Yes, I did. However, I had no personal grudge against him."

The same prisoner said the plan to kill Chaplin was abandoned because " it was disputed whether it was advisable to kill the comedian on the slight chance that it might bring about war with the United States and increase the power of the military." Another plan to provoke a war with the United States involved the murder of Joseph Clark Grew, the American Ambassador, and Arthur Garrels, United States Consul General. Sub-Lieutenant Kameshiro Ito, who revealed the plot in his evidence, was to kill the Consul General; Second Sub-Lieutenant Haruo Oba was assigned to the Ambassador. No explanation was offered or asked as to why the plan was abandoned. At the time of the Prime Minister's murder Ito was in hospital with wounds received in the fighting at Shanghai. He was tried for " contemplated conspiracy."

The weapons were furnished by officers who were not in the plot but were willing to help the conspirators. Grenades were obtained from naval vessels serving in China and brought across in suitcases. Customs men did not examine

29

the baggage of officers in uniform. The conspirators were able to get leave easily and to travel between their posts and Tokyo as often as they wanted. They met on board warships and in their quarters at naval bases.

The murder of Prime Minister Inukai was the third political crime committed that spring. On the evening of February 9, as the Finance Minister, Junnosuke Inouye, was entering a hall in the suburbs of Tokyo to address a political meeting, he was shot dead by a country youth of twenty-two. Four weeks later Baron Takuma Dan, managing director of the holding company which controls the enterprises of the immense Mitsui corporation, was killed at his office door by another country youth aged twenty-one.

A significant trinity had fallen — banker, capitalist, politician — each victim the highest representative of a class. The killings of Finance Minister Inouye and Baron Takuma Dan were isolated events, complete in themselves. The murder of the Prime Minister was accompanied by actions which constituted a "token" revolution. The attacks on banks, party offices, and police headquarters have already been described. In the evening, after the officers had surrendered, a band of civilians from the country bombed the powerhouses of Tokyo and its suburbs in an effort to throw the capital into darkness. The attack was badly planned, feebly executed, and completely futile. The raiders were the principal and some students of the Native-Land-Loving School, already referred to. Some of them had drunk blood with the brotherhood which killed Inouye and Takuma Dan.

All the crimes were part of a single plan. The murders were intended to strike terror into the governing and possessing classes, and the raids on powerhouses and banks and police headquarters were to create such confusion that martial law would be proclaimed. Some of the young officers thought martial law the same thing as military government. They believed that if they created an opportunity the army would use it to bring about what they called a second restoration, taking power from the politicians and the capitalists and returning it to the Emperor, who would thereupon entrust it to faithful soldiers and patriots. But all this did not come out until the public trials were held a year later.

Chapter II

THE TECHNIQUE OF REVOLUTION

Assassination of conspicuous individuals suspected of liberal opinions was common enough, and three Prime Ministers had been murdered in fifteen years. But uniformed officers had not till then committed murder themselves or equipped the patriot gangs from military stores.

A combination of officers and gangsters was a new and sinister development. The personal safety of statesmen depended largely on strict enforcement of the police regulations controlling the sale of revolvers. Since the exaggerated communist scare of 1928 it had become impossible for any ordinary Japanese to obtain firearms. The few foreigners who possessed sporting guns were regularly inspected. A British ex-officer who had kept the army revolver he carried on the Somme had to show it so often that he asked the police to take it away and keep it for him. They were astonished and refused. But if the army was munitioning the gangsters the police were helpless and the restrictions useless. Japan was making war in Manchuria and Shanghai, and officers (as was proved in court) could go aboard warships or into barracks and come out with suitcases filled with grenades and automatics. It was certain that in a land where " face " counts for much, the patronage of officers and gentlemen would inject new life into the death bands and blood brotherhoods of the so-called patriotic societies. Until then assassination had been an occasional risk of statesmen in Japan; thenceforward it was a constant fear, staying with every civilian statesman like his shadow and haunting the minds of mothers, wives, and children.

But stupid murders by fanatical youths in a country where patriotism goes hand in hand with crime are not at first sight identifiable as symptoms of revolution, and the older generals and statesmen undervalued the unrest. " I was once a hothead myself," said Admiral Nomura, afterwards ambassador to Washington, " and I grew out of it. They usually do." When General Araki was asked point-blank: " Who are the young officers? " that affable and ready-spoken soldier immediately replied: " They are the flower of the army." The young officers and their civilian partners were only the scum on the surface of the water. The rolling tide was the national army swinging forward into an orgy of aggressiveness, but the strength of the tide and the speed with which it was rising were still unknown and there were natural and plausible reasons why the portent of the young officers was underrated.

The youth of the plotters and the amateurishness of the plot seemed to stamp the Inukai affair as an ebullition of immature minds. The absence of preparations to follow up the opening move was inconsistent with military standards of efficiency, for the army never took one step without planning the next. The Manchurian " incident " had commenced with a faked explosion on the South Manchurian Railway, but less than two hours after the blast had been " discovered " the whole Japanese garrison was on the march and the occupation of the country was proceeding as if by timetable. When the young officers in Tokyo murdered the Prime Minister they had shot their bolt. They hastily surrendered, and when their comrades implored the War Minister to "rise," the War Minister did nothing. Elderly statesmen, taking their information from elderly generals, told foreign ambassadors that unrest in the army was confined to a small unimportant group and would soon be controlled.

The man in the street was startled but not alarmed. A Japanese neighbor was a little amused by my excitement. " The Japanese people will not be very angry about the Prime Minister's murder," he said; " many of us think the politicians needed a lesson." There had been so much propaganda about corruption among the politicians, who often were corrupt and sometimes rotten, that thoughtless people sympathized with the crime on the principle: " That'll larn 'em."

The public as a whole had confidence in the power of discipline. Faith in discipline is one of the strongest traits of the Japanese people. They do not merely submit to discipline; they embrace it. In streets as empty of traffic as the prairie pedestrians stand on the sidewalk and wait like men fulfilling a duty until the green light lifts the taboo. When soldiers espy an officer or only a fellow private in the street they preen themselves for the opportunity of performing a salute. Their eyes do not leave the recipient of the projected ceremonial until he has seen them, and when the salute has been delivered with gawky punctilio, an expression of satisfaction spreads over their faces. Grocery boys, a cynical tribe, taking military training in a primary school of an evening, post one of their number at the door and salute him with unblinking formality. In some Tokyo schools it is a ritual that pupils should give each other a military salute. Those laughing little snipes of twelve years old might be expected once in a while to thumb the nose at a parting companion; but no, heels click and the right hand is stiffly raised to the cap. Discipline is never a thing to be laughed at.

The army was Japan's great exemplar of discipline, and the public easily persuaded itself that the officers who had killed the Prime Minister were honest young men led astray by excess of concern for the country.

The outbreak was, in fact, the first symptom of a revolutionary movement in the army. We had forgotten, and the Japanese themselves had forgotten, that revolution in that singular country has a peculiar technique which repeats itself, with variations, throughout their history. Barricades do not appear in the streets; there is no mass rising or general bloodshed, no expulsion of a dynasty. The sacred and Imperial figurehead of the nation sits above the tumult like a wooden god, and just as war is an " incident," the forcible transfer of the governing power comes disguised as a restoration or a reform. The unrest expresses itself physically in conspiracies and assassinations and intellectually in a stirring of the dry bones of pseudo-history conducted by pseudo-scholars who call on the nation to arise and throw off foreign accretions which have corrupted the ancient pure spirit of Japanism. It was so before the Restoration of 1868 which came proclaiming a return to the principles of the Great Reform of 645, and it was so in the movement of 1931–41 which brought back military government. The revolution, nevertheless, is always the harbinger of imported ideas. The Great Reform of 645 was copied from China. The Restoration of 1868 brought about the wholesale adoption of Western institutions. The ideology of the young officers of today was created by the impact of Marxism upon native chauvinism. Its result has been the establishment of a Japanese form of national socialism.

The word Marxism in this connection does not mean com-

35

munism or social democracy. It means the economic core of socialist teaching — the doctrine of state ownership of wealth embodied by the early socialists in the formula: nationalization of the means of production, distribution, and exchange. Communism, which had introduced itself with a massacre of Russian royalty, was hateful to Emperor-worshipping Japanese. Social democracy was unintelligible to people who conceived of government as a magnified paternalism and thought " government of the people " only a phrase disguising the exercise of power by the ruling classes, whoever these might be — politicians, capitalists, or Jews.

Communism and democracy were obnoxious because they professed internationalism and belittled the importance of national defense. But national defense in the age of mechanized warfare required enormous budgets. A military officer who was asked what the army was thinking in the year 1936 replied: " We desire a community in which all people are able to work to the fullest degree, accepting twenty per cent of the results of their labor as their private income and turning the rest over to the government as national income."

The Marxist doctrine of state ownership of capital offered a means of providing unlimited armaments, and the Japanese twin of Hitlerite national socialism was born. The Manchurian adventure was conceived and carried out by the Japanese army as the first installment of a new order. The soldiers proclaimed that the attack on Manchuria was not an ordinary imperialistic foray. The new state the Japanese legions planned was not to be a " happy hunting ground for capitalists," but a state in which the Imperial Way would be realized.

Such was the ideology of the movement; its methods were assassination and terrorism, and its agents (besides the cranks and the criminal types) were army officers and young men who had been touched by revolutionary ideas from Europe. Some of the civilians had been socialists. They can hardly be accused of betraying their principles. In Japan there was no way of making a revolution without the army. The masses were too ignorant to rise, the political parties were hopelessly bourgeois, and the army was the only agency able to effect a forcible overturn.

The imitative, incipient liberalism which Japanese labor had adopted after the 1914–18 war, when Ramsay MacDonald's portrait hung in its headquarters, was swamped and sunk when the seizure of Manchuria released the inherent chauvinism of the nation. A labor agitator told how he had gone to Shinagawa station in Tokyo to distribute anti-war leaflets among the crowds assembled to send off reinforcements for Manchuria. " The appearance of the soldiers and the feelings of the expectant crowd knocked out of my head all the silly ideas stuffed into it by intellectual internationalists."

The movement in the army made a successful appeal to the half-baked proletarian leaders. A writer in the *Labor Magazine* of May 1931 declared labor's fear of the army had caused the movement in Japan to be sterile and indecisive: " The army is not what it was," he wrote. " Colonels, majors, and captains are not unfriendly to the proletarian parties. They are conscious of the army's mission and understand the scandalous nature of the political parties. The army is waiting its opportunity to strike a great blow against existing parties."

" How will the masses benefit by disarmament? " he asked. " It will lighten the burdens of the bourgeoisie but not ours." (He was wrong. A few years later income-tax was being levied on workers earning the equivalent of twenty American dollars a month.. It is true that millions of laborers and practically all the farmers were not liable.) He continued: " In Europe and the United States the army is the instrument of the privileged classes, and our comrades in those countries have reason to denounce it. The Japanese army is different. It is the army of the masses, with the Emperor as its central figure. Thanks to its independence, the army in Japan is a power on which we proletarians can depend in our movement for emancipation. Let us consider well before we denounce the army."

In due course the Social Mass Party converted itself into a Nazi party and excommunicated the few of its old leaders who still professed democracy.

Japanese patriots find great difficulty in expressing their thoughts, and much reading of their speeches leaves a conviction that vague phraseology is sometimes the mirror of vague ideas conceived in minds unable to think things out, and sometimes a cover for thoughts too vulpine or too naïve to be plainly uttered. An effort will be made to understand their minds by a study of their actions and ideas. Meantime let us look at some of the revolutionaries.

Ten naval officers, eleven military cadets, and twenty civilians were tried for the May Fifteenth incident. Another group of thirteen, known as the Blood Brotherhood, was placed on trial for the murders of Finance Minister Inouye and Baron Dan. Of those fifty-four persons only five were men of forty and over; none of the naval officers was older than twenty-eight, none of the cadets older than twenty-four. Few of the fifty-four were attractive or impressive physically, but that may almost be called a national characteristic. The Japanese racial blend of Polynesian and Mongolian elements is often facially unfortunate. The young officers had a wooden look, the stamp of a rigid education imposed on unformed personalities. At the age of twenty-five the Japanese are mentally less developed than their contemporaries in America and Europe, and the portraits of the young officers show a group of heavy expressionless masks.

In the student group there were some intelligent immature faces of a type with which sympathetic foreign residents in Japan are familiar — young men craving for friendship and leadership, eager for life, yet shrinking from the plunge. Given a job, a home, and a year or two, they would have steadied down. Some of the civilian prisoners were young killers, and they looked the part — village bad boys, delinquent yokels who would never grow up.

There was one different type in the gallery, Tachibana, the Tolstoyan. He had a frank glance and a weak, mobile mouth under a little unimportant ornament of a mustache. Meeting him in a train one would put him down for a good but not likely to be very successful country schoolmaster, as in a sense he was. Priest Nissho Inouye, the spiritual father of the Blood Brotherhood, had the smooth obstinate face of the one-idea'd man. A man of violent words and dull imagination, he could, like so many of the type, preach bloodshed and plan murder and yet shrink from the consequences when bolder men converted words into acts.

The story of the men and the ideas for which they were ready to inflict death and risk a hanging is as devoid of personality as a Japanese serial novel. A human background — homes, sisters, relatives — peeps out but it does not come alive; there are meetings in restaurants, journeys in the country. On his way to the murder rendezvous that Sunday afternoon one of the young officers kept an appointment with the sister of another conspirator. He had to give her the money for the school expenses of a younger brother of his friend, who anticipated that he might not be at liberty for a time. But human interest is never the theme of the story; the impression one got so often in Japan of moving in a world that thinks in clichés is persistent. The ideas for which these people were ready to kill seem irrevelant to us, as no doubt the ideas of the early Christians seemed irrelevant to the Romans. The Christians, however, endured death; they did not go about murdering those who differed from them.

Some of the young officers declared in court that they had merely wanted to ring an alarm bell to awaken the nation. They had indeed rung a bell. They were unimportant figures but they had revealed the violence of the forces stirring below the surface. They had shown that the Japanese army was infected with ideas supposed to be confined to the fanatics of the patriotic societies. The army was the one power in Japan which could make a revolution. When it appeared that the army was in the movement, the Black Dragon Society and all the others became supers on the stage. There were no more political murders by civilians. Another group of officers four years later murdered in one morning all the old statesmen they could reach. The patriotic societies relapsed into anti-foreign and pro-war mobs, the role for which they were naturally fitted. The army installed itself in power with the concurrence of a docile nation intoxicated by foreign war, its civilian leaders terrorized by assassination.

Chapter III

MARS ON THE SOAPBOX

The Prime Minister's murderers were tried a year later.
Japanese justice had moved fast; communists and dangerous
thinkers often spent four or five years in their cells awaiting
trial. All the proceedings were public. Japan looked forward
to learning the truth about the young officers and their secret
movement.

Three courts — a military court martial, a naval court martial, and the Tokyo Criminal Court — tried the soldiers, sailors, and civilians separately. There was no noticeable difference of procedure; the authorities had conferred beforehand
and agreed to allow the prisoners the fullest liberty of speech.
The boundary between relevancy and irrelevancy was tacitly
thrown open. The military court martial in the headquarters
of the First Provincial Division in Tokyo was soon the star
show of a three-ring circus. The newspapers had not struck
such a gusher of sensation and sentimentality in a quarter of
a century. They printed pages of it every day. Correspondents,
with cable tolls to consider, soon cut down on the story, for
much of it was " tripe."

But " tripe," like morals, is a matter of latitude. The Japanese nation surrendered itself to the delights of hero-worship.
Counsel for the prisoners presented 111,000 letters appealing

for clemency, many of them written in blood. Nine young men of Niigata, a quiet seaport, renowned for furnishing the prettiest girls to the Yoshiwara, chopped off nine little fingers in evidence of sincerity and sent them to the War Minister pickled in a jar of alcohol. " They broke the law but their motives were pure. We are profoundly impressed with their spirit of sacrifice," wrote the nine. Thirty thousand holders of the Order of the Golden Kite, the highest military decoration, signed a petition. A young woman cut off her hair and sent it to the judges bundled up with a note reading: " I have heard that sentences of death have been demanded. I am a young woman of twenty-two. I have cut off my hair and have decided to become a man to carry out the desires of the accused." Lieutenant Yamagishi, the man of action who had given the order to shoot, wept in court when his counsel produced a letter a schoolboy had written on a handkerchief with his blood. A German sausage-maker who had surprisingly built up a mail-order business in Hakodate sent ten yen to open a fund for a monument which should show the Prime Minister shaking hands with his murderers. A school teacher wrote asking how he could stand up before his class while the official prosecutor was demanding death for faithful patriots.

A letter was read from a little girl so very poor that the family had discontinued buying a newspaper. When the trial began they clubbed together for a paper, which the elder brother read aloud. " The young officers are greater than the three heroes whom we now call the human bombs of Shanghai. Why must such great men remain in prison? " She enclosed a small sum to buy them something. " I should like to call the attention of the court," said the defending attorney, " to the concern with which the whole nation views this case."

An exhibit which may seem more surprising to readers out-

side Japan than it did to any Japanese was a document from
the Osaka Bar Association expressing the opinion that the
actions of the prisoners could be regarded as self-defense from
the legal point of view. My mind went back three centuries.
I remembered from my school history books an old Puritan
tract called *Killing No Murder*, but the sophism came oddly
from a bar association.

To be on trial for a patriotic crime, facing a possible though
improbable death sentence, deferentially treated by a judge,
flattered by the prosecutor as he acknowledges the purity of
one's motives, watching the reporters writing and the messen-
gers hurrying to the printers with the copy, seeing the baskets
on the lawyers' table pile higher and higher with fan mail
written in blood is an intoxicating experience. Wooden-faced
young officers found their tongues, and one of the plebeian
killers, who had been a baker's delivery boy, orated for three
successive days. The prisoners were allowed to talk all the
politics they wanted and the crime of murder became a necessary but not particularly important detail. From the highest
platform the Japanese press could provide, the prisoners were
given unlimited latitude to expound their creed. They told
the story of their lives, beginning sentimentally with their
infancy. One said the first seeds of patriotism had been planted
in his mind by his grandmother.

The presiding judge sometimes allowed a smile to play on
his features (as when the proposed assassination of Charlie
Chaplin was revealed by a young man of portentous gravity),
but the procurator (who afterwards told the press that he expected to be killed for asking the death sentence) dwelt on
their patriotism. The small court was filled with sympathetic
spectators, letters written in blood (the Gallup poll of public
opinion in Japan) were coming in more than satisfactorily,

and the defending counsel wore the air of men bowed down with responsibility. Everything combined to make the prisoners speak, and they spoke.

Re-reading their speeches away from Japan and the Japanese atmosphere, I remember a conversation with a diplomat who had a remarkably good knowledge of the Japanese language and a taste for reading contemporary Japanese literature. We were discussing some particular article. " It reads silly," I said, " but perhaps it has been badly translated." " No," said the secretary of embassy, " the translation is accurate, and though the ideas do seem silly in English, they look all right in Japanese."

Reading them in Japanese was seeing them from the inside of the window; one had to some extent entered the Japanese mind. Those young officers in their evidence expressed the mind and ideas of the revolution. The crudeness of their opinions and the inadequacy of their motives disappeared in the Japanese atmosphere.

The ringleader, First Sub-Lieutenant Koga, told of his conversion to Pan-Asianism by a higher officer five years earlier while he was still at the Naval Academy. His views were definite and appallingly simple:

" The Japanese delegates to the London Naval Conference, Baron Wakatsuki and Admiral Takarabe, were influenced by financiers and therefore they failed. The political parties are the tools of financiers; the navy was asleep and Japan failed because of the lack of united force." As for his crime: " The condition of the country could not be improved unless blood was shed."

First Sub-Lieutenant Taku Mikami told how he had been influenced by his grandmother, an ardent patriot. The old lady continued to serve the cause and he was able to get leave from his post and participate in the murder of the Prime Minister with the help of a telegram she sent announcing falsely his mother's death. Mikami stated his creed in court:

" Our revolution is intended to bring about direct Imperial rule and harmony between ruler and ruled. We find it necessary to overthrow plutocrats and others whatever their station who act against the spirit of the Empire. As we aim to establish direct Imperial rule, we are neither left nor right.

" I happen to have been born in Japan and I am a Japanese subject serving in the navy. Looking around me, I find frivolity reigning everywhere. True relations between men are poisoned. Life or death does not count with me. I say to those who bemoan my death: ' Do not shed tears for me but sacrifice yourselves on the altar of reform.' "

Sub-Lieutenant Isamu Kuroiwa declared that the London naval agreement decided him to join the plot: " We were told that the ratio allotted Japan had been computed on the defensive needs of the countries concerned. Of course that was a lie. The ratio was forced on Japan by the United States."

JUDGE: " What did you think when you heard that the Prime Minister was dead? " (Kuroiwa had shot Inukai in the abdomen.)

ANSWER: " I felt sorry but I thought his death unavoidable as he had to be sacrificed on the altar of national reformation."

First Sub-Lieutenant Masayoshi Hayashi, son of a swordsmith, delivered diatribes against the educational system. " I believe that education is love, but I have found that teachers are interested chiefly in obtaining promotion. They take no interest in the spiritual welfare of their pupils. At the Naval Academy things were no better. I visited my instructor at his home. I asked what was his object in life and he told me it was to be an admiral. I felt indignant." Hayashi said he took

45

part in the murder because he believed that after the Prime
Minister was killed, martial law would be proclaimed and a
general or admiral would form a government. He understood
that this would be military government.

Sub-Lieutenant Haruo Oba, the son of a general in the
army, was relatively taciturn. He had listened to discussions of
the naval-limitation agreements and was convinced that Japan
ought to have been given parity with Great Britain and the
United States. Believing " that the trend of affairs was fixed,"
he became convinced that " reform could only be effected by
assassination of leading members of the privileged classes."
He had no notion of what was to follow the destruction of the
present system; he only wanted to see a better state of affairs.
Oba was unaware that he had committed an offense which
would disqualify him for further service. He told the court
his only wish was to finish his sentence and continue to serve
the Emperor.

Sub-Lieutenant Kameshiro Ito expounded a verbose philosophy of " constructive destruction." He said the group
that killed the Prime Minister was " an organization without
organization." They looked on themselves as " the stones that
are thrown in to form the bottom of the foundations," they
saw " an innocent population subjected to hunger and suffering merciless pressure from capitalism." But changing the
economic system would not help the situation: " My life's
desire will be fulfilled if a state is established on the principle
that the Emperor and his subjects are one."

One of the army cadets, aged twenty-two, spent an hour and
a half expounding his theory, which was then thought to be
somewhat novel (it afterwards became quite orthodox), that
the throne does not exist for the state but the state exists for
the throne.

Mars on the Soapbox

JUDGE: " Why did you, a soldier, take part in a reform movement? "

ANSWER: " Let me say a few words in regard to relations between the army and society. The glory and brilliance of the Japanese army are unparalleled in the world. This is due to conscription, because of which the relation between the army and society is very close. In fact, the army and society are one. . . . The Imperial Way should be spread through the world, the Asiatic nations being first consolidated into a unit and thereafter the rest of the world.

" We demand direct rule by the Emperor. Our center today is the imported egotistical notion of popular rights. It is wrong. Manhood suffrage and the grant of social and political rights to the people are a gigantic mistake."

This cadet expected that a military government would restrict private fortunes to 1,000,000 yen ($500,000) and confiscate all above that amount.

The accused students, each in his turn, made set speeches in the Criminal Court. The speeches revealed nothing more than the ideas idle students pick up in Japan. " The corrupt condition of the ruling class had become intolerable," said one. Another said he loved to read about heroic figures and believed that only violence could purify Japan. Another had become tired of wasting his time studying law while soldiers were fighting in Manchuria, and he left the university to devote himself to Japanism. One after another, eleven students recited the slogans of the patriots. The two killers had grudges against society and they killed. The students had been given pistols and ammunition but they showed none of the hunter's zeal. They were not revolutionaries; they were adolescents straying in a pink mist.

The leader of the group told how he had become despondent and left the Imperial University to associate himself with a patriotic seminary, where he met Priest Nissho Inouye (who will be introduced in his turn) and the young officers. He found that the reconstruction they were planning was similar to the revolution he had been thinking of and he assisted in moving a trunk full of ammunition from a naval base to Tokyo.

JUDGE: " What do you now think of your actions? "

ANSWER: " I do not regret them. That does not mean that I approve of what I have done in the past. I negate the whole of my past."

Speeches for the defense were made by young officers who had been members of the same class as the prisoners. They dwelt on the purity of their motives. " Brought up in an atmosphere of loyalty to the Emperor they believed that the country was in peril and would be lost unless they acted. In that conviction they undertook to bring about a Showa Restoration," said Lieutenant Asada, one of the volunteer defenders. He continued: " Think of the effect the conduct of the accused has had on the nation. They reawakened the Japanese spirit in a people who were drunk with Western thoughts and they have cleared the ground for revival by exposing the iniquities of the ruling class."

With a fine flow of rhetoric Lieutenant Asada described the young officers going about their duties in the Pacific: " The burning tropical sun did not daunt us; the biting cold did not cool our ardor. Our sole concern was to save the state. Meanwhile we came to doubt if the people were conscious of themselves as a nation. They were drifting towards a state of mind which would permit power to be centralized in parliament. The London [naval-limitation] treaty was signed. . . . But there are many things in this world which must be righted before peace can prevail. As the world stands today, blood is necessary. The American Naval Academy at Annapolis uses a textbook which says that the Japanese are a race which will yield if pressure is applied. The London naval agreement endorses the accuracy of that statement. . . . The time had arrived to change the situation. It was time we acted to bring about a Showa Restoration."

Before sentence was passed the prisoners were allowed to speak. Lieutenant Mikami's response was prophetic:

" What was bound to come was brought about by us. Japan had to return to her old ways and we started the revolution. Our deed was destructive but it had a constructive object."

The procurator asked the death sentence for the officer who devised the plot, for the one who fired first, and for the one whose bullet killed the Prime Minister. For the others he proposed sentences ranging from three years to life imprisonment.

A furore of indignant protest at once arose in the navy. Admiral Osumi, the Navy Minister, found it necessary to send a message to all naval stations assuring the fleet that the " sacred court martial " would pronounce a fair judgment and asking all units to perform their duties conscientiously " at this juncture when the situation is so momentous." The venerable Admiral Togo broke his habitual silence with a message exhorting the navy to remain calm.

A conference of the Navy Department, the War Office, and the Department of Justice sat for six hours, the Procurator General of Japan in the chair, to consider the sentences. Those high authorities agreed that the ringleader should suffer the death penalty. The death sentence was not given. The ringleader and the officer whose shot had killed the Prime Minister were each sentenced to fifteen years' imprisonment. The others received smaller terms. None of the sentences was fully served, and by the time the next " incident " occurred three years later, many and perhaps all of the prisoners were free. The eleven military cadets were sentenced to four years' imprisonment and were released after serving two years and eight months. They were met at the jail gate by their relatives and representatives of patriotic societies. Riding in nine automobiles, they drove to the Double Bridge at the entrance of the Palace, bowed to the Emperor within, and departed for their homes.

Courts martial are not expected to keep up with the strictest judicial standards, but one of the civil judges had lost all of his. In the court that tried the Blood Brotherhood, Priest Nissho, acting on a suggestion made by his lawyer, rose and addressed the bench of three judges. He denounced the presiding judge, accusing him of inattention, of fumbling with his papers and displaying indifference to the prisoners' assertions that they had acted for the good of the country. While Nissho shouted, the other prisoners rattled teacups and hammered the table. The bench rejected Nissho's protest, but the presiding judge suspended the trial for several days. The judge believed that he could " arrange the dispute " by a private conversation with Nissho. Before visiting him he consulted two judges of the Supreme Court. They advised him that he would lower the dignity of the court if he discussed his conduct with the prisoner. Nevertheless, the judge visited the priest in his cell. He failed to " arrange the dispute." He went to the country, saying he was suffering from neuralgia, and soon afterwards he resigned. He was forty-seven years old; he had been a judge for sixteen years and was about to be promoted president of the District Court. No explanation of his resignation was offered or invented by the press. Against the background of that trial no action was too crazy to cause surprise. What seems fantastic when written in English was as normal as the weather in Japan.

Friendly foreign observers, of whom I counted myself one, were at a loss to explain a court martial which resembled Hyde Park in London on a Sunday morning rather than any kind of court on earth. Various theories circulated. One suggested that the authorities wanted to kill the young-officer movement by ridicule and gave the prisoners all the rope they wanted believing that they would hang their cause with its own absurdity. But that was clearly too naïve. It was not the Japanese way. The army would never have connived at anything that might have got it laughed at. It was evident that the soldiers, like most of the civilians, sympathized with the young officers. They saw the Prime Minister's murderers not as harebrained youths but as heroes.

The simple truth was that the higher authorities were flabbergasted and did not know what to do. They were afraid to muzzle officers of the sacred fighting services. After all, militant nationalism was a very different thing from " dangerous thoughts." So the presiding judges shut their eyes to rules of judicial procedure and the prosecutors soon abandoned their efforts to concentrate the trial on the crime of murder. The flood gates were thrown open and the second restoration was preached with religious fury.

We had learned the truth and it was different from what we had expected. The young officers' movement was at once puerile and ferocious, and its puerility disguised its evil power. Those young officers, with undeveloped, single-track minds, not different in quality though dyed a different color

51

from minds that take to soapboxes, were typical of the mentality that was spreading through the army and navy. What we did not realize at the time was that feudal, fire-eating Mr. Hyde had become the master of the suave and plausible Dr. Jekyll, once so assiduous in his attendance at Geneva.

Chapter IV

THE BLOOD BROTHERHOOD

The civilian wing of the young officers' plot was a gang called the Blood Brotherhood (Ketsumeidan, literally the Blood Oath Band). Some of them were vicious youths, living on the borderland where patriotism and crime meet; others were idle, fanatical students. All of them were idealists, in their way. They were willing instruments, but they had hypnotized themselves with slogans and they regarded themselves as more than tools. The prospect that the army would become the active force of revolution had stimulated the patriots all along the line, and many currents met in the movement which culminated on May 15. Before their story is told spend a moment with a little naval commander, now dead and forgotten, who sowed the dragon's teeth in the Naval Academy and who finally, before a Chinese bullet killed him, prepared the crime of May 15 by bringing together the young officers and the professional patriots.

On an afternoon in June 1925 a young naval officer and a cadet walked in the grounds of the Naval Academy. The cadet was a youth of eighteen named Koga; his companion, Lieutenant Fuji, was ten years older. The older man expounded his creed of Pan-Asianism: Japan was to unite the Asiatic nations and their leaders, expel the foreigners from Asia, and become the equal of the white men. The conversation was recounted six years later to a court martial which tried the cadet for the murder of the Prime Minister. That afternoon talk fixes the earliest date that can be named for the inception of the young officers' terrorist movement.

Fuji was a born proselytizer. His own story is unknown, for he was killed in the fighting at Shanghai in 1931 and dead men cannot be tried. He had a post at the Naval Academy; many of the young officers subsequently said he had awakened them to a sense of Japan's position. He followed up converts, lent them books, and, when they were especially promising, introduced them to the big figures of the patriotic world.

One such introduction made Koga acquainted with Dr. Shumei Okawa, an intellectual malcontent, a promoter of patriotic societies, a man of many contacts who could always find money. Okawa was a national socialist, though the word "socialist" was anathema in Japan. When he heard that officers were planning a terrorist demonstration, he provided the funds. At the court martial it was found that he had given Koga 7,000 yen ($3,500). The money was used for traveling expenses between Tokyo and outlying naval stations, for visits to Shanghai and Manchuria to collect pistols and hand grenades, for houses hired in Tokyo to store those weapons in, for the organization of the Blood Brotherhood and for the maintenance of the Brothers while they prowled about Tokyo or practiced shooting.

Fuji perished without knowing what his disciples had accomplished, but his work lived after him. He had brought together the threads out of which the first murder conspiracy was woven. He had converted to terrorism the only men in Japan who had easy access to weapons, he had found them a source of funds, and he had established a partnership between them and the revolutionary patriotic societies. The formation of the Blood Brotherhood and the organization of assassination was the natural sequel.

The atmosphere in which the young officers moved during the years of incubation was like that of old revolutionary Russia turned upside down. All the slogans were inverted. The Japanese plotters called themselves patriots, but their methods were those of the nihilists and the anarchists. They raved about imperialism as the Russians had raved about liberty. They avowed their devotion to the Emperor, as the Russians did not, but like the Russians they murdered the Emperor's officials. The revolutionary ranks in Russia shaded downwards into the dark regions where spies and informers skulk, and in Japan if you scratched a patriot you often found a blackmailer. There was also a shading upwards; there were respectable patriots just as there were high-minded revolutionaries. Many officers of the Japanese army and navy knew of the activities of the terrorist group, and while they did not participate, they did not inform. The young officers' stories of smuggling pistols and bombs over from Manchuria remind the reader of Russian revolutionary tales, but they had no trouble in getting weapons from warships and barracks, and their uniforms gave them safe passage past any policeman. Patriots on the run always knew where to find shelter; public opinion where not actively sympathetic was passive.

The young officers followed the routine of their profession. The navy keeps its men moving, and in the six years between Koga's conversation with Fuji in the garden of the Naval Academy and the afternoon when he led the band to the murder of the Prime Minister he and his comrades had served in various naval stations in Japan and China.

The sentiments of their early twenties might have passed like a disease of adolescence but for controversies over arms limitation which were then stirring the navy to its depths. At Washington Japan had agreed to a sixty per cent ratio of the fleet strength of Britain and the United States. The ratio was naturally disliked by the navy, but the London Conference of 1930 confirmed it and, what was worse, the government in Tokyo overruled the Chief of the Naval General Staff and accepted the London agreement in defiance of his protests. The navy, therefore, had a grievance of an acute kind, and young officers who believed that politicians and capitalists should be extirpated were swimming with the tide.

A great air training school had been established at Kasumi-gaura almost in the center of the main island of Japan. Many young officers were passed through that school, among them Lieutenant Koga, the ringleader, and some fellow travelers. The prefecture of Ibaragi, in which it is situated, had a tradition of revolutionary violence, and in those years its principal city, Mito, happened to be the home of two revolution-ary-minded youth groups with which Fuji and Koga made contact. With a combination of Dr. Okawa's money, Lieutenant Koga's munitions, and country youths enlisted from those two groups, the murder campaign was begun.

In a suburb of Mito a business man who had grown prosperous on a street-car franchise erected a temple for the repose of his conscience and the good of his fellow citizens. Into it as priest he inducted Akira Inouye, nicknamed "Nissho." "Nissho" means "Sun-called" and the implication was that Japan (Ni-hon, the sun-land) had somehow called Nissho to his vocation. He had had little formal education and had spent a good part of his life in China as a secret agent for the Japanese army. He had been employed for a year by the army's veteran expert on China, General Banzai, who served his country by acting as unpaid adviser to Chinese war lords. After eight roving years among shady jobs in China and Manchuria Inouye returned to Japan and lived in his native town, doing nothing in particular and chewing the cud of his failure to become more than a small cog in the army's espionage machinery.

Then he " got religion " in the form of an aggressively nationalistic type of Buddhism. He spent a year in a Buddhist retreat in the mountains, and when he came down he organized a group called the National Defense Holy Society. Some of his admirers obtained for him the charge of the temple that had been built from the profits of the street-cars and he preached a fiery blend of religion and nationalism. At this temple Nissho recruited as his disciples a primary school teacher and a number of village lads in their early twenties. He contributed no ideas to the movement; his power lay in his dogged confidence in force, and he cultivated young men of the killer type. He undertook no murders himself. He was something of a Uriah Heep in the dock, professing to be an ignorant man unable to answer deep questions.

While Priest Nissho was acquiring fame as an evangelist of violent patriotism, the Mayor of Mito gave a ball. Nissho's toughs crashed the gate and made a disturbance in protest against the introduction of Western frivolity. Some naval officers heard of the noisome exploit and took an interest in the perpetrators. They attended the temple, and the priest visited their quarters. Gradually a companionship of the like-minded drew together. They talked revolution incessantly and, Okawa's money aiding them, began to make plans. The priest left his temple and went to live in Tokyo, and the primary school teacher, who was by now his second-in-command, followed.

The Blood Brotherhood was formed and the officers collected weapons. The naval officers do not seem to have actually drunk blood with the band but they financed it, munitioned it, and fitted its projects into their plans. " It was a kind of vanguard," Koga told his judge at the court martial. Two conferences were held with about thirty present, including naval officers. They discussed and discussed but nothing concrete emerged. At a second meeting it was proposed to start a magazine, but Priest Nissho vetoed it. The time of preparation was past, he said, and the time for action had come. At the third meeting the attendance was small — Nissho's thugs and four officers. There were no weaklings in the group. They agreed that on Empire Foundation Day, February 11, when all the roads to the Imperial Palace are thick with uniformed notables, the Blood Brotherhood should undertake a general battue of political and financial leaders. A conspirator was sent down to the country to get support but recruiting was slow and the rudimentary plan was dropped.

Before another meeting could be held some of the naval officers, including Commander Fuji, the moving spirit, had been ordered to Shanghai, so it was decided that the civilians would act without them. It was understood, said the priest in his evidence, that the officers would strike when they returned.

The civilians — idle students, uneducated youths, a primary school teacher, and a fanatic priest — were amateurs and some of them were shirkers. The staff work was beneath contempt. A study of the evidence leaves the impression that the movement might have produced only froth but for the fact that the officers were able to get automatics and give them to the young conspirators, one of whom admitted that at first he did not know how to use a pistol. Yotsumoto, the leader of the student group, testified that Lieutenant Mikami (army) showed him a trunk full of pistols and ammunition which he had brought from Manchuria. The trunk was left at the house of Mrs. Inouye, wife of the priest. Inouye got ten pistols from three other officers.

A list of statesmen and " members of the privileged classes " who were to be " removed," with the assassins assigned to each of them, was drawn up as follows:

BARON WAKATSUKI, Prime Minister (*Tanaka, Takuma, Mori,* and *Hishiko*) ;

BARON K. SHIDEHARA, Foreign Minister (*Kukida*) ;

JUNNOSUKE INOUYE, Finance Minister (*Konuma*) ;

DR. KISABURO SUZUKI, Home Minister (*Hishinuma*) ;

TAKEJIRO TOKONAMI, Railway Minister (*Tanaka*) ;

PRINCE SAIONJI, Elder Statesman, the Emperor's highest political adviser (*Ikebukuro*) ;

PRINCE IYESATO TOKUGAWA, President of the House of Peers (*Suda*) ;

COUNT NOBUAKI MAKINO, Lord Keeper of the Imperial Seals (*Yotsumoto*) ;

SEIHIN IKEDA, managing director of the Mitsui Bank (*Furuichi*) ;

BARON TAKUMA DAN, managing director of the Mitsui holding company (*Hishinuma and Kurusawa*) .

The band wanted to bring the list up to twenty. It was agreed to add a few more bankers and capitalists deemed ready for sacrifice, but as nobody knew who should be chosen the extra names were not put down. In the end the Blood Brotherhood's only victims were Finance Minister Inouye and Baron

Dan. The murderers were two of the priest's youngest followers. Thirteen of the Blood Brothers were afterwards tried for
murder and attempted murder. Seven were students; Priest
Nissho, four of his boys, and the teacher were the others. A
fourteenth prisoner was in the dock beside them but he does
not concern us as his only offense was that of harboring a fugitive from justice.

The priest gave no sign of intellectual capacity at his trial.
He told the judge: " I cannot understand what led me on.
I believe something welled up in my spirit compelling me to
do it. The Manchurian issue also had an effect on me. I felt
it was necessary to obtain co-operation with the military and
naval men. The desired co-operation having been obtained
and myself appointed leader, I planned a wholesale killing on
February 11, 1932 by shooting."

JUDGE: " What do you think now about the assassination
plot? "

NISSHO (*drooping his head*) : " There is nothing to think
about it. I have firm confidence that our reasons were good.
I will strive for social reforms as long as I live."

JUDGE: " What methods would you now adopt and what
reforms are you thinking of? "

NISSHO: " I am not thinking about the building of the state.
However, party politics in Japan are politics of the privileged
classes. In Germany politics of the right wing are politics of
the gods. Party politics should be corrected, and the Emperor
should give the final word. . . . I am thinking about the
future society but I am not learned and cannot decide such
important matters alone."

Tadashi Konuma, the youth of twenty-two who killed the
Finance Minister, orated in court for three days. He had a
natural gift of eloquence and the trial gave him an oppor-

tunity for expressing his soul to which his whole repressed nature responded. He had been employed by a baker in Tokyo until "oppression by the gas company," whose bills were unpaid, forced the baker out of business. Konuma went back to his native town and, under Nissho's spell, realized that his unemployment was due to the corruption of society. He dreamed of escaping from his lot by becoming a priest like Nissho and he received instruction in the doctrines of Nichiren, which combined a furious nationalism with the teachings of Buddha. "Nichiren taught that Japan is the greatest country in the world and will eventually conquer the world."

He quoted a poem by Nissho: " ' Dew taken up in the palm of the hand fades away in the summer morning.' Revolution is the morning dew; what matter if we perish? Buddhism is sensitiveness to nature. The privileged classes have no sensitiveness to nature and caused me to wish for a revolution."

Through the brawl at the Mayor's dance Konuma met the naval officers. He afterwards left the temple and went to Tokyo with four comrades. They called themselves the " Five Men Company " and attached themselves to the Japan National Party, a private patriotic society run by its president, a priest who was skilled in raising funds. Konuma named him " the reverend exploiter " and they lived on him for a time. Then, Nissho having come to town with funds supplied to the naval officers by Dr. Okawa, he joined the Blood Brotherhood and was assigned to kill the Finance Minister.

The slayer of Baron Dan was merely a killer. Nissho gave him a Browning pistol and 60 yen ($30). He went to the seaside and practiced with the pistol. Having acquired proficiency he requested instructions, received them, and killed Baron Dan according to orders.

The school teacher who became Nissho's second-in-command told how he had heard that a great man was preaching at the local temple. He took two months' mental training with the priest, gave up teaching, and followed Nissho to Tokyo. He did no work and spent his time planning conspiracies and making contacts with students. When the police were hunting for him he was sheltered in the homes of army and navy officers.

The student who was assigned to murder Prince Tokugawa had an original motive which he offered with complete seriousness. He pointed out that the Prince's ancestors had usurped the administrative power for two centuries and a half and declared that though the Tokugawas had freely restored power to the Emperor at the Restoration, the previous " act of disloyalty " had not yet been atoned for. That kind of sentiment draws a cheer from the gallery when uttered on the stage or in a court of law, but as a justification for the murder of an eminent citizen unconnected with politics or finance it smells of the madhouse. But the student, like Hamlet, was mad only when the wind was north-northwest. He went to a football match in a field next the Prince's home and did nothing further. The man who undertook to kill Prince Saionji spent two weeks looking over the Prince's garden wall but never saw his intended victim. Only two of the thirteen carried out their mission, two of the priest's village boys, aged twenty-one and twenty-two respectively.

Chapter V

A TOLSTOYAN AMONG THE TERRORISTS

Kosaburo Tachibana was haunted by dreams in his boy-hood and could not decide whether to become a statesman or a general or (sometimes) simply a good man. He had been born in the prefecture which afterwards became the site of the naval air training base and the home of the Blood Brother-hood, and his birthplace fixed his destiny.

His father was a dyer in the country town of Mito and had other sons to educate, but Kosaburo was the favorite and the brainy one and he was sent to high school. Like many Japa-nese of the period he turned his eyes left politically in his youth, but communism was unknown to him in his quiet country town and Robert Owen and Henry George were his guides. Something deep in his nature drew him to the land and the simple men who worked on it. Tolstoy was then a living prophet; young Tachibana, country-born and bred, responded with heart and soul to the message of the nobleman who wore a mujik's blouse and proclaimed the nobility of the peasant's life. When a breakdown of health ended his high-school career, Tachibana worked on the land and had sufficient persuasive power to induce his parents and his brothers and sisters — five households comprising thirty persons — to pool their holdings and start a model village on communal lines on the outskirts of Mito. The little community held together and prospered on twelve acres of land and became locally famous. Tachibana lectured enthusiastically and wrote well. In 1930 his admirers enabled him to establish a school. He called it the Native-Land-Loving School (Aikyojuku).

Everybody in Japan with a message to deliver or an axe to grind opens a school. It is the traditional method of raising supporters. The rebel Great Saigo, already mentioned, prepared for his rebellion by establishing a School of Military Arts. Every patriotic society of any pretensions runs a school. The Genyosha, parent society of the once notorious Black Dragon, sprang from such a school, which in its time had the honor of educating Koki Hirota, afterwards Foreign Minister and Prime Minister. Those schools in the hands of the patriotic societies are at once a method of training young men for strong-arm work and a plausible excuse for extorting contributions from the rich and timid.

The Native-Land-Loving School taught mathematics, national history (with a bias), bookkeeping and agricultural management, simple engineering, the use of concrete, and so on. The senior-division students were instructed in economic history, sociology, and the theory of co-operation. Anyone over eighteen was eligible provided he accepted the Native-Land-Loving Way (or creed) and promised to work for the reconstruction of Japan on the basis of the life of the soil, the life in which, as Tachibana taught, they came near to God because they lived in harmony with nature and nature's law of mutual help.

The steps by which this innocent seminary became the ally

of the Blood Brotherhood are not different except in their setting from those which in other times and places have led fanaticism to the Inquisition, the guillotine, and the Red and White Terrors. But the setting was purely Japanese. The school was in Mito and the men of Mito have a tradition of political violence. It was a gang of Mito men whose assassination of the Regent at the gate of the Palace in Tokyo in 1860 heralded the restoration-revolution. A patriotic school in Mito taught the doctrines of the 1868 restoration, but the fighting was done by the warlike clans of Choshu and Satsuma, and Mito was deprived of the spoils. It was easy for present-day Mito youths to believe that a second restoration was needed, and the depression in which the farmers were plunged sharpened their rebellious discontent.

Some eighty per cent of the Japanese conscripts come from the rural areas and therefore farming discontent acts directly on the army. Tachibana was a spokesman of peasant unrest, and army officers became interested in his views. The army itself was being permeated with the ideas of a national socialist called Ikki Kita. The idea of a combination of soldiers and farmers against the capitalists and the politicians was in the air. Tachibana delivered a course of lectures to officers at the air training school. They gave form and coherence to the idea of a second restoration that was then fermenting in the minds of all the discontented.

Tachibana said the war of 1914–18 had revealed the collapse of Western civilization. We must return to nationalism, he said, and reorganize Japan on the principle of a national social planned economy, designed for a complete national society. Marxism offers no remedy; Marx contemplated an industrialized state, whereas Japan is a state of small independent farmers. Modern Japan made the mistake of copying England, which became rich by industry though she sacrificed her farmers; but Japan is a nation of farmers whom capitalism, with its gold prices and drain of profits to the cities, is destroying.

It was easy enough to dilate on the troubles of the times but when it came to remedies the ex-apostle of Tolstoy hitched his wagon to a will-o'-the-wisp. Japan, he said, must sweep away her individualistic industrial civilization and become again a nation of independent self-supporting farmers. Foreign expansion and domestic reformation must go hand in hand. The bandits in Manchuria mattered little; it was America and the League of Nations that Japan must defeat. Many people, said Tachibana, doubt if Japan has the power to do that. " But consider the matter calmly. Japan is a debtor nation, yet Tokyo and the cities grow larger year by year. Where does their strength come from? It is clear that if the villages were released from the burden of sustaining the cities the national power of Japan would increase. At a stroke we could exclude the influence of America from the Pacific, liberate China from the yoke of the war lords, set India free, and enable Germany to rise again."

Industries and banks were to be nationalized and farm co-operatives developed into a " great organization of mutual aid." The nation was to be released from a corrupt parliament, the tool of the plutocrats. But neither communist nor fascist dictatorships would be admitted. " We need a representative organization based on self-governing co-operative municipalities. Decentralization is all-important." The present system of education should be replaced by self-governing seminaries on the principles of Pestalozzi. Tachibana excused himself from speaking about national defense on the ground that his hearers were experts. But he added that the strength of an army did not depend on technique alone. A combination of soldiers and farmers would be irresistible.

Connection was established between Tachibana and the young officers by means of his lectures. The rural prophet was flattered and his students were excited. A soft man who becomes a leader at a time of revolution is an amateur sailor who has taken his cockleshell out in a gale. Violence was orthodoxy in the circles where Tachibana's teachings had led him. His Tolstoyism was only skin-deep; he could not repudiate what his disciples believed. He lent the weight of his reputation and influence to the conspiracy. It does not appear that he joined the Blood Brotherhood, but he knew all about it, and he was present at the meetings at which plans for the rising (as they called it) were discussed. He did not shirk personal responsibility. When Koga was organizing his bloody Sunday, he asked for helpers from the Native-Land-Loving School. Tachibana allowed his students to join, and he joined himself. He regarded himself as a leader of the farmers of Japan and it was to be a soldiers' and farmers' revolution.

The priest and his tough followers had undertaken the murders which preceded the main outbreak. The officers assigned themselves to kill the Prime Minister and bomb the police headquarters. Tachibana's students were given the task of raiding the power stations and throwing the capital into darkness. Some of the conspirators thought martial law would be proclaimed and the army would then have the game in its hands. It has already been told how their comrades of the Tokyo garrison hastened to the War Office that night and pressed the War Minister to act. Others only hoped to arouse the nation by ringing a loud alarm bell. It was necessary that something resembling a popular uprising should follow the too hackneyed crime of killing a Prime Minister, so the farmer youths were brought in to attack the capital and throw it into darkness and confusion.

Tachibana came to Tokyo with nineteen followers. He did not play any active part and he left the plans to his chief assistant, a man of forty named Hayashi. Hayashi organized eight squads. Six were told off to destroy the electric-light plants with grenades; one student was sent to blow up the Mitsubishi Bank and another was given the unpleasant task of killing Reserve Lieutenant Zei Nishida, a fellow thinker whom the young officers suspected of being an informer.

The last-named assignment was the only one that was efficiently carried out. A youth of twenty-one, armed with a pistol, called at Nishida's house, was at once admitted, and, without beating about the bush, drew his gun and shot his man. Nishida was seriously wounded but he lived to share in other plots. At the trial his character was cleared by the judge, who observed that though the officers thought him a police spy he had merely tried to dissuade them from their reckless enterprise. He probably had relations with the gendarmerie but he did not reveal the plot to kill the Prime Minister. The student who was to blow up the bank hurled his bomb, broke a few panes of glass, and scurried off.

The squads sent to the power stations consisted of two or three men each. Only one man showed any determination; when his bomb failed to explode he smashed a switchboard with a hammer and temporarily checked the supply of light to one of the slum wards of Tokyo. At three stations the grenades inflicted only slight damage on the cooling system; at another the youth was seized before he threw his missile. The raid failed because there were not enough men, they were not properly led, they had not enough explosives, and some of them had not enough energy. The naval officers and the army cadets had arranged to surrender to the military police, but the civilians dispersed into hiding-places. They were traced without difficulty and arrested within a few days.

Tachibana fled to Manchuria, not for safety, as he explained, but to write a book. In his own good time he surrendered and was brought back to Tokyo by an obsequiously polite escort of military police. When questioned at the military police headquarters after his arrest he said:

" I was unable to refuse the wishes of the students at my school. Personally, I rather was dragged into the affair, but, at the same time, social conditions were such that the plot and the affair were inevitable. You officials of the law may say that our actions have availed nothing, but for my part I think that they at least indicated sincerity and the best of motives."

When he was tried with the others, Tachibana harangued the court for six days. His demeanor was dignified, as if he felt that society was on trial and he in the role of prosecuting prophet. His eloquence sometimes swept him away and he forgot to wipe the perspiration that poured from his face, but he was calm when he discussed co-operation, electric power, and farmers' debts. He thanked the court in flowing phrases for the privilege of showing that the prisoners had been moved by " fervor for the redemption of the people " and thanked his sympathizers outside for the petitions that they had sent in. Then he spread his scroll on the table and began his indictment of society. Hardly a reference was made to the crimes for which the prisoners were indicted. These were referred to as if they had been a case of spontaneous combustion. The prisoners were so carried away by the opportunity of addressing the nation that their own plight hardly entered into their arguments.

Tachibana began with his boyhood. He told of his dreams of becoming a general or a cabinet minister, but said as he grew towards adolescence he began to wonder whether it was better to be a great man like Napoleon or a liberator of the downtrodden masses. As he thought on the religious talks of his grandfather and grandmother he resolved to be a man of great character. Sometimes he was absorbed in his literary efforts and sometimes he was just a roughneck. He flunked his middle-school examination, but tried again and finally passed " out of the sheer desire to reciprocate my mother's love."

A youth who passes the middle school is usually preparing for an occupation which will not soil his hands. Tachibana, however, had fixed his heart on farm life: " There is no fake about the farmers. When man and wife, young and old, toil together, there is nothing but contentment and gratitude."

He told how he founded the Native-Land-Loving School to train men for farm work. Young men left school hating farm work because, he suggested, their education made them desire white-collar jobs. His object was to teach the pupils how to run a small farm for the living of a man and his family independent of outside help.

" What do you mean by your ' back-to-the-land principle'? " asked the judge.

" Heaven and earth — nature. The nation must stand on the basis of farming villages. Land must be the foundation of the country."

His defense of the May 15 plot was a charge that society was corrupt and the higher classes were the most corrupted. " Producing rice for the nation, the farmers were unable to obtain food for themselves. Eighty per cent of the soldiers are farmers. The politicians and financiers have strayed from the spirit of patriotic brotherhood which is the fundamental characteristic of our nation. I felt the need of awakening them and we acted with that motive.

" It is necessary to get rid of capitalism in the interests of peace, and the people should oppose capitalism. The defense of Asia must be perfected.

" The Japanese people must prepare for the day when all the men on the farms will go to the front to fight and the women will take the place of the men.

" It is no exaggeration to say that today there is not one true farmer left in Japan. The younger generation flock to the cities, and the farmers have become like merchants.

" And what a rotten educational system! Marathon runners and home-run champions don't make good farmers. Teachers are sodden with the weaknesses of civilization. They make farmers' children dance to imported tunes about foreign dolls.

" Commercialism is destined to decline. It must be replaced by Kodo, the Imperial Way of Asia, the only principle that will save the world.

" Inouye [the Finance Minister who had been murdered] threw to the winds 120,000,000 yen defending the gold standard. Two thirds of the country teachers in my district went unpaid as the result of Inouye's policy. I examined the lunch boxes of one hundred schoolchildren. Nine of them had a few salted plums buried in rice, and that was their whole lunch.

" The farmers were in a state of slavery and neither of the political parties helped them. At this moment the young officers stretched out a hand to us to stand up for better conditions." But he explained that he had joined the conspiracy because if the revolution was left to the soldiers the result

71

would be a military dictatorship. The farmers had to work out their own salvation.

" The Japanese race is superior to all others as is proved by our unbroken Imperial line.

" The Emperor is the nucleus of the Japanese nation, and the people can exist only under Imperial rule. Marxism and communism are worlds apart from the fundamental basis of the Japanese Empire."

Tachibana and the student who shot Nishida were sentenced to life imprisonment, Dr. Okawa and three others to fifteen years; the others received sentences ranging from seven to twelve years. Before the end of 1940 all had been released except Tachibana.

Punishment was no deterrent in the conditions which then existed in Japan. One of the men sentenced to ten years' imprisonment and liberated four years later was Kenichiro Honma, described as principal of a patriotic school. His after career is instructive. When he went to prison the Manchurian incident was well on its successful way; when he left prison the China affair had begun; the war party had won, the nation was being mobilized, patriotism was in flood tide, and the fighting services were enjoying the highest pitch of activity and power they had known. There seemed to be little left for civilian patriots to do except work in the munition factories.

Honma's patriotism was of another stripe. He started a new society and acquired a number of followers and some funds. Britain was at the time the Japanese army's scapegoat for its two years of fruitless warfare in China. Britain, drawing near to war with Germany, was helpless in the Far East and the Japanese garrison in North China was gaining great " face " by its blockade of the British concession and its rough treatment of British men and women in Tientsin. It is possible that the government in Tokyo did not entirely approve of the army's methods and eventually the British Ambassador arranged a conference in Tokyo at which he was able to have the blockade called off in return for a temporary closing of the Burma Road and some local financial and policing concessions in Tientsin.

The army in China was dissatisfied with the negotiations in Tokyo and Honma saw an opportunity for direct action against the "pro-British" statesmen in Japan. His society planned to murder "a certain important statesman close to the throne" (the name was not divulged, but there were indications that Tsuneo Matsudaira, former Ambassador to Washington and London, was meant). He was to be bombed as his automobile was on its way to his office in the Imperial Palace. With funds provided by Honma, dynamite was bought and placed in custody of a patriotic tailor. The janitor of a fashionable fruit store on the Ginza undertook to throw the bomb. He failed to identify the automobile of his prospective victim and the plan miscarried. Last year Honma and his accomplices were still in detention awaiting trial.

Chapter VI

THE YOUNG OFFICERS

The story of a disciplined army driven forward by its young officers is a strange one. Who are the young officers? Are they organized, and if so, how? How do they make their influence prevail? How has such a movement been allowed to grow inside the army?

The question leads into some dim recesses of Japanese racial psychology. Explanation is not easy nor can it be tendered with much confidence. A foreign observer in Japan begins at last to realize the Japanese attitude by a process of absorption. He recognizes it and learns to allow for it, but never quite understands it. A few trivial-looking anecdotes will illustrate the mental background.

At the annual grand maneuvers of the Japanese army a few years ago the foreign military attachés saw a lieutenant step up to the Minister for War, salute smartly, and begin a conversation on political questions. One foreign officer, who happened to be within earshot, had an instant vision of what might happen to a subaltern of his own service who attempted to pump the head of the army on politics, and he watched the scene with interest. But the Japanese lieutenant was not blasted from the sight of men. The general listened attentively and answered freely. An army in which a callow lieutenant can walk up to the Minister for War and engage him in a political discussion is different from other armies. The foreign officer was puzzled.

Some British naval officers were entertaining Japanese naval officers who had come aboard the flagship of the British Far Eastern squadron to pay a courtesy call on a new admiral. They were taken over the ship and shown the admiral's office. " And there's his desk all ready for work," said the cicerone, pointing to the admiral's pens and pencils and paper. The Japanese smiled. " Ah," said one, " it is different on our flagship. Our admiral does not need pencils and pads. We do all the work for him."

The difference between Japanese ways and ours often seems only a matter of a shade or two. Any admiral might ask his staff to work out the details of a problem; any statesman might ask his secretary to draft a speech. But in Japan the custom goes very far and sometimes it would be hard to say whether it is a case of assisting a chief or exercising a chief's authority. I have seen the President of the Upper House, when confronted with an important but not unexpected point of procedure sit silent until his official assistant had passed him a slip of paper telling him what to do. He did not need to be told, but he conceded his assistant's right to tell him. It was figurehead government in action. The Emperor, divine, all-powerful, but an automaton in the hands of his servants, is the supreme example of the system. It pervades the whole of the administrative machinery. The Japanese Foreign Minister has walked into a conference and read as his own a statement he had never seen before, and with which, as answers to questions subsequently showed, he did not agree.

I have known the Navy Minister's own words, given to a

correspondent whom he had invited to his office for the purpose, to be suppressed by a subordinate whose action might have remained unknown if the correspondent, surprised by the absence of reaction, had not flashed an inquiry to his paper. An instance occurred in which a War Minister's utterances in parliament were repudiated by a staff officer who stated, on his own account, that the general had meant something else.

There was a notorious case in which two American airmen, Clyde Pangbourn and Hugh Herndon, purposing to fly the Pacific on a voyage round the world, were held up in Tokyo for six weeks on the fiat of a young official of the Communications Department. The Vice-Minister for Foreign Affairs went in person to beg for a lifting of the ban in view of the unfavorable impression the affair was making in the United States and received a lesson — very politely given, of course — on minding his own business. Only the signed and sealed order of the Minister of Communications could have moved that young official before he was ready. The Minister did not give the instruction nor did the Cabinet ask him to do so.

The young officer, or official, in Japan not only expects to do part of his chief's work, but thinks he has a right to do it. Just as his chief's authority is derived from the Emperor, so is his derived from his chief and up to a certain point he expects freedom to use it as he thinks best. Japanese officials are never told to exercise their discretion; on the contrary, when a new regulation is issued which the government desires to enforce strictly, the cabinet minister responsible issues an instruction that no deviation will be allowed without a special order bearing his own seal.

The Tokyo *Nichi-Nichi* once offered its readers a reasoned explanation of the power of the young officers. It said that in any organization the person who actually handles an affair has the right to a say regarding the methods to be adopted. It applied this rule to the army and declared " the officers of the middle stratum of the army, who directly attend to the disposal of concrete problems, have their own right of talking to their superiors.

" The great propelling force of a strong army," the journal continued, " emanates from its middle stratum. The actual central force of the Japanese army is found there. The question is whether the authorities are able to direct it into a proper channel."

The explanation is incomplete; the " middle stratum " of the army, the captains, majors, and colonels, deals with all kinds of concrete questions but not with high policy. The Japanese writer only restated the problem; he did not explain it. But his effort was true to national psychology. The custom of seniors depending on their assistants does give the juniors power. When the spread of revolutionary politics among the young officers became known, the generals lacked confidence in their own authority. They dealt with officers who were dabbling in conspiracy as if they were erring sons. Divisional commanders and officers in charge of garrisons were instructed to see that their young officers abstained from politics.

The orders were accompanied with a promise that the chiefs of the army would make the army's influence felt in national policy. The promise was kept and the old policies were one by one reversed. The naval-limitation agreements were scrapped; the Lytton Report was rejected and Japan left the League of Nations. China policy was turned over to the army. The statesmen gave the army its head, deeming aggression abroad a lesser evil than military revolution at home. A national mobilization law turned all the nations' resources above the most meager subsistence standard into preparations for the gigantic war Japan is now waging.

A novel practical step was taken to keep the chiefs informed of army opinion. An officer was appointed to each division with functions which might be described as those of a public-relations counsel inverted. He did not convey the views of the government to the officers; he faced the other way round and conveyed the " public opinion " of the officers to the War Office and the General Staff. It was a practical device and it reveals, with a national touch of topsyturvydom, the peculiar nature of the Japanese army.

The young-officer movement was not confined to the fanatical groups that joined hands with the patriotic murder societies and organized assassination and revolt. It permeated all the younger ranks of the army and navy and was expressed in an incessant political agitation. It would hardly be an exaggeration to say that between 1931 and 1936 more political meetings were being held in officers' quarters than in the rest of the country. At these gatherings demands were made and sentiments uttered which would have caused an ordinary public meeting to be abruptly closed by the policemen in attendance. The speakers would have been marched to the police station and cooled down by a night in the cells. The young officers were able to obtain the attention of their commanders for hours at a time. A few examples out of hundreds will show how political the services had become.

At the Yokosuka naval station near Yokohama thirty naval lieutenants and lieutenant-commanders called on the commander of the base and urged him to " work for a new cabinet." They condemned the appointment of Admiral Saito as Lord Keeper of the Seals to the Emperor and demanded the dismissal of the President of the Privy Council. The admiral did not order them back to their duties; he listened for three hours and a half and replied " in an abstract manner."

A little later " medium-ranking officers " at Shanghai held a meeting and demanded that the Japanese Ambassador cancel his projected visit to Nanking " because of the insincerity of the Chinese government."

Young naval officers at Yokosuka held another meeting at which resolutions were passed attacking their official chief, the Minister of the Navy, Admiral Osumi, for having said in the House that the naval-limitation agreement did not create a crisis for Japan, and for revealing " military secrets " (some details of the naval building program) in a secret session of the Diet.

These were relatively innocent intrusions into politics. Others less innocent were rigidly censored, and even in private conversation Japanese would only refer to them obliquely as " the October incident in the First Division," or " the March affair." Sedition in the army became a topic like a lady's lost virtue; there were hints and innuendoes but no one knew enough, or defied the consequences enough, to speak plainly. Besides being dangerous — for who knew what might come out if the gendarmerie gave a listener the third degree? — it was bad form, and no one is more the thrall of conventional good form than a Japanese gentleman. But when a formation of six planes belonging to the Ninth Division scattered leaflets over the countryside summoning the nation to awaken and defend its rights in Manchuria, the exploit could not be hidden.

A year after the flying officers' performance a manifesto signed " Officers' Group of the Imperial Army " was sent to hundreds of officers. It reviewed the outbreak of May 15 when the Prime Minister was murdered, and vehemently attacked Count Makino, the Emperor's closest adviser, and General Ugaki, a powerful moderate. The police claimed that premature publicity given to the manifesto enabled them to nip in the bud a flamboyant demonstration, to include murder, which the " Officers' Group of the Imperial Army " had planned to carry out under the Emperor's nose at the Grand Maneuvers a month later.

Military officers were accustomed to exercise their power in many fields. From masses of evidence a few examples are selected:

Junichi Fujioka, a publisher specializing in books on labor and socialism, announced that he would cease publishing such works and would devote himself to books promoting the spirit of nationalism. He stated that army leaders had persuaded him to make the change.

When rival seamen's unions discussed a merger, the commander of the Osaka garrison intimated that the army wanted two conditions to be carried out: first, that the amalgamated union should sever relations with the Social Mass Party and the Labor Union Conference because both these advocated democracy; and second, that it should dismiss the vice-president of the seamen's union, who had said that the Manchurian " incident " was an imperialist invasion.

The army issued a " goodwill warning " to cement-makers not to sell cement to the Soviet Union, which might use it to build fortifications along the Manchurian border.

When an American automobile factory leased land for an extension of its premises near Yokohama, an officer of the General Staff objected to the transaction on the ground that the automobile industry, being a vital element in national defense, should not be in the hands of foreigners. The Ministry

of Commerce obediently issued notice that it would intro-
duce legislation prohibiting foreign interests from owning
more than forty-nine per cent of the shares in such enterprises.

At military instigation an oil law was passed making it
obligatory on oil companies to store a perpetual reserve of
six months' supply in addition to the reserve normally needed
in their business.

A project for the establishment of a national news agency
(now known as Domei) was delayed until officers of the General Staff were satisfied.

The Department of Education was compelled to dismiss a
number of professors because they did not accept that interpretation of the Constitution which the army and navy
thought proper.

The army in China took the lead in all matters of policy
concerning China and there is evidence that this was done
with the consent or submission of the Tokyo Cabinet. The
most striking example was the reception given to the British
Cabinet's proposals for financial assistance to China at the
time that the drain of silver was threatening the monetary
system of that country with complete collapse. The British
government did not desire to ignore Japan's interest in China,
and its financial adviser, Sir Frederick Leith Ross, was sent
to Japan to explain the plan and ask for Japanese co-operation. He brought a letter to the Emperor and he stayed in
Tokyo for some weeks discussing the plan with Japanese government, financial, and military leaders. No opinion was expressed by the Cabinet or the Foreign Office, but when Leith
Ross went to China the Japanese military attaché at Shanghai,
Major General Rensuke Isogai, issued a statement denouncing the plan as one intended to " exploit the blood and sweat
of the Chinese people " and bring them " under a protector-

ate of British capital." Such a situation, he said, could not be tolerated by Japan. The War Office in Tokyo issued a statement repeating those views and the Foreign Office followed suit. The Chinese went ahead with the plan the British recommended and it succeeded.

When the Japanese Legation in Peking was raised to Embassy status the China section of the General Staff objected on the ground that they had been promised that no important decisions would be made regarding China without consulting them. Mr. Shigemitsu, Vice-Minister of Foreign Affairs, replied that the change concerned the Foreign Office only and did not call for consultation with the army. The War Minister, who had approved the change, did not know of the alleged promise. The China section agreed to overlook the affair but said it must not happen again.

In 1935 officers of the army in China demanded that China carry out the terms of the Tangku truce. From this demand the North China " incident " of 1935 began. The officers said that the truce was a military matter and they did not need to consult the government regarding it. The interpretation of the armistice clearly involved delicate national policies. The staff in China had spent a month collecting data for the demands they made; they had plenty of time to consult Tokyo but did not do so.

Army control of policy functioned openly in China while it was still camouflaged in Japan by a façade of Cabinet supremacy. And even in Japan, while business men deprecated army interference in civilian affairs, they accepted it. Defense was the army's prerogative and the army was the judge of what concerned defense. A few editors, commentators, politicians, and business men occasionally criticized specific instances of military interference when these seemed to go too far or when they clashed with established interests, but no one questioned the right of the soldiers to butt into any matter provided they hooked up their action with defense. The boundaries of defense expanded every year. It was just as natural in Japan that the army should poke a finger into all kinds of questions as that the majority party in an American state should choose the local office-holders. The young officers were the active militant members of a party permanently in power.

Chapter VII

THE IDEA–MONGERS

The philosophers, the idea-mongers, of the movement were Ikki Kita and Seikyo Gondo. They were not a team; they may not even have known each other; they are brought together because their teachings furnished the movement with its thin coating of political idealism. Kita was young and Gondo old. Their philosophies had been taken down from different trees in the European forest. Gondo was a library follower of Prince Peter Kropotkin, the old Czarist exile on whose gentle books the dust now lies thick. Kita's spiritual father was Marx, and his creed a mixture of communism and nationalism. Both were borrowers but more than mere copyists; they understood their Japan and knew how to adapt imported ideas to the Japanese situation.

Ikki Kita was the first Japanese nationalist who found a way to combine socialism with imperialism. He is sometimes given credit for having converted the Japanese army to national socialism. It is an exaggerated award; the army was driven to national socialism by the needs of its insatiable ambition, but Kita's propaganda had great influence among the young officers of twenty years ago who are the generals of today.

When he first appears on the stage, Kita was in Shanghai,

84

"helping the Chinese revolutionaries" — in other words, stirring up trouble in China — and he had some underhand connection with the Japanese army. The Black Dragon Society was at that time thrusting its assistance on Sun Yat-sen, and Kita was one of its emissaries. His real name was Kazuteru Kita, but he had taken "Ikki" as his pen name. Whether he entered the stage from the right or the left wing is uncertain, but by 1919 he was known as both a nationalist and a socialist.

Dr. Shumei Okawa, a noted promoter of patriotic societies, concluding that old-style nationalism had lost its pull, had left the Black Dragon Society and founded a new patriotic organization with a red tinge which he called the Yusonsha. He went over to Shanghai and persuaded Kita to write the book which subsequently became notorious — *A Reconstruction Program for Japan.* It quickly obtained a vogue among the restless young officers of the Japanese army.

One year later the police prohibited the *Program* and thereby increased the desire of people to read it, with the result that it was mimeographed for surreptitious circulation. It was something new in patriotic literature and was much talked of in both the red and the white camps. Japanese labor was becoming self-conscious and its advance guards were dividing into two streams, one following the British trade unions towards social democracy, the other attracted and assisted by Moscow. It was the age of the "Marx boys" at the universities, and of inflated scares about the Japan Communist Party.

Kita's *Reconstruction Program* brought socialism and Japanese imperialism under one umbrella. His opening sentence was: "The maker of a reconstruction program for Japan must be the builder of a great revolutionary empire." He declared that Japan faced an unprecedented crisis, a statement which commanded the assent of all the discontented, the red, the white, and the merely blue. " The life of the people is unsettled," he wrote. " The Japanese are following the destructive examples of the Western nations. The possessors of financial, political, and military power are striving to maintain their unjust interests under cover of the Imperial power. We should bring about a great combination of the nation to ask the Emperor to use his Imperial power and complete the basis of reconstruction with the Emperor at the head of the nation.

" Seven hundred million brethren in India and China cannot gain their independence without our protection and leadership.

" History in East and West has been a record of the unification of feudal states after the age of civil wars. The only possible international peace which will come after the present age of international wars must be a feudal peace obtained by the emergence of the strongest country, which will dominate all other countries of the world."

Kita proposed revision of the Constitution and " removal of the barriers between nation and Emperor." This meant the abolition of Parliament, which, in the theory of the discontented, was standing between the people and their sovereign. The Cabinet was to be replaced by a " conference of patriots." The vote was to be conferred on heads of registered families, and a national consultative soviet established with soldiers and reservists as leaders. Private property was to be restricted and no individual allowed to accumulate more than 1,000,000 yen ($500,000). Important industries were to be nationalized. Dictatorship was upheld. As for the woman question: " Women shall be faithful wives, modest and virtuous, cultivating the ancient Japanese arts of flower arrangement and the tea ceremony."

Kita's *Program* was summarized as follows:

Affirmation of the right of revolution and the *coup d'état* as used by Napoleon and Lenin.

Denial of parliamentarism, the source of many abuses by political parties.

Affirmation of dictatorship, as it is an Oriental custom that the masses should be ruled by the wise.

The Emperor shall be the representative of the nation.

The vote shall be restricted to the heads of houses, as the family system is a most important traditional organ.

Restriction of private property. Fortunes in excess of 1,000,-000 yen ($500,000) shall be confiscated. Enterprises with over 10,000,000 yen capital shall be nationalized. Important industries shall be nationalized.

Political criticism shall not be allowed. Opposition shall be strictly suppressed.

Representatives of the reservists shall form a national conference in place of the Imperial Diet, but it shall be only a consultative organ.

Koreans shall receive the vote in ten years and independence in twenty years.

Feeble and imitative as it seems, Kita's book had great influence. It circulated surreptitiously in every officers' mess; it was one of the books given by Fuji to his converts; it split the rising labor party into democratic and nationalist factions. Many of Kita's ideas are in operation in Japan today; the leading industries are state-controlled; the government is a military dictatorship; fierce efforts are being made to confer new masters on the " seven hundred million brethren " of

Asia. The political parties have been dissolved and a " National Co-operation Council " has been formed with functions similar to those of the Fascist Grand Council — " to convey the desires of those below to those above, and the instructions of those above to those below." It has been proposed that the right to vote should be conferred only on reservists and heads of families. Kita was not imitating the Nazis; his book was written in 1919 and first circulated in 1920.

The Yusonsha patriotic society was dissolved in 1923 when Okawa and Kita parted company, but the influence of the book remained for many years. When Lieutenant Colonel Aizawa was arrested for the murder of Major General Nagata in 1935, four copies were found among his papers.

Seikyo Gondo, the other ideologist, preached a peasant empire. The farmers of Japan were at the time suffering from a severe depression, and the idea of a soldiers' and farmers' movement, suggested by the soldiers' and workers' movement in Russia, was buzzing in the brains of the young officers.

Gondo was a man of sixty-five. He owned some property and lived in a suburb of Tokyo, cultivating his garden, going fishing, and writing books. His past wore an engaging air of mystery. He had been a journalist, a mining man, a stock farmer, and in his youth had made himself useful to the army at the annexation of Korea. Such figures are not uncommon in Tokyo, and no one is so impolite as to inquire into the source of the comfort in which they live. Patriotism, like politics, has its secrets. When the Queen of Korea was murdered by order of Viscount Miura, the Japanese envoy accredited to her court, the instruments employed were members of Japanese patriotic societies and they were given facilities by the Japanese army. More than one Japanese owed his start in a public career to services rendered to the army in Korea, services which were modestly left undescribed.

Gondo called his doctrine " communalism." It was a Japanized version of philosophic anarchism. He applied some of Kropotkin's ideas to Japanese history and produced another of the borrowed philosophies which the Japanese easily persuade themselves are their own. What Kropotkin called anarchism Gondo called village self-government; Kropotkin's mutual aid became natural assistance in a village community.

The abolition of central government and its machinery was a leading idea with both. Being a Japanese, Gondo retained the Emperor, but he devised a theory of the Imperial origins and functions which caused the first chapter of his first edition to be almost entirely suppressed. He treated the history-book statement that the first Emperor was the descendant of the Sun Goddess as a myth. He described the first Emperor's conquests as the triumphs of a chief leading his tribe into new lands. He argued that evolution was the law of nature and that Japan's emperors had always helped on " the changes ordained by Heaven " — for example, the Emperor Meiji in becoming the figurehead of the revolution of 1868.

The two pillars of his doctrine were, first, that it is the Emperor's function to assist the evolution of the nation and, second, that the productive mass of peasants is the foundation of the state and that production should be so regulated that security and equality are assured to the mass. He was against central government, against bureaucrats, against money, against big cities, and he found plenty of illustrative matter in pictures of the Japanese farmer toiling from dawn to dusk to pay the interest on his mortgages. Money was the root of all evil, said Gondo. Formerly the people in the villages met all their needs with village products, but now they have to sell their produce to get money, and the farmer's life has been completely destroyed by fluctuation of prices and consequent exploitation and insecurity.

He held that the growth of cities had sucked the lifeblood out of the countryside. He saw no need for any state authority; Japan should be a nation of self-governing villages with the Emperor at its head. Every village adult was to have a vote in the election of a communal council which would regulate wages, housing, the distribution of food, and the marketing of produce. Rich villages were not to compete with poor villages, but to assist them.

" A village where a very rich farmer resides cannot be called happy when the other farmers are comparatively poor. Land is the gift of nature like air and water. Farm land should be the common property of the village, but the landlord should be repaid its cost price. It is unnatural that landlords should have the right to sell crops without the approval of the other farmers."

There is nothing specially dynamic in such ideas, and Gondo might have remained in obscurity if the young officers had not been interested. His argument that the restoration had taken the wrong track when it introduced capitalism, landownership, and bureaucratic government and that Japan needed a second restoration-revolution was grist to their mill and he was invited to give a course of lectures which the officers attended.

Their minds were open and Gondo was flattered to find such influential converts. The conspirators held meetings in his house, and he gave them an empty house in which they stored weapons and sheltered the young killers. His ideas bore fruit which he had not foreseen when he spent interesting hours adapting Kropotkin's ideas for Japanese use.

Leaflets scattered by some of the young officers on May 15 advocated a dictatorship of soldiers and peasants. From Gondo's Communalists' League another body called the Farmers' Conference for Self-Government was developed. It spread in the farming districts around Tokyo. Priest Nissho's young men associated themselves with it, and its members entered the conspiracy. They were not tillers of the soil, but wastrels and thugs and professional agitators from other patriotic gangs. Threads from this movement, the Native-Land-Loving School, Priest Nissho's group, and the army and navy were woven into the plot of May 15.

II. *The Army*

Chapter VIII

MURDER IN THE WAR OFFICE

Lieutenant Colonel Sabura Aizawa, who had come from his provincial barracks in obedience to " an impulse from on high," as he afterwards told the court, drove up to the back entrance of the War Office in Tokyo at half past nine on the morning of August 12, 1935.

The War Office is a dilapidated and untidy old building, two stories high. No government office in Japan was less formal in its ways. Callers walked in by the back door, which they often imagined to be the principal entrance. The doorkeepers were decayed pensioners who spent their time squatting around the charcoal brazier, making tea and smoking Golden Bat cigarettes — two and a half cents for ten. The China war changed the old ways, but at the time of this narrative nobody bothered about visitors who seemed to know where they were going. They crossed the faded courts on stepping-stones, the relics of old gardens, and rambled along the verandas till they found the room they were seeking. It would have been easy for anyone to go in and commit a murder; for an officer in uniform with the stars of a lieutenant colonel on his shoulder, it was ridiculously simple.

Aizawa asked to be shown the room of Major General Shigeatsu Yamaoka, Director of the Military Equipment Bureau, with whom he had no business but who had been Commandant of the Military College while Aizawa was a student and whose name he suddenly thought he would give. While they sat chatting, a passing messenger boy was sent to see if Major General Tetsuzan Nagata, Chief of the Military Affairs Bureau, was in his room.

Nagata had more power in the War Office than anyone except the Minister himself. A purge had been going on among officers connected with the Showa Restoration movement. Several of Aizawa's friends had been dismissed from the service. The August transfers, promotions, and appointments, for which Nagata was responsible, were designed to disperse and discourage the revolutionary faction. General Jinsaburo Mazaki, Inspector General of Military Training, and, by virtue of that post, one of the triumvirate which rules the Japanese army, had opposed the purge and been dismissed. The young officers regarded Mazaki as their leader; his dismissal, for which they blamed Nagata, had shown that none were safe. The Showa Restoration movement, which was to be a kind of national socialist revolution, seemed in danger of being aborted.

While the messenger boy went to see if Nagata was in his office, Aizawa and his old commandant had a peculiar conversation. Major General Yamaoka pressed Aizawa to tell him why he wanted to see Nagata. Yamaoka knew Aizawa's views and knew that three weeks earlier he had come to Tokyo to threaten Nagata, but had changed his mind and gone back to his barracks. Aizawa answered in riddles which Yamaoka could read. He said the situation in the country was grave and trusted that Yamaoka would do his best to cope with it. Yamaoka advised him not to force himself on Nagata and thereby make more trouble. Just then the boy returned to say that the Director of the Military Affairs Bureau was in his office.

Aizawa went in without being announced. Nagata was sitting at a table talking with two officers and did not look up. Aizawa drew his sword. Nagata saw him with the tail of his eye and rose. Aizawa lunged but missed. A second thrust reached Nagata and wounded him slightly. He turned to a door leading to the next room and Aizawa ran him through from the back. As he leaned on the table, Aizawa rushed round and brought him down with two savage cuts on the neck. One of the two officers who were with Nagata attempted to protect his chief and was severely wounded, but Aizawa had no recollection of striking him.

" Then someone called my name," he told the court martial. It was like the knocking on the door in *Macbeth*. A spell was broken. Aizawa walked out of the room and returned to Yamaoka, his old commandant, and told him he had executed Heaven's judgment. His finger was bleeding and he was taken to the medical department to have it bound up. In the corridor he met a party carrying a stretcher from which blood was dripping. " I then remembered," he told the judge, " that I had failed to dispatch Nagata with one stroke of my sword, and as a fencing instructor I was ashamed."

A strange silence covered the actions of the other officer, and a report that he had afterwards committed suicide was hushed up. It would not have been nice for the public to think that an officer of the Imperial army had stood gaping while his chief was murdered.

Aizawa had just been transferred to a regiment stationed in Formosa. He had left his cap in Nagata's room and wanted to go back for it in order that he might leave for his post. A plain-clothes gendarme who had taken him into custody refused to fetch his cap or to stop at the Military Club, where he might buy one. Aizawa thought he would be put through a brief examination by the gendarmerie (military police) and then he would go to Formosa. This confidence faded after he had been in a military prison for several days under examination. He then thought that he would not be brought to trial but secretly killed by the gendarmerie.

It might have been better if the higher authorities had used Oriental methods. They were too civilized, or too shaken by this fresh revelation of the furious passions that were boiling up in the army, and they followed routine.

The first step was posthumous promotion, a method of showing that the murdered man had deserved well of the Emperor. Nagata died at eleven thirty, two hours after the attack, but the official announcement said he died at four. The delay was invented in order that he might be promoted Lieutenant General. The Emperor promoted him on receiving a request from the Prime Minister, the War Minister and the Minister of the Imperial Household. The detail is interesting for the glimpse it gives of the Palace mechanism. The War Minister was the proper person to make a formal request for promotion. It was not necessary that he should have the support of the Prime Minister. The Household Minister, ex-Ambassador Tsuneo Matsudaira, had nothing to do with military changes. He was one of the politically irremovable officials who assist the Emperor, and he was there as one of the " statesmen close to the throne " of whom much was to be heard before the trial ended. Thus did those high statesmen encourage each other and divide responsibility.

The preliminary examination of the murderer was conducted by military procurators. They presented their report, a thousand pages long, on November 2, and on that date

Aizawa was charged with the crime of murder under the civil code and with armed assault on a superior officer under the military code. The civil code had to be invoked because the military code had not anticipated that kind of murder. It dealt with armed assault by a soldier upon a superior officer and made a distinction between assault committed in front of an enemy and one committed in other circumstances. For an attack on a superior officer in the presence of the enemy the punishment is death or not less than ten years' imprisonment; for an assault in any other circumstances the penalty is imprisonment for any term between two years and life.

The trial began in the barracks of the First Division in Tokyo before a court martial of four judges: Major General Shozaburo Sato, two colonels, and one lieutenant colonel. The procurator of the First Division took charge of the prosecution. Lieutenant Colonel Sakichi Mitsui, an instructor in the Staff College, volunteered to defend Aizawa. Dr. Somei Uzawa, a prominent Tokyo lawyer and president of the Meiji University, was civilian counsel for the prisoner.

Aizawa was not a great man but he was an emblematic man. It is as a type of the young officers, declaiming their ideas before his judges with passionate sincerity, that he is noteworthy. His trial was a microscopic section of the revolutionary ideas then near to explosion point in the Japanese army.

The trial and the defense exhibited the arrogant mentality of the young officers and the perplexity of their superiors. Re-reading the prolix records, one is suspended between two doubts: either the court was sympathetic with the opinions of the killer and connived at his intention to use the trial as a loud-speaker or it feared to provoke an explosion by applying the ordinary rules of a formal tribunal. The latter was the correct interpretation; the presiding judge's supineness was the role the highest authorities had enjoined. If they hoped that they were providing a safety valve they were mistaken. Before the trial was over, a military rebellion broke out from the barracks where it was held.

Lieutenant Colonel Mitsui, volunteer counsel for the defense, would have been a formidable figure at the bar if he had chosen the black gown instead of the khaki coat. By leading the court into an examination of Aizawa's patriotic motives he was able to convert the trial into a platform from which the murderer and his advocate preached revolution. The presiding judge only interrupted him when matters arose which might be injurious to the prestige of the army. These were taken *in camera;* his attacks on the government, on the Emperor's advisers, on the " financial clique," and on the " military clique " (generals who disagreed with the young officers) were reported in many columns. When the procurator wanted to pin the business down to the charges in the indictment, Mitsui threatened the court with dire consequences if it tried the case as a common murder.

Aizawa accepted the report of the preliminary examination as to facts, thereby pleading guilty, and asked to be examined fully concerning his motives. This was permitted and the trial ranged far and wide over the corruptions of the Japanese government and the sins of statesmen and capitalists. Mitsui took the fight into the enemy's territory at the start, demanding a suspension of the trial until the omissions in the thousand-page record of the preliminary examination had been made good. He said that the accused had not been examined about social conditions, nor about " the disturbance in the army caused by statesmen close to the throne and financial circles." The court formally rejected the request, but the heads of the army decided to give the accused officer and his fiery soldier-counsel all the rope they wanted. Next morning the chief procurator invited Aizawa to explain his motives " to his heart's content."

In Japanese disputation, stock phrases, unimpeachable in sound and purposefully vague in meaning, are used to express and also to disguise the ideas under discussion. The parties, being Japanese, understand one another well enough; but the implications of those phrases must be explained if the foreign reader is to understand. The following account of the trial therefore includes a commentary intended to place the foreign reader as nearly as possible in the place of those who followed it in the vernacular.

Aizawa explained the " foundation of his mental outlook " as taught by his father: " Those born in Japan should return everything to the Emperor in times of emergency." " Returning everything to the Emperor " is a reference to the 1868 restoration when the feudal lords relinquished their fiefs. In its modern application, as Aizawa used it, it means that financiers and politicians are to surrender their powers to the Emperor, who will thereupon incorporate them in the new structure which the Showa Restoration is to establish. In other words, national socialism.

Then he made a declaration of faith which he often repeated: " The Emperor is the incarnation of the great god who made the universe. The Emperor is absolute; he has been so in the past, he is so now, and will be so in the future." In those phrases Aizawa declares that he acknowledges the Emperor's power alone. The statesmen who exercise power are intruders between the sovereign and his people, and he does not recognize any responsibility for obeying their orders. This thought characteristically is unfinished; it does not expect the Emperor to become an active executive ruler; it assumes that he will have new advisers who will carry out the policies of the young officers.

Aizawa was taken through an account of his political convictions: " The country was in a deplorable state, the farmers were impoverished, there were official scandals, diplomacy was weak, and the prerogative of the supreme command had been violated by the naval-limitation agreements. When I thought of these things I could not merely pass the time in giving gymnastic instructions. That was the motive of my interest in national reconstruction."

Aizawa told the judge he had held those opinions since 1916. The date is interesting. Japan had entered the First World War in virtue of her alliance with England. She had captured the German colony of Tsingtao on the coast of Shantung. Japanese warships were escorting Australian troops across the Pacific and a detachment of destroyers was assisting the British fleet in the Mediterranean. Those useful but not onerous services were rewarded by a flood of war prosperity and a secret treaty giving Japan the German islands in the Pacific, a prize of enormous potential value. Its ultimate effect was to change Japan's naval strategy from its originally defensive role to the aggressive role of today, in which those islands are of major importance.

The cause of the Allies nevertheless was unpopular; Britain and France in 1916 were far from victory and many Japanese were lamenting that the British alliance had brought them into the war on the weaker side. Japanese soldiers were dazzled by the German army, its strategic traditions, its iron efficiency, its position in society, and its power in the state. The thundering series of defeats which Foch, Haig, and Pershing were to inflict on Hindenburg and Ludendorff were still distant. After the war the suggestion that Germany's downfall was not due to military defeat but to civilian collapse was unhesitatingly accepted, and it was manifest to every Japanese officer that the sufferings of Germany were due to the injustices of Versailles instead of to the waste and losses of war.

Aizawa said that his convictions had drawn him into the circle of young officers who carried out the assassination plots of 1932. He had studied Ikki Kita's forbidden book, *A Reconstruction Program for Japan,* and four copies were found in his room, though the War Office had forbidden officers to read or possess it.

" What grievance had you against Major General Nagata? What had he done that you should kill him? " the procurator asked Aizawa.

The question made Aizawa uncomfortable and he shuffled. He said: " Instead of guiding the younger elements in the army he brought pressure to bear on them."

When he was asked to come down to cases the only instance of pressure Aizawa could remember was the dismissal of two young officers who had been circulating mimeographed criticism of the higher authorities.

Even in the revolutionary-club atmosphere of that court martial the charge was too trivial and Aizawa under further questioning accused Nagata of having " plotted with statesmen close to the throne " for the removal of General Mazaki from his post as Inspector General of Military Training.

As the trial rolled forward on floods of irrelevance, it became clear that this was the true motive. The murder was an act of vengeance and a threat.

Its background was a mild purge by which the government was endeavoring to break up the young officers' revolutionary movement. Disaffected officers were being placed on reserve or transferred to country and colonial garrisons, and safe men were being put in key posts. Nagata, as chief of the Military Affairs section of the War Office, planned and directed the changes. A strong-headed soldier of the old school, General Senjuro Hayashi, afterwards Prime Minister, had become War Minister to carry out the government's policy.

He was opposed by General Jinsaburo Mazaki, Inspector General of Military Training. Mazaki's position enabled him to exercise a veto. The Japanese army is controlled by three high officers: the Chief of the General Staff, the War Minister, and the Inspector General of Military Training. Changes and promotions are arranged by the War Office, but they must be approved by the triumvirate. The routine half-yearly shake-up was being used to effect the purge. Mazaki, a fellow traveler with the young officers, blocked every punitive change.

At this time the triumvirate was really a government of two. The Chief of the General Staff was Prince Kan-in, a soldier of modest abilities who had been installed in the highest post at a period when internal feuds in the army were too bitter to allow of a normal appointment from among the senior generals. The triumvirate makes its own changes; before a member resigns or is transferred he agrees to the appointment of his successor. At a meeting of the three the War Minister proposed that Mazaki resign, seeing that he was out of sympathy with the policy of the government. Mazaki refused. The seventy-two-year-old Imperial Prince doubtless deemed it wise to keep the Imperial family out of the quarrel and did not intervene. Thereupon the War Minister obtained the Emperor's approval for a successor to Mazaki, and the new appointment was announced.

It can be assumed that the Emperor was not brought into the matter directly except to give formal assent to the new appointment. The War Minister's dealings with the throne were conducted through the Lord Keeper, the Emperor's responsible intermediary in such matters. Saito was a cautious and experienced official and there can be no doubt that he informed the Emperor faithfully of what was going on. The Emperor knew and approved. When he sanctioned Mazaki's dismissal he created unknowingly the motive for the crime. The revolutionary-minded young officers not only saw their careers in danger; they had been given a grievance similar to that of the young officers of the navy a few years earlier when the Prime Minister overruled the Chief of the Naval General Staff and advised the Emperor to sign the second naval-limitation agreement. In each case a fundamental principle had been violated, in the opinion of the fanatics of the fighting services. The Prime Minister and the Emperor's advisers had interfered with the " prerogatives " of the supreme command; they had acted as if the army and navy were subject to the central government.

The prosecution was reluctant to bring that motive into sharp focus; the defense was determined to exploit it. Aizawa's soldier-advocate, Lieutenant Colonel Mitsui, was not concerned to get an acquittal but to have it known that the murder was the consequence of an unforgivable sin that had been committed against the army. That sin was interference in army affairs by " statesmen close to the throne."

The occupant of the throne was, of course, not mentioned. Hirohito was a divinity, the living incarnation of the eternal dynasty, a distant and sacred personage, not a human sovereign exercising political functions and the office of commander-in-chief. The human persons assailed were Lord Keeper Saito, the Emperor's adviser; Admiral Okada, the Prime Minister; and General Hayashi, the Minister of War. In keeping with the deep-rooted Japanese system of delegated responsibility, Saito was held responsible for the acts of the Emperor, and Nagata was held responsible for an action effected by the War Minister.

Mitsui admonished the court to " remember the fundamental spirit of the army." He did not shrink from menaces nor did the presiding judge stop him. " If an error is made in this trial it will have serious consequences. . . . If the court fails to understand the spirit which guided Aizawa, a second and even a third Aizawa will arise." " The time has come to rescue the army from corruption," continued the military advocate. " I hope the court will give serious consideration to the consensus of opinion in the army. A large majority of the younger officers are determined to oust outside influence, and the nation sincerely desires that the army will prove itself to be the army of the Emperor."

Mitsui named the " outside influences " to which the army objected. The chief of them was Admiral Viscount Saito, Lord Keeper of the Imperial Seals. His was an important and confidential office. Without the seal no order or edict or law was valid. The seal could not be affixed to any document without Saito's knowledge and approval. He was continuously closer to the Emperor than any other high officer of state. He had his office in the Palace and he was first in the small group of politically irremovable officials who form what may be called the Palace private cabinet. He had been appointed by the Emperor and he had authority to speak for the Emperor. It would have been as logical to call the United States Secretary of State an " outside influence " in American government. An incisive prosecuting counsel would have torn Mitsui's preposterous pretentions to shreds. If the Emperor's representative was an outsider, what was the Emperor?

The answer was known to everyone except the simpletons,

though it could not be spoken. The Emperor was a figure-head, and his representative could be nothing more. Saito's offense was that he had tried to exercise real authority in be-half of the Emperor and the government. But the army was a sovereign state within the state. Interference with its auton-omy could not be allowed. That was the case the defense was setting up — not, of course, in these words, which would have made everybody in court shudder with horror, but in the claim that " interference " from any quarter outside the army was an intolerable " violation of the prerogatives of the su-preme command." It was implicit in Aizawa's admission that he had killed Nagata because Nagata was " plotting with statesmen close to the throne," but Aizawa was obviously a simple-minded man who could not see below the surface and he became little more than a lay figure in the dock, half ig-nored by the keen-witted men who were battling for a cause and not for his insignificant life.

Major General Sato, who presided, was as supine as the prisoner. It seemed that the bench itself tacitly admitted the validity of Mitsui's claims and the prosecutor hardly even tried to keep the proceedings pinned down to the crime of murder. The legally trained procurators and the military judges were not shocked by Mitsui's arguments. Reality was present in that shabby courtroom though heavily veiled. All knew that the Emperor can act only on the advice of those who have the right and power to advise him. If the Chief of the General Staff has the sole right to advise the Emperor on army affairs, it follows that anyone else who presumes to do so is " interfering with the prerogatives of the supreme com-mand."

This aspect was expounded at length by Dr. Uzawa, the em-inent jurist who appeared for the defense. He drew a dis-

tinction between " administration " and " command." Many
people, he said, confused the administration of the army with
the supreme command, but the principles underlying the supreme command in Japan differed greatly from those in other
countries. Even Japanese constitutional scholars, he said, had
mixed up the administration of the army and navy with the
supreme command, with the result that they had incurred
general criticism.

Everyone in court knew what he meant. The London naval
agreement had been signed by the Emperor on the advice of
the Prime Minister and against that of the Chief of the Naval
General Staff. Constitutional lawyers had stated that in cases
where there was a difference of opinion between high authorities the view of the Prime Minister, as head of the government,
should prevail. The young officers asserted that the advice of
the Chief of the Naval General Staff should alone be taken
on the question of naval strength, a matter belonging solely
to " command." In their view, which was afterwards found to
be the view of the entire army and navy, " command " includes virtually everything except finance. Preparing the
army's (or navy's) budget and getting it voted is " administration " and the War Minister (or Navy Minister) can
negotiate with the Cabinet, the Treasury, and the Houses and
can make concessions if necessary in order to get it passed. But
changes of personnel were " command " business, according
to Uzawa, and only the triumvirate had the right to handle
them.

As the Emperor had sanctioned Mazaki's dismissal this part
of Uzawa's argument had to be presented delicately in muf-
fled phrases, but his hearers were able to read between the
lines. He continued: " A set of regulations is maintained by
the army in which the strongest emphasis is always placed on

the rights of the supreme command. The Mazaki affair is the first violation of the supreme-command prerogatives since those regulations were made. The question of personnel has an important place in the army. Viscount Saito's remark that the August transfers in the army were 'worthy of praise' is very significant. Senior statesmen are apt to interpret the supreme-command prerogatives of the Emperor in the light of Occidental practice. I hope the court will examine Viscount Saito on this point." Before the court got round to him Viscount Saito was murdered.

Those remarks were not addressed to a jury but to a court martial which was able to understand the concrete idea veiled in that discreet terminology. In saying " the supreme-command prerogatives of the Emperor," counsel was using the prescribed form of words. The trope was not only conventional usage; it was a necessary veil. The argument rested on the contention that the Emperor exercised this prerogative only with the consent of the army. The prerogative was the Emperor's, but the army (and navy) chiefs decided when he was to use it.

The public was enjoying a sensational murder trial and did not realize the issue at stake. Lieutenant Colonel Mitsui was in his element and he gave the Japanese people the melodrama they dearly love. He produced a long epistle which a second lieutenant of reserve had written with his blood. The sincerity of the document was guaranteed by its precious ink, a considerable quantity of which had been shed. It demanded that the court examine all the circumstances connected with the dismissal of General Mazaki and said if these were hushed up there would be more murders. The judge was exhorted not to adhere to " legal trifles " but to " reach his decision with the reasons and the feelings of a father who expostulates with his

children." The letter ended with a flowery peroration about
the plum that blooms in winter without knowing why and
compared Aizawa to an early-blossoming plum. " I entreat the
court to understand how natural was his action."

The court heard without comment or sign of impatience
the statement that the premeditated murder of one officer by
another for political reasons was a beautiful action.

Mitsui accused the higher authorities of trying to suppress
the truth: " My desire that our intentions be carefully considered was rejected at a conference of the War Minister, the
Vice-Chief of the General Staff, and the Vice-Minister for
War. It is with grim determination that I am here. I have ig-
nored pressure from many quarters." With tears welling from
his eyes Mitsui besought the court to appreciate the loyalty
and patriotism of the accused man.

Nagata was doomed as soon as it became known that Mazaki had been removed from the triumvirate. Aizawa learned
of the dismissal on July 16. " I was so concerned," he told the
court, " that I could hardly eat my meals. I requested permission to go to Tokyo; permission was granted and with it a
warning that I should act with great care."

Aizawa admitted that he had determined to kill Nagata on
that visit, and his first act on arriving in Tokyo was to buy a
dagger. But during the train journey he was haunted by fears
that he would fail and at night he could not sleep. In the
morning he heard a voice whispering " as from the sky," telling him not to act hastily. He was not ready then for murder.

He saw Nagata at the War Office and told him that the
steps taken to dismiss Mazaki had been improper and he
should resign. Nagata asked him to be more concrete, but it
did not appear from the evidence that either of them was
inclined to be frank. Nagata gave him smooth words and

Aizawa came away feeling, as he said afterwards, that he could not trust Nagata to be sincere.

His friends may have been disappointed that the dagger was unused; at all events two young officers with whom he spent the night gave him more " inside information " about Mazaki's dismissal, and after he had returned to his post he was bombarded with communications about the manner in which Mazaki had been removed from his key post. He told the court:

" After reading these letters I realized that the senior statesmen, those close to the throne, and powerful financiers and bureaucrats were attempting to corrupt the army for the attainment of their own interests; the Imperial army was thus being changed into a private concern and the supreme command was being violated. If nothing was done I was afraid the army would collapse from within. The senior statesmen and those close to the throne are indulging in self-interest and seem to be working as the tools of foreign countries who watch their chance to attack Japan.

" Allow me to say something about the people too. Young girls now dislike to work on the farms. Young men in the country are not serious. They spend their time in cafés and mahjong parlors. Internal conditions are deplorable. When I observed the state of the country, the teaching on which I was brought up — that I must give up everything for the Emperor — burst forth and encouraged me.

" I marked out Nagata because he, together with senior statesmen and financiers and members of the old army clique like General Minami and General Ugaki, was responsible for the corruption of the army. The responsibility for the army rested on Nagata, the Director of the Military Affairs Bureau. He was the headquarters of all the evil. If he would not resign there was only one thing to do. I determined to make myself a demon and finish his life with one stroke of my sword." Aizawa denied that he was a national socialist. " The young officers are not national socialists," he said; " they place the Emperor above everything."

Nowhere in the world is the connection between words and things so tenuous as in Japan. The officers " placed the Emperor above everything," but they refused to obey him. The case was a perfect example of young-officer mentality. The War Minister had recommended that the Inspector General be replaced when he refused to resign. The Prime Minister and the Lord Keeper had concurred, the Emperor had approved and on the Emperor's authority the Inspector General was removed from his post and transferred to the Supreme Military Council where he was still eligible for command of an army in the field or for any high post. This procedure was " converting the Imperial army into a private concern," that is to say, an army governed by the civil power. Soon after Aizawa and his military defender had proclaimed those ideas an outburst of assassinations, the first victim being the Lord Keeper, and a mutiny which was intended to inaugurate a revolution proved that Aizawa's creed was that of many other officers.

The real proposition of the defense, as Uzawa clearly understood though he stopped short of stating it in blunt words, was that the army regards itself as a self-governing independent body controlled by a self-perpetuating oligarchy of three, whose members are not to be changed without their own consent. This autonomous body is the " army of the Emperor "; any attempt to bring it under Cabinet influence is " converting it into a private army." It follows that the Emperor, in the thought though not in the language of persons like Aizawa, is but a figurehead dressed in Imperial robes. A thousand years of history attest that this is really the Japanese conception of the Emperor. He is a divine person, a symbol of the eternity of the state; he is an automaton who accepts advice without demur when it is offered by the proper person; he is a high priest, but he is not a king ruling the country. The restoration of 1868 might have created that position for him; the murder of Nagata was part of the army's counter-revolution.

The presiding judge invited Aizawa to explain the Showa Restoration movement. He replied: "The Emperor is the incarnation of the god who reigns over the universe. The aim of life is to develop according to His Majesty's wishes, which, however, have not yet been fully understood by all the world. The world is deadlocked because of communism, capitalism, anarchism, and the like. As Japanese we should make it our object to bring happiness to the world in accordance with His Majesty's wishes. As long as the fiery zeal of the Japanese for the Imperial cause is felt in Manchuria and other places, all will be well, but let it die and it will be gone forever. Democracy is all wrong. Our whole concern is to clarify the Imperial rule as established by the Emperor Meiji. Today is marked by arrogation of Imperial power. The Premier has propounded the institutional theory of the Emperor."

The Prime Minister, Admiral Okada, had asked the nation to co-operate with the government, thereby, according to Aizawa, revealing that he believed in the institutional theory of the Emperor.[1] Aizawa gave another illustration. When General Jotaro Watanabe was appointed to succeed

[1] For an account of the institutional theory of the Emperor see Chapter XVII: "The Suppression of a Scholar."

General Mazaki in the ruling triumvirate he gave a press interview in which he said that army control should be exercised by the War Minister and that the army should unite
around the War Minister. These words, said Aizawa, reveal
him to be a supporter of the institutional theory of the
Emperor.

The institutional theory holds that the Emperorship is the
highest organ of the state; those who deny this legal interpretation of the Imperial function have not offered another
except in mystical variations of Aizawa's words: " The Emperor is absolute, he is divine, the state and all within it
are his."

Aizawa continued: " Greedy craving for wealth is preva-
lent. An Osaka merchant has sold barbed wire to the enemy.
School teachers say that their salaries are paid not by the
Emperor but by the people. At least so my child is taught.
The Showa Restoration would be the return of financial and
political power to the Emperor."

The Emperor would thereupon hand these powers over
to a new set of servants agreeable to Aizawa and his fellow
thinkers. This is the " Emperor-centric " theory of the constitution as opposed to the institutional theory.

When he was asked to explain why he thought he could kill
his superior officer and then go to his new post as if nothing
had happened, Aizawa's assurance was broken down.

PROCURATOR: " I believe you knew that to murder your
superior officer was a crime under the law of the country? "

AIZAWA: " Yes."

PROCURATOR: " You must have known that you would be
charged with murder? "

AIZAWA: " I am not trying to evade the issue. I assassinated

Major General Nagata to save the nation from a crisis. I was guided by that single conviction."

PROCURATOR: "That was your motive. But your action broke the law. Did you know that you would be punished in accordance with the law for killing your superior?"

AIZAWA (*shouting*): "I broke the law."

PROCURATOR: "Why did you not think of the consequences before you committed the act?"

AIZAWA: "I broke the law."

PROCURATOR: "You feel your responsibility, don't you? I fail to comprehend what made you decide to go off to Formosa after you had killed the major general."

AIZAWA: "I was a fool."

PROCURATOR: "The Emperor gave the laws to the people, and the people must respect them?"

AIZAWA: "Yes, I understand."

PROCURATOR: "If you break the law you are acting against the wishes of the Emperor?"

Aizawa made no answer, but his civilian counsel, Dr. Uzawa, interposed with the objection that it was improper to cite the law while the court was examining the facts.

With reference to his idea that financial and political powers should be returned to the Emperor, the procurator asked if he meant that subjects should not possess those powers or that they should be considered as borrowed from the throne. Aizawa thought they had been borrowed.

PROCURATOR: "How then could subjects bring about the Showa Restoration?"

AIZAWA: "Men with absolute respect for the throne will serve near the Emperor and strive to have the august wishes of the throne pervade the nation. Army officers will unite to uphold army prestige, and army and people must co-operate and become as one in living up to the wishes of the throne."

The procurator found the reply ambiguous and asked for something more concrete.

Aizawa said economic power could not be returned because of Japan's relations with foreign countries. Education, however, could be renovated.

PROCURATOR: " Your answer is not to the point. I am asking you as a soldier about the ways and means to bring about the Showa Restoration."

AIZAWA: " An officer is an elder brother to privates, and a company commander is their father. The army exists to scan the general situation in the world and eradicates social evils through its leadership of privates and reservists. The relations between the army and society are so delicate that I cannot comment on them."

This part of the examination petered out in metaphysical sands as Aizawa tried to explain that renovation could only be carried out by the Emperor in whom all power dwells and that to have it effected by subjects would be detrimental to the prestige of the throne.

The hunt for motives led the court to ever wider horizons. Nagata's murder had been left far behind; the court martial had become a witch-hunt. General Hayashi, the War Minister who dismissed Mazaki, was called and examined in private, and then Mazaki was summoned to be questioned about the conference of the triumvirate which had ended in disagreement over the August transfers and had been followed by his dismissal. Mazaki was an honorable officer and, whatever his views may have been, he never uttered them in public. He obeyed the summons of the court martial but refused to answer Mitsui's questions on the ground that he was one of the high officials who may not divulge, without the Emperor's sanction, matters they have learned in the course of their duties. After fifty minutes Mazaki strode out of the court making no effort to conceal his anger. When reporters went to his home he would not see them.

Emboldened by their success in extending the issues, the defense next asked that Viscount Saito, the Lord Keeper, be summoned for examination on the report that he had promised to guarantee Hayashi's future if he dismissed Mazaki. He was also to be questioned, said Uzawa, about the truth of a story that he had said the August transfers were " worthy of praise." Not to be outdone, Lieutenant Colonel Mitsui asked that Seihin Ikeda, managing director of the great firm of Mitsui, be examined about his political views and asked whether he had given financial assistance to Nagata or his bereaved family. Mitsui informed the court that he would ask Viscount Saito if it was true that he had persuaded Prince Saionji, the Elder Statesman, to recommend Admiral Okada to the Emperor as Prime Minister, and if he had asked Okada to bring about the success of the London naval-limitation conference and suppress the Showa Restoration movement. He also wanted to summon Marquis Kido (a friend of Prince Konoye and now Lord Keeper) to explain an organization called the Breakfast Club, which he described as a brain trust trying to bring about an understanding between the court and the army. The real cause of the affair, said Mitsui, was the conflict between the conservative forces near the throne and the radical elements in the army who wanted the Showa Restoration. The conservatives had the upper hand and had nearly poisoned the Imperial army.

Mitsui's closing address was an eloquent dissertation about rural poverty and the unequal distribution of wealth. It took the whole morning and the presiding judge asked him if he could put his views on those matters in writing briefly. Mitsui answered that he wished for a few more hours in order to explain vital conditions in the army. In the afternoon he gave an address on conditions in the country, the relations between young officers and the young men of the rural villages, the evils of plutocracy, financial panics, the government's inadequate measures to relieve rural distress, the monopoly of capital by the big interests, and the close relations between financial interests and statesmen close to the throne. The court listened stolidly and adjourned at five p.m.

It did not meet again. During the night the army broke into open mutiny.

A new court martial was opened after the mutiny had been suppressed. It was held in strict secrecy and the proceedings were concluded in five sessions. Aizawa was sentenced to death. He was executed on July 3, 1936, after the higher court martial had rejected his appeal. His body was returned to his family, but elaborate memorial services were forbidden and a general order prohibited the erection of shrines or monuments to his memory and the use of his story in cinema or stage dramas.

Chapter IX

"BUT THIS IS MUTINY"

The ideas of the young officers had been displayed at the trial as on a gigantic screen before the people of Japan, and the people had applauded the picture. A more stirring drama was being prepared for them.

White-collar workers coming into Tokyo on the morning of February 26, 1936, deep in the reports of the unfinished trial, jerked their noses out of the newspapers when policemen ordered the buses to make a detour because the streets around the Imperial Palace and the government offices were filled with troops. The Houses of Parliament, the Prime Minister's residence, the War Office, the Metropolitan Police office, and the Sanno Hotel were occupied by 1,400 soldiers who at midnight had sallied from the barracks where the Aizawa court martial-forum had been sitting. Separated from the rebels by the width of the street, the Imperial Guards division held all approaches to the Palace, where the angry, astonished, and impotent Hirohito sat and listened to the news as it was brought to him in penny numbers. What thoughts passed through his mind can only be guessed, but Hirohito knew the history of his own house, and the skeleton in the Imperial cupboard was the dread of a new shogunate in khaki uniforms. How can any Japanese emperor forget the humiliations his ancestors suffered from military chieftains who, with false loyalty, professed to govern in their name and relegated them contemptuously to shabby poverty in leaky palaces?

The mutineers were led by captains and lieutenants of the First Division. The division was under orders for Manchuria, and before going off for a cooling period its young officers wanted to light a fire at home. Their thoughts cannot have been a secret from their seniors, yet no precautions were taken and the only attempt to restrain them was an oral appeal from a major as they were leaving the barracks. He committed suicide a few days later.

The motives that impelled the young officers to revolt at that moment were not disclosed by the secret court martial that afterwards tried them. Private reports had it that they had seized the War Office believing that in the murdered General Nagata's files they would find evidence of his collusion with Admiral Saito and other " statesmen near the throne." Aside from this possible though unprovable object, their evident purpose was to repeat the May Fifteenth incident on a larger scale. They intended to strike terror into the government by slaughtering a batch of the highest men in the country and to create such a situation that the army chiefs would be compelled to take charge.

While the soldiers marched through the snow, murder squads in military trucks went to the homes of Admiral Okada, the Prime Minister; Korekiyo Takahashi, Minister of Finance; Admiral Kantaro Suzuki, Grand Chamberlain to the Emperor; Admiral (and Viscount) Saito, Lord Keeper of the Imperial Seals; General Jotaro Watanabe, Inspector General of Military Training (he who had succeeded Ma-

zaki); and Count Nobuaki Makino, formerly Lord Keeper
of the Seals and the Emperor's principal adviser for many
years. The last of the Elder Statesmen, Prince Saionji, was
hastily taken to a place of safety by the Governor of the prefecture where he lived, and if the rebels intended to kill him
they were baffled. It does not appear that they tried.

The weapons used were sub-machine-guns and the old men
were murdered with ruthless brutality before the eyes of their
families. The Prime Minister concealed himself in a toilet
and the killers, who did not know him, murdered his brother-
in-law. Two days later, dressed as a mourner, he followed his
own coffin, in which his brother-in-law's body lay, out of the
residence under the noses of the mutineers. Mr. Takahashi, a
man of eighty, was shot with an automatic and brutally
hacked with a sword by hysterical murderers. Admiral Saito,
who had returned late from a dinner followed by a picture
at the American Embassy, was butchered in the presence of
his wife. That courageous and beloved lady tried to shield
her husband, crying: "You shall not kill Saito; he still has
work to do for the country." She was wounded in the arm as
a stream of bullets was pumped into the old admiral. General
Watanabe was shot dead in his suburban home. Admiral
Suzuki, the Grand Chamberlain to the Emperor, was slightly
wounded, and recovered. It was said that the officer assigned
to kill him had received kindness from him and deliberately
shot him in the arm only.

Count Makino had a miraculous escape. He was staying
at a country inn with his wife and granddaughter when, at
night, a captain and a squad of reservists armed with rifles
and a heavy machine-gun came to the front door. A policeman detailed to guard Makino shot the captain dead without

wasting a moment and was shot himself. Count Makino, with his granddaughter, went out by the back door, which opened on a steep hillside. " If I am to climb that hill," he said, " I may as well stay and be shot, for it is more than I can do." An unknown man appeared from the inn and took his arm, and, supported by the man and his granddaughter, a beautiful girl of twenty, Makino scrambled a short way up the steep bank. They had not gone far before the killers appeared, but the slope was such that they could not bring the machine-gun to bear and one of them fired a rifle at the Count. The shot wounded the man who was helping Makino and they both fell. The leader of the soldiers signaled with his hands and shouted the Japanese word meaning " success " and they decamped, menaced with rough treatment by the villagers.

There was no more killing. The rebels made flags out of tablecovers commandeered from the dining-room of the Peers' Club and paid for with hundred-yen notes (of which they had a mysterious supply) and hoisted them over the Prime Minister's residence. They made no effort to extend their positions and had nothing to suggest or attempt when they had come to the end of their prepared plan. For four days they remained in possession of the buildings they had seized. The Emperor held family councils in the Palace. The War Minister and the members of the Supreme Military Council, evicted from the War Office, sat in the Military Club, heavily guarded, and negotiated with the rebels. The parleys came to nothing and the mutineers did not attempt to break the ring of steel that was being slowly drawn around them. As on the former occasion, they waited for their official chiefs to " rise " and their chiefs sat tight. Officers of the mutineers occasionally harangued the populace, but, as I saw myself, only curious groups of shopkeepers and local residents

listened to them. They distributed a manifesto which could
only have been written in Japan. It read:

MANIFESTO

The essence of the Japanese nation consists in the fact
that the Emperor reigns from times immemorial down
to the remotest future in order that the national glory
be propagated over the world so that all men under the
sun may enjoy their lives to the fullest extent. This fundamental fact has been from the earliest days down to
the present time the glory of Japan. Now is the time to
bring about an expansion of the power and prestige of
Japan.

In recent years many persons have made their chief
purpose in life the amassment of wealth regardless of the
general welfare and prosperity of the people, with the
result that the majesty of the Empire has been impaired.
The people of Japan have suffered in consequence. Many
troublesome issues now confronting our country are due
to this situation.

The Elder Statesmen, the financial magnates, the government officials, and the political parties are responsible. The London naval agreement and the unhappy
events which have occurred in the Japanese army in recent years prove this statement. That Prime Minister
Hamaguchi was assassinated, that a Blood Brotherhood
arose, that the May Fifteenth incident occurred, and that
Aizawa killed Nagata last summer are not without
reason.

Those incidents, however, have failed to remind men
of their responsibility. The recent strained relations between Japan and the other powers are due to our states-

men's failure to take appropriate measures. Japan now confronts a crisis. Therefore it is our duty to take proper steps to safeguard our fatherland by killing those responsible. On the eve of our departure to Manchuria we have risen in revolt to attain our aims by direct action. We think it is our duty as subjects of His Majesty the Emperor.

May Heaven bless and help us in our endeavor to save our fatherland from the worst.

February 26, Eleventh year of Showa.

> [*Signed*] SHIRO NONAKA, Captain
> and his colleagues

All round the square mile where mutineers and Imperial Guards faced each other life went on. Shopboys plugged through the snow on their bicycles delivering the groceries. The newspapers came out every morning with all kinds of news except the news the people wanted. The press called the revolt an " incident," an " affair," anything but its true name, until a story went round that the Emperor, very angry, had said to the War Minister: " But this is mutiny." Afterwards the reporters would sometimes call it " mutiny " but their favorite word was " rising." To stigmatize the Imperial army was something Japanese writers just could not do.

The fleet steamed into Tokyo Bay. The old generals sent to country barracks for tanks, guns, ambulances, and troops under reliable officers. They drew a ring of steel round the mutineers. Civilians were evacuated from their houses in the rebel zone. All the while the generals were working for a bloodless finish. Their problem was one of discipline. The soldiers had been trained to obey the orders of their officers as if they were the orders of the Emperor. Could they now be told to disobey and desert their officers without destroying discipline at its foundations? A Major Okubo, who had a literary gift, devised a method. He drafted the following message to private soldiers and non-commissioned officers:

"Hitherto you have obeyed your officers believing their commands to be just. His Majesty the Son of Heaven (Heika Tenno) now orders you to return to your barracks. If you fail to obey you will be traitors. If you return you will be pardoned. Your fathers and brothers and all the people are praying you to return. Come back to your barracks."

Announced by radio and dropped from planes, the appeal confirmed the doubts that had begun to sprout in the minds of the soldiers. From three high windows of my house on the top of Reinanzaka Hill, just outside the rebel zone, we watched the closing scenes. The city was lifeless under the grimy snow. All the familiar figures had vanished from the streets. The schools were closed. No trains were entering the city and no street-cars were running. The telephone exchanges were forbidden to operate and the telegraph offices were closed. Tokyo had been isolated for the last act. Major Okubo's appeal, signed by the commander of the Tokyo garrison, Lieutenant General Kashii, was reaching the soldiers. Groups of them began to emerge from the Prime Minister's house and walk down the hill to the barricades where the loyal troops waited. They surrendered their arms and were packed into trucks and rushed to their barracks.

At two o'clock the tablecover over the Prime Minister's residence was hauled down. For one hour and forty minutes nothing more happened. The citizens of Tokyo were not impatient, for all of them understood the solemn pause. The generals were silently giving the rebels a chance to commit hara-kiri. The invitation was not accepted. At twenty-five life is sweet. Only one leader, Captain Teruzo Ando, shot himself in his room in the Sanno Hotel. The excuse offered was that the rebels thought that a trial by court martial, like that of Aizawa, would give them an opportunity to propagate their opinions. It may have been so; if their leaders had ordered them to commit suicide they would doubtless have obeyed. The order was not given; they were allowed to think for themselves and they did nothing. Fifteen of them were tried by secret court martial and shot on an unannounced date in Tokyo military prison.

The Emperor, his advisers, and the people in general were so glad to see the rising safely subdued that not much attention was paid to some significant developments that followed it.

The Supreme Military Council disavowed any desire to alter the form of government and proclaimed its intention to co-operate with a civilian cabinet. Before allowing a War Minister to be appointed, however, the generals exacted certain assurances. One concerned foreign policy. The soldiers would not allow the Prime Minister, Koki Hirota, to make Shigeru Yoshida his Foreign Minister. Yoshida was stoutly opposed to any policies which would lead to a break with Britain or the United States, and he was son-in-law of the strongest statesman on the " liberal " side of the hedge, Count Makino. Mr. Hirota was obliged to take foreign affairs himself in addition to the Prime Ministership.

The army also insisted that it be consulted on the new Cabinet's declaration of policy, and the declaration when issued bore signs of dual parentage. It endorsed many of the ideals of the young officers and at the same time it avowed respect for the Constitution and the people's will. Its foreign policy undertook to obtain the fruits of " Japan's position as the stabilizing force of eastern Asia." The search for " clarification of the national polity " (see Chapter XVIII) was to be resumed. Defense was to be strengthened and more money found for the fighting services. Foreign policy was to be " positive and independent."

It is probable that the civilians assented to those somewhat vague promises in the belief that the trouble would blow over and they would not be called on to redeem their promissory notes. It is also likely that the senior generals were then limiting their aggressive plans to the acquisition of what they called a " corridor " in North China to round off their defense of Manchukuo against Russia. By that corridor they meant control of China north of the Yellow River. They were confident that China could not resist, confident also that Britain, in the shadow of Hitler's growing power, could not interfere and that the United States would not. Though they attached importance to isolationist sentiment they did not rest on that alone, but on the knowledge that the American fleet was at the time little stronger than their own and that their hundreds of " anchored aircraft carriers " in the Pacific could more than offset any numerical advantage the United States fleet possessed.

Only a year later General Terauchi, the War Minister who represented the army in its negotiations with the Cabinet, took command of the great Japanese army which invaded North China expecting to destroy the forces of Generalissimo Chiang Kai-shek in a six months' campaign. He was successful in a way. In six months the Chinese armies had been defeated in battle after battle and the Chinese government driven far into the interior. But the shortsighted Japanese militarists

127

had aroused something new in the world — a fiercely nationalist spirit in the peace-loving Chinese — and they had committed their country to a policy which was to lead them into a war of survival with the United States and the British Commonwealth of Nations.

Chapter X

THE MIND OF THE ARMY

The Japanese people had been taught that the army of the Emperor was different from the armies of other countries. Mutiny and murder had now shown them that it was different from what they themselves had supposed. It was not the servant of the civil power, but the master. Its officers considered themselves the modern samurai, the ruling class.

Not in one half-century can a feudal Oriental society change its ways. To know the Japanese army today it is necessary to understand its social and spiritual inheritance.

In the Japanese state until one lifetime ago the samurai, or warriors, were the privileged class, the gentlemen. The other classes, the farmers, artisans, and traders (in that order) were the common people. The warriors were also the administrators; the army, politicians, and civil servants were one class in that feudal society. This system — the warrior caste identical with the ruling class — continued until the restoration of 1868. The aim of the restoration leaders was national unity under a centralized government. They abolished the clan system with its hordes of two-sworded samurai and introduced conscription. The sons of peasants, carpenters, and shopkeepers became soldiers. " It was the greatest reform of a thousand years," wrote General Araki; " once the

129

warriors were a privileged class, now all are equal." Healthy young plebs were drafted into the ranks impartially, but the strong Choshu clan, one of the victors in the restoration struggle, retained the command, and its samurai were the officers. Its rival and colleague, the Satsuma clan, was given the navy. For the first thirty or forty years nearly all the generals of the new army were Choshu men and at their head was Prince Aritomo Yamagata, greatest of all the Choshu clansmen. The title "Shogun" (barbarian-subduing generalissimo) had been abolished, but Yamagata till his death was in fact though not in name generalissimo of the Japanese army. He was also, from time to time, Prime Minister, and as Elder Statesman in his old age he made and unmade governments.

While Yamagata lived he controlled the army. When he died the new system of universal service was producing its results. Generals might be members of any clan; the clans themselves were becoming shadows. The conscript army had grown up, a new "clan" had been created. The officers regarded themselves as the samurai of new Japan. The public had forgotten the insolence of the old samurai. Writers threw a halo of romance around them. The stage played dramas of chivalry from year-end to year-end. A name — Bushido, the way of the warrior — was invented for a code of chivalry discovered after the thing itself had passed into limbo unregretted.

Conscription brought the new army close to the masses. Its officers were drawn predominantly from the thrifty and self-respecting rural middle class. Their minds had more in common with those of the soldiers under them than with the new commercial bourgeoisie stretching out tentacles into the modern world and sending its sons to American and English universities. Their religion was state-worship; their highest virtue was loyalty to the state; they were inspired with a fierce desire to extend the power and glory of the Empire; they believed their country to have few equals; when they looked around them in Asia, they saw only nations far inferior to their own in armaments and they saw the riches of Asia in the hands of foreign conquerors who had appeared on the scene while Japan was still asleep.

If not wholly an illusion it was a distorted picture. The rubber, oil, and ores of Asia could be bought in the open market and the Japanese bought them like others. They acquired mines in Australia and mines and rubber plantations in Malaya. Davao in the Philippines became a Japanese city, its industries in Japanese hands. But they were liable to be deprived of these in the event of war, especially after the League of Nations had been formed and economic sanctions invented. The Japanese military mind could not endure a state of things in which its fleets and armies might be immobilized by an international authority.

The new army had modeled itself on that of Germany. The policy of blood and iron with which Bismarck welded and aggrandized the Hohenzollern empire was one after its own heart. In the early stages of the China war Japanese generals declared that Bismarck's war of policy against Austria was the model they followed. Chiang Kai-shek, like Francis Joseph in 1866, was to be taught who was master and was thereafter to be a docile and honored collaborator. Drawn from a lower social grade than the German officer, the Japanese officer admired and envied the standing of his Prussian opposite number and his arrogant self-assertion. Partly because of his poverty and partly because the tone of society was set by the new bourgeoisie, infatuated, as he thought, with the commercial civilizations of America and Britain, he never acquired the same position as his German confrere. Considered as careers, banking, commerce, industry, even politics, offered richer prizes than soldiering, and more of them.

In the normal course, a Japanese officer could expect to become a major at the age of forty, and a lieutenant colonel at about forty-five. Three years later he might expect to be retired with the rank of colonel and a pension of about 100 yen ($50) a month. A Japanese writer computed that of the 800 cadets who annually entered the Military Academy, one became a general, thirty lieutenant generals, and fifty major generals; the rest were retired before reaching the age of fifty. Some found employment, some joined patriotic societies or busied themselves with youth movements, but the majority settled down, like elderly Frenchmen, in suburban retirement.

When the warrior of the new era looked around and compared his place in society and his personal lot with what he believed to be due to his importance in the state, it is not surprising that he began to think that the glorious restoration had somehow gone astray. He saw politicians of his own age who had started life as jackals for party bosses rise to be ministers of State, plastered with decorations, admitted to the presence of the Emperor. His contemporaries who had succeeded in business had mansions in Tokyo, villas by sea and mountain, secondary wives demurely tucked away in little houses on quiet streets; he had genteel poverty on a shabby pension. It was easy to believe the voices that were telling him that the politicians and the capitalists had filched the prizes of the modern Empire.

A minor professional irritation was festering within the army itself among that large class of officers who saw themselves doomed to early retirement. Graduates of the Staff College wore with pride a small bronze plate adorned with a star. It was worn low on the right side, as if to exert some efficacious action on the liver, and was inconspicuous except to those who did not have it.

The officers who had the right to show it were the intellectual elite of the army. They got the staff posts at home, they were attached to the embassies abroad, they had the field-marshal's batons in their knapsacks. The others spent most of their service in the dismal knowledge that they would end as colonels. "Those non-graduates," says the Japanese writer already quoted, "are the backbone of the army, but when their services are no longer required they are dismissed. Every disarmament conference brings nearer to them the shadow of unemployment." A non-graduate lieutenant colonel who had been made fencing instructor in a colonial garrison drew his sword in the War Office and killed the graduate who had appointed him to that unattractive post. Graduates were then forbidden to wear the brass badge.

The Japanese army, as a political entity, is not the million peasants who spend a couple of years in barracks. It is the corps of officers, the men who have made military service their profession. That army is a hierarchy on a democratic base. The officers are ambitious, energetic youths from good poor families. General Araki, who was made a Baron for his services, began life as an apprentice in a pickle factory. General Gen Sugiyama, the only man who has held all three of the highest posts in the army, is the son of a country schoolmaster.

Racial character and the system of education combine to discourage individuality and produce uniformity. A Japanese statesman thus illustrated the national ideal: "Compare American woods with our state forests. In them a great tree rises here and there and dominates the scene. We don't like that. We prefer making our trees grow like a government afforestation scheme, in straight rows uniform in height and girth."

Japanese wars have produced no great commanders. The strength of the army is its staff work, its capacity to produce long-pondered plans in which everything foreseeable has been taken into account. The execution of such plans requires implicit obedience, and the rank and file are trained to believe that the orders of their officers are the commands of their Emperor and that to die fulfilling them is a glorious consummation.

The biographies of Japanese generals are usually colorless " Who's Whos." The greater the success attained, the more completely has the hero conformed to the standard pattern. The method produces immaculate plans and early successes. Whether it develops initiative and resourcefulness against strong adversaries trained in a freer school is a question that remains to be answered.

On the equalitarian base of national service a rigid hierarchy has been erected. It was necessary because it is a Japanese habit to attach oneself to a leader, obtaining protection and promotion in return for loyalty, and the army was honeycombed with cliques. The need of unity caused a centralized system of control to be evolved. The rule of the army is now focused in a triumvirate of generals: the Inspector General of Military Training, who prepares it for war; the Minister for War, who administers its affairs and is its link with the Cabinet and the channel through which it obtains funds; and the Chief of the General Staff, who, in war, uses it. The post of Inspector General of Aviation was created in 1940, and a General-in-Chief of the Air Force was appointed in May

1942, but so far as is known the supreme control of the army is still vested in the holders of the three high posts just named.

The triumvirate is self-perpetuated; it chooses its own successors as vacancies occur. The only frequent change is that of the War Minister, who comes and goes with cabinets. The War Minister is the agent by which the army controls the administration. By withdrawing him the triumvirate can disrupt any government; by refusing to appoint a War Minister it can prevent a cabinet from being formed. In the days of party cabinets some advanced politicians advocated a change by which a civilian could be head of the War Department as in the United States and Britain. The first party Prime Minister, " Kei " Hara, once took over the war portfolio temporarily, and optimists believed they saw an entering wedge which would loosen the army's grip on the government. But Mr. Hara, a practical politician, soon returned the post to the army. Another method of reform which seemed more attainable was the appointment of retired generals who would not be under the domination of the active army. But the army saw the danger and forestalled it.

Revised regulations, approved by the Cabinet and sanctioned by the Emperor, prescribe that the Minister for War must be a general or lieutenant general on the active list. Those officers are under the orders of the triumvirate. When a new Premier wants a War Minister he asks the triumvirate to nominate one. The request is usually made through the retiring Minister, who can be reappointed. If any officer should accept a Prime Minister's invitation to become War Minister without the consent of the big three, they could immediately remove him from the active list. By that action he would cease to be qualified and his career would close.

In times of peace a decent air of reserve was usually worn over the army's power. There is nothing secret about it and the army marches on to the political stage without hesitation when it meets resistance on matters it considers vital. Two recent cases displayed the system in action.

When the fighting services decided that the time had come to join the Axis, the army dismissed a Prime Minister with little more ceremony than a corporation would use in changing its janitor. The Prime Minister, Admiral Yonai, had been in office for six months; he was popular with the public and he had made no blunders. Handsome, laconic, genial, and always ready with an observation which lowered the temperature of any discussion, he had been a success in parliament and in the Cabinet as Navy Minister in two previous administrations. His appointment to the highest post was unexpected and the manner in which it was made turns a striking light on the haphazard methods by which Prime Ministers were chosen after military interference had stopped the normal growth of representative government. It was, as it turned out, the last effort of the civilian statesmen to find a safe Prime Minister who would be content with war in China only. Yonai was spending a Sunday with his daughter and her children in their small Japanese house near Tokyo Club. An Imperial chamberlain came to this house in the evening with the Emperor's command to form an administration. The admiral was wearing easy Japanese dress; before going to the Palace he had to send to his suburban home for his formal clothes.

During his administration the " phony war " in Europe ended and the blitzkrieg began. Holland was overrun, Belgium and France defeated. French generals who had hardly taken their hands down were comparing Britain to a chicken

which would soon have its neck wrung. To the Japanese army
it seemed that the French, Dutch, and British colonial estates
in Asia were theirs for the taking. Japan's day had dawned.

Yonai held that Japan's business was to win the China war
before seeking fresh adventures. He opposed an alliance with
Germany. The army was dissatisfied and early in July 1940, a
few weeks after Dunkirk, General Hata, the War Minister,
brought matters to a head.

First he consulted Generals Terauchi and Sugiyama, two
senior generals who could be expected to support him. He
next had an interview with the Prime Minister, whose answers he found unsatisfactory. On the third day he sent his
chief assistant, Major General Akira Muto, a notorious fire-
eater, to give the Chief Secretary of the Cabinet a detailed
statement of the army's wishes. On the seventh day he presented the Prime Minister with his written " advice " in favor
of a " new structure " at home and a new foreign policy — in
plain language, military socialism and an alliance with
Germany.

The Prime Minister replied that he did not share the War
Minister's views, was prepared to accept his resignation, and
desired the army to name a new War Minister. Hata resigned
at once, and in the afternoon the triumvirate met. In the
evening General Hata told the Prime Minister that " in view
of the circumstances " the army could not find a qualified
officer willing to serve as War Minister. Admiral Yonai, his
Cabinet thus broken up, presented his resignation to the
Emperor.

The Emperor's advisers recommended Prince Konoye as
next Prime Minister. Before accepting the Imperial mandate
Konoye asked that War and Navy Ministers be furnished.
This was done; the army appointed General Hideko Tojo,

who afterwards became War Premier; the navy made no change. Konoye then named Yosuke Matsuoka, who was believed to understand America well, as Foreign Minister, and the four decided the new government's policy before Konoye troubled to appoint the other members of his Cabinet. In a few weeks the result of those consultations was seen. An alliance was signed in Berlin and a commission was appointed to prepare a " new structure " of totalitarian design.

Konoye believed in a " new structure." He thought that an authoritarian type of state would work better among a politically immature people than a representative system. He wanted to bring the army into the " new structure," hoping thereby to end its interferences with the central government. The army preferred to retain its autonomy and refused. General Tojo conveyed its refusal. Konoye's interest evaporated; the " new structure," which was born after a short gestation had little appearance of viability. But Konoye, " the last ace of the Constitution," remained at his post. He was willing to go a long way with the army; he knew that not otherwise could the semblance of civil government be kept up; but he was unwilling to go to war with the United States, and when the navy and army were ready and determined for war, he resigned and his War Minister succeeded him. Military government had come into the open at last.

Besides dismissing cabinets the army could and did refuse the Emperor freedom to choose a Prime Minister. In 1937 the Emperor gave General Issei Ugaki the mandate to form a government. Ugaki was a moderate; he was the friend of politicians and capitalists. In his time as War Minister his clique was all-powerful in the army and he was the enemy of the Nazi officers' faction. The triumvirate feared the power which that bold and astute soldier-statesman would wield if he became head of the government.

Ugaki received the Emperor's command while he was staying at a hot spring fifty miles from Tokyo. He hastened to the capital after notifying the Palace that he was on the way. The Emperor sat up to receive him. Towards midnight, as Ugaki's car was bowling along the broad road by the Palace moat, a gendarmerie officer stepped out and signaled the car to stop. Lieutenant General Kesago Nakajima, general of the gendarmerie, approached and gave General Ugaki the army's " advice " that he should not become Prime Minister. Nakajima afterwards explained that he was acting on the orders of the War Minister, General Hisaichi Terauchi, the same who later figured in the dismissal of Admiral Yonai. (Terauchi commanded the Japanese armies in the first stage of the China war and attempted to repeat among the plains and lakes of rural North China the operation by which Hindenburg destroyed the Russian armies in the Battle of the Mazurian Lakes. It would have been a grand maneuver but the Chinese slipped out before the pincers had closed.)

Ugaki listened stiffly to his junior telling him what he should say to the Emperor, intimated that he did not require advice, and went on to the Palace, where he undertook to form a cabinet. The army triumvirate would not furnish him with a War Minister. He struggled for a week. Every possible effort was made. Many sympathized with the strong and ambitious old man thus barred from a prize that was to be thrust on many smaller men. Old generals went to the triumvirate and implored them to allow their former commander to attain the goal of his life. Generals of high standing on the retired list offered to serve under Ugaki if the regulations could be waived. The triumvirate would not budge. The final scenes were stormy. Ugaki swore he would never wear Japanese uniform again. But he did nothing. The hive spirit was stronger than human anger.

A political general, who had reduced the army in conformity with general policy during the disarmament era, had not been allowed to head a Japanese government. So much the public saw, but the story was incomplete. From the triumvirate's point of view their resistance to Ugaki was a heroic effort to enforce unity on an army divided into cliques and given to bestowing its loyalty on separate chiefs as in feudal days. Ugaki played with the capitalists and the politicians, with whose help he hoped to rise to power, but he also was feudal-minded. A significant and heavily censored incident occurred in the General Staff Office in March 1931. General Kanaya was Chief of the General Staff; Ugaki had just ceased to be War Minister after holding that office in several successive cabinets, during which time his supporters were rewarded and his opponents left in the cold. Kanaya was due to retire and Ugaki aspired to succeed him. One day a group of young officers of the Ugaki faction entered General Kanaya's room and " advised " him to make way for Ugaki. This revelation of faction and insubordination was placed under triple seals of secrecy while the public was diverted with quarrels in the House between members and the War Minister.

The army responded by invoking the time-honored method of figurehead government. An Imperial Prince aged 67 was appointed chief of the General Staff and he was kept in the post for ten years. Brains are at least desirable in high executive posts, and the worthy Prince Kan-in's endowments were moderate. The situation was met by always appointing a clever general as Vice-Chief. The arrangement lasted until 1941, when, as war with America loomed nearer, a professional soldier, General Gen Sugiyama, was appointed Chief. A new clique ruled the army; unity had been achieved by ten years of war, with more wars to come.

The instrument by which the army can veto the formation of an administration is the regulation which ordains that the War Minister must be a general or a lieutenant general from the active list. This provision makes the War Minister's post the keystone of any cabinet; if the stone is not in its place an administration cannot be formed; if it is pulled out the administration falls.

The regulation was later reinforced by an important and little-known state paper in which the War and Navy Departments define their relations with the Cabinet. The circumstances in which that document was issued are a complete example of the military mind and methods.

In 1931 a party government of liberal complexion was in power. The Prime Minister was Yuko Hamaguchi, subsequently assassinated, the Finance Minister was Junnosuke Inouye, subsequently assassinated, and the Foreign Minister was Baron K. Shidehara, who, though often in danger, fortunately escaped the attentions of young officers and patriotic gunmen. The government's policy was economy, arms limitation, and conciliation in China. On August 5 of that year the War Minister, General Jiro Minami, made a speech at a divisional generals' conference denouncing arms limitation, declaring that the situation in China was going from bad to worse, and directing army commanders to " counteract those tendencies," an instruction which was interpreted as a hint to agitate against the policies of the government. Foreign diplomats were startled; they waited to see whether the Foreign

Minister would resign or the War Minister retract. Neither of them did anything.

Minami is the type sometimes called, unflatteringly, a good soldier. He is bull-necked, domineering, capable, and jovial. Ambition and hard work carried him from a roistering youth in a cavalry barracks to the highest posts. He could lead men well in the field and — a rarer gift — instruct others how to do it. His speech was the first indication that the army had a China policy of its own. In making it Minami seemed quite unconscious of any responsibility to the Cabinet, which had a different policy. He regarded himself as the army's agent in the administration; when he spoke in public, he was the voice of the army. When his speech was criticized in the House he said: " No restraint can be placed on the utterances of the War Minister by other ministers."

Civilian politicians did not then admit that the army was an independent institution and a serious effort was made to obtain an authoritative definition of powers. When the papers were published two years later, the definition was there but it was not the one the Cabinet had written. In a document the tortuous phrasing of which revealed the struggles that had entered into its composition the Cabinet stated: " In matters concerning the strength of the army and navy, the government is to discharge its duty of advice to the throne in thorough co-operation between the government and the organ of the supreme command. A unified decision is to be attained through perfect collaboration between the government and the organ of the supreme command. As far as the administrative phases are concerned, the government is to bear the political responsibility."

The statement was intended to mean that the Cabinet was bound to " co-operate " with the heads of the fighting forces but could, in the last resort, reject their proposals. This had been done in 1930 when the Emperor, on the advice of the Prime Minister, signed the London naval treaty and disregarded the contrary advice given to him by the chief of the Naval General Staff. Before tendering his advice to the Emperor the Prime Minister consulted Dr. Tatsukichi Minobe, the greatest Japanese authority on constitutional law. Minobe reduced the issue to simple terms. Both the Prime Minister and the Chief of the General Staff, he said, have the duty of advising the Emperor. If their views differ, the Prime Minister, as head of the central government, is entitled to advise that his advice be accepted.

Dr. Minobe paid a heavy price for his loyalty to the civilian interpretation of the Constitution. His story will be told in its place. The Prime Minister was murdered.

The fighting services did not accept the government's formula. Their reply drew a distinction between the " Cabinet " and the " government " and demanded " concise and definite terms " instead of " the vague word ' government.' " " In determining the defense strength," they said, " the matter is first to be considered by the Chief of the General Staff and the Chief of the Naval Staff, who constitute the organ of the supreme command. The War and Navy Ministers, who are simultaneously state ministers, negotiate with the government on behalf of the defense forces. Therefore, by the word ' government ' is meant the other party in the aforementioned relations."

It was thus made clear that the general staffs deal with the government as independent bodies. Only an agreement of the two can produce action. It is also clear that the supreme command is not the Emperor but the two chiefs of the two general staffs, " who constitute the supreme command in which the War and Navy Ministers participate." The army and navy, in short, are autonomous organizations treating with the central government on terms of equality.

The Cabinet published both statements and allowed the matter to rest. Japan was at war in Manchuria and was defying the League of Nations and the United States. The fighting men were on the crest of the wave and the liberals in the trough. The chronological record now stands thus: in 1931 the War Minister asserted the right to say what he liked regardless of the Cabinet. In 1933 the War and Navy Ministers intimated their independence of the Cabinet in matters affecting armaments, as just described. In 1941 the Navy Minister told the House: "The Prime Minister cannot participate in the prerogatives of the supreme command in any way."

The soldiers dominated public policy, and to all questions they brought minds steeped in a terrifying blend of Prussian and Japanese false philosophies. Their training was modeled on a devout study of modern Germany superimposed upon an Oriental groundwork which inculcates treachery, stratagem, and cruelty and teaches that all others are preparing to practice those arts.

The barbarities of the China war soon demonstrated the kind of conduct that flows from such a false philosophy. I am not speaking of Nanking, which a few shamefaced humane Japanese try to think of as an isolated outbreak, but of the general practice of the Japanese high commanders. They took few prisoners in China. After the first Chinese armies had been defeated the Japanese engaged in operations which were known as slaughter battles. In these "engagements" official statistics carefully reported the number of men slaughtered and the number of rifles taken. The discrepancy would often be greater than a hundred to one. It would be reported that a specific number of Chinese dead, sometimes as high as 14,000 or 15,000 had been counted on the field, and that six or seven hundred rifles had been captured.

An explanation was needed, but none was offered. Either the Chinese had been allowed to go back over the field of battle and collect the weapons, which was incredible, or the men whose corpses were counted had never had weapons. A Japanese officer, who seemed to be a sincere Buddhist, aware of the Buddhist canon against the taking of life, admitted in a magazine article his dislike of those massacres, but excused them on the ground of necessity. An ordinary battle between regular troops would not be called a " slaughter battle." What were such battles if not mere battues of unarmed Chinese peasants? Harsh and hellish as war is, it had felt the effect of human progress. The wounded were no longer dispatched where they lay; the defeated were no longer massacred. But that part of civilization, it seemed, had passed the Japanese army by. " Slaughter battles " were recorded among its triumphs in China. Yet General Araki could write: " What massacre, what idle fighting can there be when the Imperial army takes up arms in the proper spirit? It is very annoying to us to have our army spoken of in the same breath as the armies of other powers "!

Minds trained in cruelty and treachery are by the same process trained to distrust. Incapable of an objective analysis of the naval treaties, the young officers were convinced that the Washington ratio had been fixed because the United States was planning to dominate Asia. A strange sign of the times was the insistence of the Japanese fighting services that a crisis of unprecedented gravity was about to confront the country. The words " *hijoji* " (crisis) and " *kokunan* " (national emergency) were in all mouths. The date of the crisis and the emergency was fixed at 1935 or 1936 and it was associated with the naval-limitation agreement, which Japan did not renew. The crisis the army and navy expected was that the United States would commence a preventive war while it still had a margin of naval superiority before Japan's new secret program was completed and that the United States would be assisted by Soviet Russia.

To calm the public, a former Prime Minister and chief naval delegate, Baron Rejiro Wakatsuki, had an official conversation on the question with the Prime Minister, Admiral Saito, at the beginning of 1934. He told the press that they were agreed that " a crisis between the United States, Russia, and Japan can be averted by diplomacy."

The suggestion that there might not be a crisis gave great offense to the soldiers. To the Japanese military mind their view was a normal and realistic reading of the situation. The stronger country would always wage a preventive war. All relations between nations were decided by power. First it had to be established who was strongest. The strongest would then grant such concessions and rights as seemed proper. If the United States and Britain would recognize Japan's special rights in China, Japan would in return recognize their " legitimate " interests. If China would place itself in Japan's power Japan would allow China to " co-operate." To the American and Briton, with centuries of commercial civilization behind them — and commercial civilization, whatever its faults, teaches patience and respect for the prospective customer's point of view — this Japanese philosophy seemed a bad joke. But the Japanese officer only understood force.

Chapter XI

THE WORDS OF THE ARMY

The effort to understand the mind of the army by reading what soldiers write is hampered and often baffled by the Japanese propensity for veiling actions and intentions in misty phraseology and cloudy imagery. It is not conscious deceit or hypocrisy. It is inseparable from Japanese ways of thought, and these have been conditioned by a language which specializes in indefiniteness. It is not a case of devious approach before coming to the point. The point is there and the Japanese see it, but it is wrapped in wool. The difference between words and things is so great that what the soldier says often seems to have little relation to what he means.

" Is it true," I once said to General Araki, " that you are a dictator as some foreign newspapers say? " " Dictator! " said Araki. " What does a country which possesses the three sacred treasures [the mirror of truth, the jewel of mercy, and the sword of justice] want with a dictator? Japan needs no Hitler or Mussolini." We have to translate the general's thought as well as his words. What he meant was that the army's power, drawn from the limitless reservoir of the Emperor's prerogative, made a formal dictatorship superfluous.

A soldier who has risen to be full general, Minister for War, and a peer of the Japanese Empire should have a good mind.

If he is, moreover, a fluent speaker and a ready writer we must presume that he can express what is in his mind. Let us listen to General Araki in an article published in *Kaikosha,* the monthly magazine of the Army Club in Tokyo, and follow the thread of his thought. Internal evidences show it to be the manuscript or stenographic report of an oration such as the general was always ready to deliver.

First there is a rhapsody about the vital energy of Japan: " Imperial Japan has made her own place, unassailable like Mount Fuji soaring severe and resplendent. When we contemplate the august form of Mount Fuji and compare it with the spirit of our race, a lofty sense of elation and pride rises in our breasts." The " peerless mountain " in Japanese oratory is an infallible cheer-raiser.

General Araki discards the Buddhist doctrine of equality: " Everything in the world has its mission. The sun, the moon, and the stars have their mission. Pekingese dogs are for petting and pointers for hunting. The Japanese have their own destiny and the Chinese have theirs." The fundamental cause of the trouble with China, he says, is that the Chinese look down on the Japanese. They do so because the Japanese have immersed themselves in frivolity: " Before we can impress upon the world our importance as a nation, we must discard our frivolous ways of thinking and living. We have been despised by the Chinese and despised by the League of Nations because we do not value ourselves enough. China, unfortunately, does not understand the true spirit and strength of Japan; it relies on Americans and Europeans."

General Araki protests that the view of Japan as a warlike nation is " ill-natured and superficial ": " Japan's ideal is the realization of eternal peace. The Japanese are scrupulous, as no other nation has ever been, not to use arms where their use is unjustified. The Imperial Way does not allow us to engage in wars of aggression. That is why we are always united in an emergency."

Yet even to some Japanese it was apparent that the China war was unnecessary and they regarded it as a blunder, though the overpowering conformity of the hive made them afraid to say so. " Why do they call it a sacred war? " I asked a Japanese publisher. " What else can they call it? " he contemptuously replied, meaning: " What is the good of it? "

Interwoven with these lofty thoughts was a business-like explanation by General Araki of why Japan was at that moment making war in Manchuria. First, Manchuria and Mongolia are the gateway for the propagation of Japan's fundamental principle; second, these regions are economically inseparable from Japan; thirdly, their natural resources are necessary for the existence of the Japanese nation. But these factors, says Araki, are secondary. The urgent thing is that the Japanese should establish their prestige in Manchuria and Mongolia firmly and eternally; otherwise they may forever be deprived of the opportunity to extend the national spirit of the Empire.

The foreigner who tries to study the creed and the philosophy of " Japanism " encounters continual references back to the injunctions which Jimmu Tenno, the first human Emperor, is said to have given to his followers. Jimmu Tenno was engaged in conquering central Japan and driving out its original inhabitants. His edict, if it actually was ever uttered by him, was not recorded until some eight centuries after the event and cannot be called a historical document. Jimmu Tenno nevertheless was a historical personage; he was the chieftain who led the tribes into the fertile lands they coveted. His words are archaic and hard to translate. He bade his followers " make and stabilize this drifting land." General Araki once summed up his philosophy to a Japanese writer thus: " We are born Japanese and must consider what is our duty in the world as Japanese. The mythology of every country reveals national characteristics, and the Japanese mythology teaches us our duty. Those words of the god: ' Make and stabilize this drifting land,' uttered at the creation of the Empire, teach us our mission."

It is the perennial excuse of the aggressor. Where there is confusion, let there be order. Hitler drowns Europe in blood to unite it, and Japan devastates Asia to form a " co-prosperity sphere."

The military mind dwells fondly on the thought of a unique army in a unique nation. " Our army is matchless in the world," writes General Araki. " When the military authorities are attacked for being arrogant and interfering in politics, it is very annoying to us because those who make such criticisms are looking at the Imperial army as if it were like the armies in Europe."

General Mazaki, that tactiturn fellow traveler with the young officers, once explained why the Japanese army is unique. " Armies abroad exist on a legal basis, but the Imperial army is founded on that which is infinitely more precious than law." A certain difficulty of defining " that which is more precious " unfortunately troubles all generals and all exponents of Japanese uniqueness.

Lieutenant General Shinji Hata showed such intellectual capacity in his Staff College days that he was sent to Germany for post-graduate study. He responded splendidly to his German training. In a book which by its form seems to have been at first a series of lectures to the Staff College, Hata expounded his philosophy. He starts with the idea of a unique state.

Japan "possesses a permanent and unique characteristic," which, however, "defies analysis." In default of a positive definition Hata builds up a negative one by comparing other countries with Japan. China, it seems, is a society but not a state, a "conglomeration of peoples" which will never become a state — "we advise the Chinese to cast away their nationalism and take pride in their culture." Another eminent nationalist, Ambassador Toshio Shiratori, put this idea in more concrete form when he advised the Chinese to entrust their foreign policy and national defense to Japan.

In Japan, says General Hata, "state and society are one." It is curious how the idea of oneness haunts the Japanese. Centuries of Buddhism, teaching that the supreme end of man is reabsorption into the All, as rain is reabsorbed in the ocean, may explain the fascination of oneness to a nation in which individualism is discouraged; but the army's assertion of a unity contrary to ordinary human experience has a practical motive. The soldiers know that they are setting back the clock. They have revived the claim of a military caste ruling the nation, they know that an intelligent minority deeply fears the results of their policy, and they are under compulsion to convince themselves and others that the nation is united with them.

Other countries, continues Hata, are bound together by force or contract, but "Japan is neither a monarchy nor a democracy but a unique state where ruler and ruled go along in perfect harmony." He says other definitions of a state base it upon sovereignty, territory, or people, but omit the supreme and vital element. This vital element which Japan uniquely possesses is the eternity of the state and its consequent duty of continuous expansion. National defense in

Japan therefore means " the eternity of the state and the ever fruitful growth of natural resources . . . it means the defense of the possibility of the development of our posterity. We must protect the extensive possibilities of our children. Whoever thinks that national defense ends with the guarding of our present boundaries is ignorant of the basic idea of the state. In order to guard our ever prosperous growth, national defense must pass over our legal and geographical boundaries."

Divagating into unmilitary fields General Hata states that the immortality of the soul is also an idea peculiar to the Orient. Western individualism, he says, believes that death is the end of everything, but the Japanese regard their children as " an extension of themselves," hence " the Japanese state is eternal and requires continuous growth of resources."

This is the theory of the Japanese state and its destiny as Japanese soldiers and nationalists conceive it. It is linked to the primitive mythologies recorded in the earliest Japanese books, and, like the Hitlerite doctrine of a master race, it is an example of twentieth-century mythology. Briefly the doctrine is this: The Japanese emperors (some say the whole Japanese nation) are the descendants of the Sun Goddess. The Imperial dynasty is therefore " unbroken for ages eternal " (as the Constitution has it) and the continuity of the Imperial house for twenty-six centuries is proof of the unique character and destiny of the Japanese Empire. Such an Empire, Hata argues, has a mission of eternal expansion. And who could be better fitted to conduct this expansion and fulfill this destiny than the Japanese army and navy, so much more powerful than any other army and navy for thousands of miles around?

The conception of immortality, like that of divinity as

attributed to the Emperor, becomes curiously diluted in the Japanese mind. The immortality that the general contemplates is impersonal: we are to live in our children. We shall hardly be our familiar selves in such an immortality, but the children also will be something not themselves. It is an immortality of the hive.

General Hata regarded the United States as the inevitable enemy. Analyzing what he called the basic principle of America's Far Eastern policy, he wrote: " America is always on the alert to gain economic supremacy in the Far East. She does not hesitate to use every opportunity to block the progress of a powerful state in that region. . . . She considers the rise of a formidable power a menace to her economic aspirations and does not spare efforts to place obstacles in its path. . . . It stands to reason that America will always obstruct Japan. . . . Against what power America's armaments are directed is only too plain."

General Yoshitsugu Tatekawa, afterwards Ambassador to the Soviet Union, defended the continental policy in two sentences. First, he said, the Japanese have the right to remove every cause which might menace the existence of the Empire; and second, the Japanese are the most active and diligent people in the world today; their resources are limited, their population is increasing by a million a year, and they possess only four out of the twenty-five essential raw materials. With equal brevity General Tatekawa explained why Japan needed a large army: first, to force China to stop anti-Japanese agitations; second, to repulse the southward advance of the Soviets; and third, to maintain order in Manchuria.

A younger officer, Major T. Takashima, of the General Staff, expounded military socialism: " There is, or at least there has been, a number of nations which valued money and believed in its power. Substantial races like the Japanese and Germans value the state, honor, prestige, above material things. We have different ideas about economy. We prefer to mobilize the land, resources, man-power, and potentiality into a workable unit. When these assets are harnessed for the good of the state they will become a lever to move the world."

Those ideas of Major Takashima's are embodied in the National Mobilization Law, which for years before the attempt to conquer the Pacific began, was converting Japan into a community of 70,000,000 persons organized for total war. The major's debt to Germany is obvious. But the Hitlerite doctrines were so congenial and so closely akin to the principles of Japanese nationalism that where Japan imitated Germany it was in matters of form. The substance was there already, latent in the doctrine of a unique, ever expanding state.

The rank and file do not express political ideas. A Japanese soldier wrote a diary of his thoughts during his service in China which was afterwards published and became a best-seller. It was a kindly book, full of the misty sentimental introspection which pervades Japanese fiction, and the public devoured it eagerly. It helped to soothe minds made uncomfortable by grapevine stories of the atrocities of Nanking.

Another Japanese soldier, First-class Private Taro Tanaka, attempted to explain the Japanese soldier in an article published in *Nichi Nichi* in 1941. At first reading I supposed the writer to be a literary youth doing a piece under the stress of warlike emotion on a civilian mind. I was mistaken; according to the *Nichi Nichi*, he was a soldier in the ranks who had served for three years in China, apparently with his eyes shut. But it was interesting, alarming, and humiliating to see how an educated and intelligent youth could drug his brain.

The Japanese soldier, he wrote, is not a pagan. Though seldom a Christian, he has faith in a divine omniscient being and in the absolute values of virtue and sacrifice. He is not " the Nietzschean superman nor the reincarnation of Sparta," he is "a unique being, strong, noble, and beautiful, from whom much can be expected for the destruction of evil in the present and the progress of humanity in the future." When he enters the army the Japanese soldier gives his soul and body, his all, to the Emperor. " No longer is his ego his own; it is the Emperor's. He is now one in a great endless force reaching back to the era of his god-ancestors and forward to the infinite perfection of his Emperor's godlike idealism." The Japanese soldier accomplishes his ideal only in death; hence he willingly enters the suicide bands which undertake desperate enterprises. After death he expects to become " a demon-who-guards-his-country." He is not complete until his spirit rests in the military shrine in Tokyo.

Another Japanese writer, himself a Christian, explains this attitude of mind. " To the Japanese," he says, " a dead-and-gone feeling about the dead is beyond the pale of common sense." They believe their ancestral spirits still live in the land, as they shall live after death.

The soldier-writer described the ideal death of a Japanese soldier. He asks his comrades to turn his face towards the Imperial Palace and his last words are " Long live the Emperor! " A quaint story is told to illustrate the working of this belief in his naïve mind. The regiment had marched all day over hot mountain trails in the blazing sun. A soldier accidentally ripped his trousers. When fifteen minutes' rest was ordered he brought out his needle and thread and began to repair the damage. His comrades asked why he did not rest like the others; a hole in his pants wouldn't hinder him from fighting. He replied: " We do not know when we shall die. How can I die with a hole in my trousers? " He was thinking, says the narrator, of the time when he must face east and, dying, bid farewell to his Emperor.

There in its primitive simplicity is the racial instinct which gives Japanese generals the blind obedience of their cannon fodder.

Pamphlets poured from the War and Navy offices in Tokyo during the decade 1931–41. The army's brochures were the more interesting of the two. They reflected the ambitions and ideas that had taken possession of the minds of the young officers and were crystallizing into a national policy. The pamphlets were not born out of the emotions of the China war. They preceded the China war and they prepared the way for the greater war that followed. Re-reading them today with the advantage of hindsight is like turning to a fulfilled prophecy. The ideas they publicized — an armed nation and total war — have incarnated themselves in the war now raging in the Pacific.

A regular date of publication was March 10, Army Day, the anniversary of the Battle of Mukden, in which Japan defeated Russia. The budget is voted at the end of March and the pamphlets were part of the propaganda for ever increasing estimates.

The stock theme was usually the need for greater armaments against Russia. The pamphleteers believed that war with Russia would come earlier than the war with America and Britain. This lapse of prophetic power is explained by Hitler's devious Russian policy. The advantage Japan expected to gain from association with Germany was at first only an opportunity to invade Siberia while Germany assailed Russia in Europe. Later Hitler converted the Anti-Comintern Pact into the Axis alliance by showing Japan the far grander prospects of loot that would follow the downfall of Britain.

The pamphlets show that plans for total war were engaging staff officers even before the China war had begun. Russia, America, and Britain were held up to the public as the potential enemies Japan must one day fight. The United States was accused of seeking to dominate the Pacific. England was reviled for having discarded the Anglo-Japanese alliance at the bidding of America. Both America and Britain were exhibited as Japan's enemies in China. The Japanese people were told that Britain and America were continually interfering in Asia to check their rightful expansion. The word " encirclement " had not yet been imported from Germany, but the thing itself was persistently held before the public. Only by stronger and stronger armaments, they were told, could the nation live and progress.

The pamphleteers promulgated the idea of impending crisis. They had Japan at the crossroads of fate years before General Tojo used the phrase. " It is possible," wrote the 1934 pamphleteer, " that the 1935 naval conference will lead to a head-on collision between Japan and America and Britain. As this is the decisive point for the whole future of our country, we must satisfy the navy's demands at all costs. Our dignity cannot tolerate another treaty based on the ratio system. The solution of the Pacific problem and our success in China depend on naval strength."

The " crisis " years passed without any sign of action from the democracies, who were by then too deeply concerned about Hitler to pay much attention to a Far Eastern power whose strength they underestimated. The Japanese army's eyes were also turned to Berlin, and the army's philosophy began to be explained in terms borrowed from the Nazis. Future wars will be " symphonies of armed force, economic power, and ideological warfare," the public read. To emerge victorious the nation must in time of peace organize a synthesis of all its forces. Administrative renovation was required because unless individualistic institutions and liberal politics were fundamentally changed there could be no hope for advancement of the national fortunes. " The state must be rebuilt on the basis of the Japanese spirit and in accordance with the needs of modern armaments. A state reorganized on a totalitarian basis has latent power in time of peace which would prove the decisive factor in an emergency. Thus administrative renovation and adequacy in armaments form an inseparable unity." Need it be explained that " administrative renovation " is a characteristic euphemism for the kind of state structure that then existed in Germany, Italy, and Russia and that now exists in Japan?

As signs of storm in Europe multiplied, the pamphlets began to focus attention on the opportunities that would open before Japan when Europe went to war. The opportunity would be so vast that it would need armaments beyond the financial capacity of Japan, as then organized, to provide, and from then on the army advocated national socialism.

" It is impossible to get sufficient armaments from the present system. The attempt would bring about national bankruptcy and dissolve the unity of the nation. We must set up a new economic system which can provide the expenditures necessary for defense without threatening the national life."

This pamphlet was circulated among business men and

they did not like it. Questions were asked in the House. The War Minister in a sedative reply pooh-poohed the activities of his subordinates. Documents issued by the Press Section of the War Office, he pointed out, were not so important as documents bearing the signature of the Minister: " The pamphlet describes ideas current in the army. National policy is being studied by my subordinates, but the study has not been completed. The pamphlet contains some stiff words about reform of the economic structure, but the true intention of the army is far from such radical thoughts." The Minister was mistaken; it was the opinions of the youth officer pamphleteers, not those of the old generals, that prevailed.

The red coloring in the thought of the young officers began to show up boldly. The Japanese people were urged to " liberate their minds from the idea of an individualistic economy." " In order to attain full efficiency of the human factor in national defense and also to make possible total mobilization it is necessary that every Japanese should have an equal chance to share in the material wealth of the country. A situation in which economic superiority is enjoyed by only a few while the masses are sunk in poverty gives rise to class struggles. Such a situation can no longer be overlooked from the point of view of defense."

The army denied that it wanted a military dictatorship or a fascist regime; all it wanted was " a national-defense state," in which all the resources of the nation would be organized for use in war. This particular pamphlet (November 1936) showed a prophetic insight and revealed the line of thought which led inexorably to war. European war was deemed inevitable and the Japanese were warned that they were approaching the real crisis this time. It was still assumed that Russia would be the principal enemy. The Japanese were shocked when Hitler made his spider-and-fly non-aggression pact with Stalin. Much persuasion and the German victories in western Europe were needed to convince them that they too should shake hands with the unspeakable Soviets. Hitler's propensity to make the swastika a double cross helped to delay the war.

III. *The Murder-and-Hokum Societies*

Chapter XII

THE PATRIOTIC THIEVES' KITCHEN

The patriotic societies of Japan are the nurseries from which young fanatics are sent forth armed with bomb and pistol. They are a native growth with no exact counterpart in other countries. Like the Chinese secret societies they prey on the rich under a pretense of defending the poor; like the Sicilian Mafia they make murder a business; and like the Ku Klux Klan they exploit tribal prejudices; but these are only incidental behaviourist features. The Ku Klux Klan in its highest heyday could never be called a part of the political system of the United States. The Imperial Kleagle — if that is the correct title — was not invited to the White House, but not long ago the Tokyo newspapers announced that Mitsuru Toyama, the patron saint of the Black Dragon Society, had lunched with Prince Konoye. The Japanese patriotic societies are an integral element of Japanese political life and are accepted as such by the government, the politicians, and the public.

It was difficult for any adult foreigner to take those societies seriously. When their leaders wrote or spoke in public they exhibited themselves as stuffed shirts. In the lower range the societies are a mixture of ward politicians, poolroom loafers, gang leaders, and racketeers. In the upper reaches they proclaim a lofty interest in high politics, domestic and foreign, but especially foreign. Their leaders obtain funds from the government, from politicians, and from big business. The typical patriotic society of the higher class is a group or gang of intensely nationalistic temper with a belief in direct action. In a list of the personnel of one well-known society there appeared the following illuminating item: "—— chief of executive section; can mobilize a large number of ruffians in an emergency." The Japanese word I have translated " ruffians " is " *soshi* "; it once meant a stout follower or strong fellow, now it means a thug, a gangster. Such ruffians are always ready to sacrifice their lives for the cause, by which they mean they are prepared to commit murder and take the consequences. These were never deadly. Nobody has ever been hanged in Japan for murdering a prime minister.

The self-announced mission of the patriotic societies is to see that weak-kneed statesmen do not deviate from the path of glory. The path of glory is always bloody; war abroad and dictatorship at home are the essential elements of national greatness in the simple creed of the Japanese patriots. Their claims to have influenced policy are exaggerated, but they at least yelled loudly and murdered when necessary for the policy which eventually won.

The patriotic societies exist in a state of perpetual flux, eternally dissolving and recombining. Any list that is made of them is obsolete in a year. I once investigated a list which included ninety-nine societies with names and addresses. The registered addresses were sometimes the suburban home of a secretary, sometimes merely the number of some cheap office block with a mobile clientele. A good many high-sounding titles were but the trade names of enterprising rascals who lived by soliciting contributions and got them from people who would rather part with money than be haunted by bullies. Some societies had offices and staffs and some maintained dingy hostels where patriots of thuggish appearance came and went. The office of the Black Dragon Society was also the home of its president, Ryohei Uchida, and he had a number of secretaries and assistants. In general a patriotic society, even the biggest, was one man with a group of adherents and followers, these ranging from fellow thinkers and fellow travelers who could write and speak or collect funds to moronic youths who could be sent out to threaten or to kill.

The Japanese language lends itself with facility to combinations of ideographs with a lofty sound. Characters signifying nation, empire, patriotism are the commonest titles of patriotic societies and Great Japan is much in use as an adjective of number and quality, though the membership may be like that of the three tailors of Tooley Street who proclaimed themselves " We, the people of England." A few characteristic titles selected from a long list will show how it is done:

" Dai Nippon Kokusui-kai (Great Japan Spirit [or Essence] Society) ; object: imperialism.

Yamato Minro-kai (Japanese National Society) ; object: guidance of general thought and promotion of military arts.

Kenkoku-kai (Foundation of the Country Society) ; object: imperialism and realization of the spirit of Japan.

Kokuhonsha (Basis of the Country Society) ; object: guidance of thoughts.

Naichi-Gaiko-Sakushin Domei (League for the Improvement of Administration and Diplomacy) ; object: improvement of diplomacy, imperialism.

Daiko-sha (Great Work Society) ; object: imperialism, foundation of a new Japan.

165

Kenki-kai (Imperial Flag Society) ; object: extermination of anti-Japanese thought of right and left.

Dai Nippon Seigi-dan (Great Japan Justice Society) ; object: morality first, improvement of society.

Meikoku-kai (Illustrious Virtue Society) ; objects: fundamental extermination of anti-Japanese thoughts, re-establishment of moral Japan.

Kokkyo Semmei-dan (National Principle Society) ; objects: prevention of Jewish intrigue, explication of the national principle.

Daiko-sha (Great Unification Society) ; objects: clarification of nationality, co-operation of Asiatic races.

Goko-kai (Society for Protection of the Emperor) ; objects: exclude European thoughts, display the originality of the Japanese race.

Aikoku Taishu-to (Patriotic Mass Party) ; object: social patriotism.

New groupings spring up like mushrooms when the situation seems to require them. During the agitation over the London naval-limitation conference an All-Japan Patriotic Conference for a United Front was organized, and from it sprang a smaller group called the Advance Guards. The advance guard was a death band, or murder gang, and its members performed the rite of blood brotherhood at a temple in Tokyo. A similar gang called itself the Volunteer Union of Empire. When the young officers and the rural patriots were planning the murders of 1932 a society appeared called the Conference of Patriotic Farmers for United Action. Another of the same period was the Patriotic Love-Country Blood and Iron Band. In the years preceding the war, posters denouncing America, Britain, and Russia would suddenly appear on the vacant walls of Tokyo overnight. A telegraph pole near the American Embassy was a favorite place for pasting them. These posters were signed by an "Association of Fellow Thinkers on the Present Situation." Such conferences and associations were temporary affairs, but the men who organized them and worked in them were members of the patriotic societies. The patriotic societies formed a permanent reserve of political malcontents ready for use by unscrupulous leaders in any crisis.

Why Japanese politics of the extreme right should have taken the form of bosses and gangs working in darkness is explained by certain social conditions that existed naturally within the feudal shell Japan has so recently cracked. The political structure of old Japan was some three hundred clans, each ruled absolutely by a hereditary chief, and over them was a military government headed by a hereditary generalissimo (shogun) who ruled in the name of the secluded and powerless Emperor. The social structure consisted of five hereditary classes ranking in the following order: nobles, warriors, farmers, artisans, and traders. The warriors (samurai) were maintained in idleness by their lords; they alone had the right to carry weapons; much has been written of their chivalry, but they were less admired by the people who had to live with them than by subsequent writers in the romantic tradition; many were bullies who abused their right to carry arms and the immunity their position gave them. The plebs formed clubs and gangs in self-defense — "associations of chivalrous men" who professed to defend the oppressed.

A singular institution of the time created a reservoir of plebeian man-power from which those associations drew recruits. The military government ordained that the feudal lords should spend half of the year at the generalissimo's court in Tokyo and half on their estates, a device which successfully prevented the growth of conspiracies and combinations among the clans. The main roads of Japan were thronged with the processions of the chiefs traveling between their distant domains and the administrative capital. The color prints of Hiroshige have depicted in imperishable art the armies of burden-bearing coolies that traversed Japan carrying the banners and baggage of the feudal lords. Those coolies had bosses who farmed them out and received in return rations of rice. Each boss had his own gang; they were called Otokodate, and their master was the Father of the Otokodate. The system survives today; the processions have long ceased to move on the roads, but modern contractors require gangs of coolies and they employ them through labor bosses. Deadly feuds, ending in murder, still occur between rival bosses and their thugs even in so modern a thing as the moving-picture industry.

Two Tokyo gangs each claimed the exclusive right to " shake down " a motion-picture company for a percentage of the profits accruing from films starring Torazo Hirozawa, Japan's leading " naniwabushi " singer. A Kobe gangster known as the Korean Tiger was sent up to Tokyo by a Kobe gangster syndicate to " mediate " in the dispute. The Korean Tiger met with the chief of a Tokyo gang in a room of the Naniwaya Club. He was attended by two henchmen; the negotiator for the other side was similarly guarded and had posted two more outside the door. All carried two-handed swords. The Tokyo chieftain had no intention of accepting the Tiger's mediation, and he brought on a quarrel. The Tiger leaped to his feet, drawing his sword from under his cushion on the floor. At that moment the two plug-uglies who had been lurking at the door burst in. The Tiger bounded out of the window, and his two henchmen were forced to follow him, fighting all the way. The Tiger stayed out of the fray till one of his followers went down with a mortal cut in the belly. Then he went into battle and killed the Tokyo leader with a deadly crosswise slash from the waist to the navel. A second later his sword arm was hacked off at the shoulder. The police arrived in answer to a telephone call from a shopkeeper and found three gangsters dead or mortally wounded and four others bleeding on the sidewalk.

After the restoration the samurai lost their privileged position and associations of brave men were no longer needed to defend the plebs against the arrogance of the warrior caste. But when opposition to the new government developed, it embodied itself in the old forms. Associations of the discontented or the adventurous had played a great part in destroying the old system, and the custom continued in the new; it was the only political technique the Japanese knew. The new Imperial government was in substance a group dictatorship of the victorious clans. The gates of opportunity were suddenly opened wide to their members, but the lesser clans, or those which had failed to climb on the victor's band-wagon, were no better off than before. The first patriotic societies were formed in Fukuoka, a district swarming with *ronin,* dispossessed samurai, unemployed warriors, who found, when the restoration struggle was over, that the two powerful clans which conducted the revolution had seized the fleshpots. Out of this discontent the patriotic societies were born. Mitsuru Toyama, the son of a penniless Fukuoka samurai, was the first to organize *ronin* gangs in modern Japan. They could not change the new regime, so they professed a loud devotion to the restored Emperor and preyed upon the victorious clans.

Toyama's admirers compared him to Robin Hood, taking from the rich to give to the poor:

> For they shall take who have the power,
> And they shall keep who can.

Exactly the same motive appears in the patriotic movement today which asserts that the politicians and capitalists have stolen the fruits of the restoration.

Another Fukuoka man felt aggrieved by the dominance of the two victorious clans. He was a modern-minded man and he chose new methods as Toyama had chosen old. He assailed clan government by speech and agitation and rallied the public to the cause of liberty. "Itagaki may die, but liberty never," was a saying of his that became as famous as Patrick Henry's. But the liberals and the gang leaders shared the same grudge against the monopolizing clans. The political parties which arose at Itagaki's summons were too near the feudal age to have any true comprehension of the liberalism they wore as a garment; they preyed on the bureaucrats in their way, and Toyama and his henchmen preyed in another way. The patriots were the kind of men who loved war and aggression; their chauvinism was real and it welled up from deep native springs, but it was also a cloak they wore to blackmail the clans newly rich in power. The politicians wore a cloak of democracy, but they also devote themselves to extracting their share of the advantages which the bureaucrats possessed. And the clan statesmen compromised with both, and used both. The public conscience admitted both methods, and sometimes in its fitful way condemned both.

That is the background of the patriotic societies. They carried over into the politics of new Japan the feudal methods of the old. The clan leaders of the Empire recognized a certain " sincerity," or legitimacy, in the movement, and instead of extirpating it, they traded with it. It opened a back door to a political career and more than one future cabinet minister got his start by making himself useful to a local boss. The custom was tacitly accepted, like bootlegging; and as bootlegging brought gangsterism along, so *roninism* in Japanese politics was a wide-open door to professional patriotism, murder, and blackmail.

Japanese nationalism is the cloth from which all patriotic societies are cut. Their titles and their professed objects are affected by the political fashions of the day; nationalism, imperialism, chauvinism are the constant element in their creed. It has been combined at times with agitations for the " rights of the people " — votes and a parliament; in more recent years it has demanded the dissolution of political parties, the establishment of a military government and a national socialist state. In foreign policy the patriots were always aggressive, agitating for war. They always demanded bigger armaments; always denounced the " weak-kneed diplomacy " of their own government; hating all foreigners, they disliked England and America most and they admired the Germany of Bismarck as much as the Germany of Hitler. They are weak in debate, either written or spoken, and wholehearted in their dislike of " government by talk " considering that reason and persuasion are weak instruments unworthy of strong men armed. They have evolved a loyalty of their own by which they reconcile devotion to a divine Emperor with disregard of his edicts and injunctions, and make mutiny, murder, and revolt permissible.

Their continuous decay and reappearance in different form reveals the fermenting, yeasty mind of new Japan, bewildered between the worship of the old, so heavily impressed on the plastic intelligence at school, and the acquired experience of a world where everything is new. I wandered wearily and vainly through reams of patriotic society prospectuses seeking for concrete programs and statements of principle in plain language. I found myself in a collection of strange shibboleths such as I had never before encountered. The patriots deal only in untranslatable platitudes: they demand " Clarification of the National Polity," " Promotion of the Foundation Principle of Japan," " Government according to the Principle of One State, One Family," " Oneness of Emperor and People," " Oneness of Man and Land." But the permanent element — the yeast itself — is the urge to conquest and expansion. Since the army took charge, the Black Dragon Society and the rest have found their occupation as professional jingoes gone, though they have the satisfaction of knowing that their policies — war, conquest, and military government — have triumphed.

Chapter XIII

THE PATRON SAINT OF THE BLACK DRAGONS

A young Japanese nobleman, wearing "a suit of green armor and the headdress appropriate to his rank," rode into history in 1867 leading a troop for the Emperor in the restoration wars. In the city of Fukuoka a sturdy, unruly urchin was then peddling sweet potatoes. The green-clad youth became Prince Saionji, the Elder Statesman; the other, Mitsuru Toyama, became the most powerful of Japan's gang leaders and is today the patriarch of its professional patriots. Through lives prolonged past the ordinary span both followed their stars with perfect consistency. Both became venerated public men, but the gangster had the greater success. When Saionji died, the liberal Empire he had worked for was in dissolution. Toyama has seen even more wars and invasions than those he demanded. He will die in his bed; it was not the fault of his followers that Saionji died in his.

Those long, coeval careers exhibit the Jekyll and Hyde strains of Japan.

Saionji's public services were open and, so to speak, commonplace. He was nobleman, Governor, diplomat, Cabinet Minister, Prime Minister, confidential adviser to the Emperor.

Toyama was a man of mystery. The Japanese are an inquisitive people, avid for personal details about their heroes and accustomed to regard the most intimate details with medical nonchalance. Thousands of pages have been published about Toyama, yet in this Mississippi of words you will fish in vain for facts. We are told that he is a great man, but his most devoted disciples cannot say why; he has done great things for his country, they assert, but none will plainly say how. Reading those praises, one at last senses an inner conflict so deep that the writers are perhaps scarcely aware of it, a conflict between the conviction that Toyama is a great Japanese hero and a feeling that if the truth were faced the idol would be seen as no hero but a medieval-minded freebooter.

In a tyrannical feudal society Toyama might have "tempered despotism with assassination" and deserved the fame that legend and ballad would have transmitted to posterity. Toyama, bringing the methods of the Mafia into a country which had adopted Western standards of public conduct, was an anachronism and a blot. He seemed a hero to immature, unreflecting minds because they did not understand the use of the votes that had been given them and still considered assassination a heroic method of redressing the wrongs and the errors of governments.

Toyama never held any public office, never made a speech or wrote an article. If he influenced governments it was as a master of assassins and bullies. He escaped the fate which his medieval prototypes usually suffered. He once remarked that a true patriot would never starve. He was thirty-five years old before he possessed a silk suit such as comfortable Japanese would wear. But in the remaining two thirds of his life he never lacked comfort or money to give his retainers. In his old age he was honored by the court and entertained by prime ministers. He had after all been useful; more than once he had been able to call off the pack that followed him. He could, in his day, control the patriotic brotherhoods, and by doing so he served the government.

He is not to be judged by Occidental standards. He is a purely Japanese figure, projecting the Middle Ages into the modern era, which had overtaken Japan with lightning suddenness. The feudal survivals were there, cheek by jowl with the modern age, lurking, dagger in hand, behind the ballot boxes, and Toyama was as truly a representative figure as Saionji. Neither of them was of heroic proportions. But everything is relative. To the liberal West one was an angel of darkness, the other an angel of light. That valuation was unjust; each was a type of modern Japan. Saionji, like the Emperor Meiji, for whose restoration he fought, was a type of that modern Japan which sought knowledge throughout the world and proclaimed government by public opinion. Toyama was a type of the vague, undefinable " Japanism " which lay like a hot core under the suave new surface.

Toyama, the son of an obscure samurai in reduced circumstances, was born in Fukuoka in 1855. He is a famous man in Japan and is even known to the world in a dim way. " A Japanese schoolboy might not know the name of the Prime Minister," wrote an admirer, " but he knows the name of Mitsuru Toyama." Yet while his admirers agree that Toyama's character is greater than that of ordinary men, they do not produce evidence or illustration.

A biographer, Mr. Toshio Yoshida, sat like another Boswell at Toyama's feet almost daily for twenty-five years, but all that came of such industry is a collection of trivial anecdotes. The *Japan Times* published a supplement in Toyama's honor which contained thirty-two articles written by men who had first-hand knowledge of Toyama and of the inner political history of his day. The writers agree that he is a very great man, but by tacit consent they are all silent on the actions which made him great.

A witness who commands respect is Mr. Taketora Ogata, chief editor of the Tokyo *Asahi*. None knows better than Mr. Ogata the importance of facts, but he dealt delicately with facts when writing about Toyama: " Toyama is often represented abroad as if he were the chieftain of some secret society for political assassination. But he who has met him but once can never fail to discover in him a big heart, a heart like a deep mountain lake filled with clear water. The depth and breadth of his kindly nature may be seen in every little thing he does. As he sits in his living-room in summer he is often annoyed by mosquitoes, but none of them is ever mortally punished." Evasion of a question is a way of answering it and when the ablest editor in Japan, having raised the question whether Toyama is or is not a " chieftain of assassins," answers it with talk about mountain lakes and mosquitoes, we can draw our own conclusions. Toyama in his active days was a commander of bullies ready to engage in violence and murder for political causes. His mastery of this trade is the secret of his fame.

To be a bully was in Toyama's young days a recognized and not dishonorable way by which an under-privileged ambitious youth might enter a political career. A slightly younger contemporary was Kenzo Adachi. He began by participating in the intrigues which culminated in the barbarous murder of the Queen of Korea and ended as Home Minister and " god of elections " in a " liberal " Japanese government. His last exploit was a political coup which resulted in Japan going off gold. It was popularly believed that millions were made by financiers who knew what was coming. Soon afterwards Adachi built himself a temple dedicated to eight great sages, including Jesus, Buddha, and Mohammed, and there in tranquillity he spends the evening of his days.

Those strong-armed practitioners of medieval politics were known as *soshi,* a term which has been flatteringly translated as " strong gentlemen " and " daring characters." It soon came to mean bullies and gangsters and became unsavory. Then they were called by the politer and more romantic term " *ronin,*" literally " wave-men," the term given to samurai or feudal retainers who for one reason or another had become men without a master. The samurai was a licensed killer; the ronin was an unlicensed but equally honorable killer. The political ronin of whom Toyama is the type was accepted as a legitimate figure in Japan's public life. To prove this it is but necessary to observe the position enjoyed by Toyama in his old age. At public meetings he makes no speeches but is given the honor of leading the " Banzai " for the Emperor. He was a guest at the marriage of the Crown Prince Hirohito and at the coronation when Hirohito became Emperor. Prime ministers call on him and Prince Konoye invites him to luncheon. One such invitation was given and accepted just after a member of the Black Dragon Society had shot at Baron Hiranuma, Home Minister in the Konoye Cabinet. Obviously Toyama had nothing to do with the crime. It was nevertheless an example of his methods.

It is impossible to know from any written or recorded words of Toyama's whether he is a man of intellectual capacity. " One is at a loss to know in what his greatness really consists," wrote Ryohei Uchida, Toyama's foremost disciple and president of the Black Dragon Society; " he is an example of a man who refrains from using his mental and physical faculties." Panegyrists pay tribute to his great courtesy. Mr. Takejiro Tokonami, Cabinet Minister and leader of a political party, wrote: " When I meet Toyama I feel the potency of a person to whom money, honor, and life do not mean anything."

In old age a venerable beard conceals half of his face though an emphatic lower lip is seen. His eyes behind his spectacles beam with benevolence like those of a Cheeryble Brother. His looks and demeanor inspire confidence, and even a hostile observer like myself receives in his presence a strong impression that Toyama is a man with whom to go tiger-shooting.

Toyama has told his Boswells little about his early days; his mother is not mentioned, and no detail gives life to that doubtful label pinned on his father, " a samurai in reduced circumstances." Besides his potato-peddling there are stories of an unsuccessful apprenticeship to a clog-maker. The only detail recorded about a sketchy education is that he attended a seminary kept by a masculine dame who wore a sword and told her pupils tales of national heroes. Japan was smoldering with revolution, and crank academies were common.

By 1875 the first flush of revolutionary enthusiasm had died away. The victorious clans were doing very well by their adherents; the others, including Toyama's, were treated like poor relations. There was much discontent, and the invasion of Korea was advocated as a means of distracting the people's minds from their own troubles. Groups were formed among the discontented, the ambitious, and the idle to push this agitation, and young Toyama began his career by joining the local group.

The agitation culminated in three rebellious outbreaks. The gravest of them, known to history as the Satsuma rebellion of 1877, led by the " Great Saigo," was bloodily put down by the new government after several months of fighting. Toyama was thrown into prison, but released when Saigo,

defeated, killed himself. When the eminent restoration statesman Okubo, father of the present Count Makino (whose life
has been many times attempted by the patriotic gangs), was
assassinated, Toyama was again arrested, but by that time he
had a considerable following and the government allowed
him to go after a short detention.

The government's conscript armies were contemptuously
called farmer-soldiers. They defeated the samurai, however, to
the amazement of the multitude. Rebellion and violence were
temporarily discredited and the soshi were at a loose end.
Toyama consulted another young man of the region, who
afterwards became Count Itagaki and acquired fame as a liberal leader and founder of a premature liberal party. Itagaki
told him that speech and agitation were the proper instruments to use in the modern Empire and Toyama agreed. A
" Society of Patriots " (Aikokusha) was founded. Many other
societies sprang from its loins. They united in one called
" Society for the Attainment of Parliament," with 90,000
members. The government promised to grant a constitution and establish a parliament and in 1891 the promise
was fulfilled. Toyama was asked to become a candidate for
the House of Representatives, but he refused. He knew his
vocation.

Following a traditional practice which still flourishes and
provides at once a cloak, a livelihood, and a recruiting ground,
he founded in his native town a seminary to train youths. It
was at first, according to Toyama's friends, " the center of the
liberal movement in Fukuoka," and it sent delegates to the
" Society for the Attainment of Parliament." Later, in one
of the incessant and untraceable mutations of such groups, the
seminary and society coalesced into a new organization called
the Genyosha. Its platform was three sounding phrases: " Rev-

ere the Imperial House "; " Love the Fatherland "; " Protect the Rights of the People."

Its most famous pupil was Koki Hirota, afterwards Ambassador, Foreign Minister, and Prime Minister. Mr. Hirota remained loyal in sentiment to those early days, but his public career had nothing in common with the teachings of the Genyosha.

The Genyosha displayed its true colors in the election of 1892. It was a contest between the government and the popular parties. Toyama allied himself with the government; gangs of his followers were sent out to the constituencies to terrorize voters; 35 people were killed and 395 wounded. The government nevertheless was defeated, and resigned when the enraged new House assembled. The conduct of the Genyosha's bravos had not been in keeping with the society's professions, and apologists afterwards explained that Toyama had sided with the government because he thought a strong foreign policy more important than popular rights.

At the moment the advocates of a strong foreign policy were demanding increased armaments in order to chastise China. A year earlier they had demanded abolition of the extraterritoriality imposed upon Japan when she first opened her ports to foreign trade. Toyama visited the Prime Minister, Prince Ito, and remonstrated with him; Ito and his Foreign Minister, Count Okuma, were at the time trying to negotiate an agreement with the treaty powers. They stuck to their guns and the next move was an attempt to assassinate Okuma by a member of the Genyosha. Okuma lost his leg; the bomb-thrower committed suicide and became a popular hero, and the effort to reach a compromise with foreign powers on the question was dropped.

Toyama was arrested and released for lack of evidence, but,

writes one of his biographers, "after this he was feared by all statesmen." The government tried to deal with him on the lines sometimes adopted in China when a war lord accepts a million for traveling expenses and departs on a trip to Europe. It was suggested that Toyama make a journey to the South Seas, but the offer was refused.

During the years between the Satsuma rebellion (1877) and the attempt on Okuma (1892), Toyama was making his way upwards through the hierarchy of ruffians who flourished in the dark alleys of Japanese politics. He was ostensibly on the liberal side, shouting with those who agitated against the dominant clans and demanded a parliament. But Toyama's liberalism was merely a protective coloring adapted to his surroundings. He conceives of himself today as a man of the people who has risen to eminence; something survives of the tough little boy peddling potatos and embittered because his people were deprived of the prizes that had fallen to the victorious clans. In his old age he supported the agitation for manhood suffrage. He was in general prepared to support whatever the mob supported.

His own ideas, so far as they can be judged from his infrequent utterances, are the crude notions that appear by a kind of spontaneous generation in the muddy depths of society. When the Emperor Meiji died in 1912 Toyama signed a manifesto calling on the Cabinet to "immolate itself" in retribution for its failure to "give the Emperor advice when he neglected his health." The allusion is to His Majesty's liking for French wines. Toyama opposed the visit to Europe which finished the present Emperor's education; there was talk of his followers laying themselves on the rails in front of the royal train; but after Prince Saionji's son had been attacked the agitation died away.

On the other hand his admirers give Toyama credit for extricating the court and the government of the day from a singular dispute over the marriage of the present Emperor and Empress. Prince Yamagata, the venerable field-marshal who controlled the army and the Choshu clan, opposed the choice of a bride. No reason except one was given for opposition to a marriage which has proved happy and fruitful: it was alleged that the buxom young Princess was color-blind. The real reason lay in Yamagata's fear that the influence of a rival clan would be strengthened by the wedding. Yamagata eventually withdrew his opposition. Toyama's eulogists allege that he told Yamagata that his personal safety could not be guaranteed if he continued to disturb the tranquillity of the Imperial household. Yamagata was not the man to be scared by such threats, and the claim made on Toyama's behalf is probably untrue, but it illustrates the material of which Toyama's fame is built and the kind of activity his followers believed him to exercise.

Toyama was a lifelong chauvinist; apart from that he had no political ideas. He was not interested in ideas; he was a stuffed shirt — stuffed with the patriotic platitudes he dispensed to his foreign visitors.

The accounts of those unrecorded years which Toyama's admirers have preserved follow the well-worn heroic tradition. He sojourned in the mountains living on herbs, giving himself mental training and becoming fearless of death and indifferent to comfort. He walked barefoot and scorned the luxury of a mosquito net. He engaged in an endurance test with a Zen priest as to who should longest lie awake and motionless. It ended in amicable agreement that both had won. Which of the two first detected the other sleeping has not been recorded.

Those ascetic exercises were interspersed with periods when he drank mightily and competed successfully with cabinet ministers for the smiles of fashionable geisha girls. He had visions of a successful money-making career. When he first met the late Count Soyeshima, then Foreign Minister, Soyeshima asked what he could do for him and Toyama replied that the most urgent business at the moment was to make him a rich man. Soyeshima treated the remark as a joke, but it was an age of easy riches for people who could be useful to the new rulers. Through the unexplained kindness of a prefectural governor or, as some say, by borrowing at the time of the Russo-Japanese War, Toyama became the owner of mining rights which he sold for 700,000 yen. Many queer stories are told of fortunes made in Japan's early wars when the utility of the printing press for turning out money on a large scale had just been discovered.

If wealth came lightly, it went lightly. Toyama distributed his money to his followers with a lavish and careless hand. The editor of the *Asahi* as a child saw Toyama handing out bundles of banknotes to needy followers without troubling to count them. They were wrapped in paper just as they had come from the bank, and he estimated the value of a package by its thickness.

Today Japanese policy wants to establish a co-prosperity sphere for Greater East Asia; in Toyama's days it wished to promote the peace of the Far East and it caused the war with China in 1894 and the war with Russia in 1904. The agitation for expansion began with the rebellion of 1877. The peace party won and seventeen years of peace followed. But the victory was only temporary. The effete Korean government was never out of difficulties. A Korean malcontent named Kim fled to Japan and was taken up by Toyama. He was decoyed to Shanghai by emissaries of the Korean government and killed. The murder of one whom the Genyosha had undertaken to protect gave its leader a grievance. The society sent representatives to General Kawakami, then War Minister. Toyama's biographer records the interview and its consequences in terms which can never be verified, but they ring true.

The War Minister told the deputation (according to their own account) that the civilian Cabinet was against war, but that if someone started a fire it would have to be put out and he would gladly be the fireman. The deputation " understood his meaning"; they reported to Toyama and he organized a band called Tenyukyo or " Fire-setters," fifteen in number, who went to Korea and established relations with the rebels. Toyama, the boss, remained behind and, " calling youths to him," organized a " rear guard " to send over if the fifteen failed. The Korean government forces attacked the rebels, were surprised to find Japanese aiding them, and asked China for help. " China dispatched forces to Korea, and General Kawakami was able to persuade the Prime Minister, Prince Ito, to send an expeditionary force, and the war of 1894 with China commenced." So runs the Genyosha's claim.

This is not a complete account of the origins of the first China war, but it illustrates Toyama's view of his activities. The " Fire-setters " were arrested when they returned, but they were acquitted for want of evidence. They claimed later that their services had been " recognized " by Japanese generals.

The war ended in China's defeat. Marquis Inouye was sent to Seoul to represent Japan, which had become by force of arms the paramount power. He produced reforms faster than the Koreans could digest them and he was too moderate for the chauvinists at home. He was succeeded by General Viscount Miura, a " passionate patriot " who (again quoting the Toyama biography) " with the help of Japanese patriots and soshi belonging to the Genyosha conducted a *coup d'état.*"

The mission of the " passionate patriot " was short. He went to Korea in September 1895, and in January 1896 he was placed on trial in Japan for the murder of the Queen of the country to which he had been accredited. The preliminary court in Japan found that Miura had been greatly troubled by discovering that Japanese influence in Seoul was less powerful than he expected. He came to the conclusion that this was due to the Queen, a woman of masterful character, and he decided that the only remedy was to have her killed.

Arrangements were secretly made with the Korean faction opposed to the Queen; the Japanese officers of the Korean guards were instructed to facilitate an entry into the palace and give assistance if necessary; and in due course a mixed gang of Korean and Japanese ruffians entered the inner rooms of the palace and murdered the Queen, the ladies in attendance, and the guards who tried to protect her. They were savagely slashed to death, their bodies were thrown into the courtyard, drenched with kerosene, and burned. Miura and his staff were recalled to Japan and tried, but the trial was a farce and they were acquitted on the ground " that there is no sufficient evidence to prove that they actually committed the crime meditated by them." Miura lived in Japan for many years afterwards in retirement, but not in disgrace nor uninterested in politics. He had influence with the army and he was consulted by governments and party leaders throughout his life.

Toyama and his associates next turned their attention to Russia. The Czar's Far Eastern policy was aggressive, but

Prince Ito, the Prime Minister, did not believe that war was the only solution and his powerful hand restrained the war-mongers.

Toyama visited Ito and gave an " advice " urging immediate war. A noted jingo group at the time was known as the Seven Stalwart Doctors. One of them, the late Dr. Terao, left an account of a conversation he had with Toyama. " Well, Toyama-san, the time has come when the nation must ask for your help," he said. Toyama replied: " Whom should we get rid of first? " Terao mentioned a name which a cautious editor subsequently disguised in the words: " a great leader who was opposed to war." Prince Ito is meant. Toyama told him everything had been prepared. But war came soon after-wards and Ito was not " bumped off."

Toyama understood the value of " inaction." Too many as-sassinations would have brought him to the gallows. He kept himself in business by not using the instruments at his com-mand, and statesmen found that his fanaticism was tempered by discretion. So the Genyosha flourished and had a numerous progeny and Toyama lived to an honored old age. By that time direct action had become a weapon of army and navy officers, and the murder societies had no longer a monopoly of " patriotism."

Aside from his " advice " to Ito, Toyama's main service to war was an agitation conducted by an anti-Russian society he launched. When the war began his young men were recog-nized in a curious manner. Some twenty members of the Genyosha went to Toyama and asked how they could " die for their country." Enlistment would have been the obvious course, but Toyama chose another. He went to the War Of-fice and got twenty of them attached to the army as " in-terpreters " though they knew no language but their own.

They were employed to establish connections with Manchurian bandits and organize espionage and guerrilla warfare. The value of their services cannot have been great. The Japanese war correspondents called them the " deaf and dumb interpreters," but the Genyosha profited by the fact that the army had used them. The official biography observes: " Toyama had now gained such political influence that even Ito was afraid of him. He was always behind the scenes, but he had many followers prepared to risk their lives for him and he became the ' superintendent ' of the government."

Toyama is not fully explained by describing him as the organizer and master of terrorists. He considered himself part of His Japanese Majesty's loyal opposition, unconstitutional but faithful to the national spirit, and he was so accepted even by the statesmen whose lives he threatened. Toyama tells that when he visited Ito to warn him that the government must make war on Russia he offered to sit closer to Ito, who was speaking in a low voice. Ito said: " You are near enough." Although one of his followers had thrown a bomb at Okuma, who walked with a wooden leg for the rest of his life in consequence, Okuma did not refuse to receive him. When he visited him, " Okuma did not refer to the incident [of the bomb] but paid him a flattering compliment."

One of Toyama's biographers, Hiroo Sasa, the son of one of his earliest and closest associates, described the relations of Toyama and Japanese cabinets in terms which in the West would be applied to open and honorable political opponents: " Toyama's power stimulated, castigated, and compelled the statesmen who held power throughout the Meiji era. If those governments acquitted themselves without glaring faults it was largely thanks to the presence of so cool-headed a watcher and so daring a condemner. The political history of the Meiji era is largely the record of the activities of the ronin behind the scenes. Theirs was hidden but active power." Mr. Sasa regards the position so described as quite normal. He continues: " No doubt the ronin were extreme and hasty whether they stood for liberty and popular rights at home or a strong policy abroad and it is to the credit of the governments of the time that while they were constantly pushed and pressed by those ronin, they knew how to control them."

Mr. K. Mochizuki, one time Home Minister, wrote: " There are scarcely any grave national matters during our modern existence in which Toyama has not played an important and decisive role, but he has not been decorated for his efforts for they were always made behind the scenes."

Toyama's methods were enveloped in darkness and everything that has been published about him in Japan is so grossly adulatory that exaggeration must be allowed for. But his power was real and it was great enough to make governments obey him even at the cost of international embarrassment.

In 1916 the British government was at war and Japan was also at war as Britain's ally. Rash Behari Bose, an Indian malcontent, had come to Japan. He was more than an anti-British propagandist. He had taken part in the attempted assassination of Lord Hardinge, the Viceroy, and he boasted of the exploit in the account of himself he contributed to the Japanese *Who's Who*. At the request of the British government, who desired to try Bose for murder, the Japanese authorities ordered him to leave the country. Bose knew that if he went to Shanghai port he was liable to be arrested. His Japanese friends took him to Toyama, who posed as the protector of Asiatics against the white oppressors. Toyama concealed him in his house. The police knew he was there but they did not dare to enter nor did the Japanese government dare to order them. The Foreign Minister apologized to the British Ambassador, Sir Conyngham Greene, and told him that Toyama was so powerful that the authorities could not remove Bose from his house.

Bose is at present performing in the role of Japan's potential Quisling for India. Until Japan entered the war he was an insignificant individual and his career had been humble. After eluding British efforts to bring him to trial for conspiracy to murder he became a naturalized Japanese. He married the daughter of a Japanese who kept a popular restaurant in the busy and unfashionable district of Shinjuku and eventually he succeeded to the business. The restaurant has been his source of livelihood for many years. He was at one time correspondent for the Indian newspaper *Forward,* but he did not attend the Foreign Office conferences nor was he ever detected gathering news. He had no cable privileges. He lived by his restaurant, kept in touch with his reactionary Japanese friends, and kept himself before the public by organizing a " Japanese Friends of India Group," which from time to time passed verbose resolutions against Britain drawn up by Bose.

It was not the only occasion on which Toyama's house has sheltered murderers. When Nissho Inouye, spy, military agent, priest, and organizer of death bands, was wanted for his share in the murder of a Japanese Prime Minister in 1932, he fled to Toyama's house and was sheltered there for many months.

Toyama's eulogists make much of his services to Sun Yat-sen and the Chinese revolutionists. Many Japanese adventurers fished in China's troubled waters then. Those who believed they were serving their country's greatness by fomenting conspiracy and rebellion in China were relatively respectable. There were also swarms of camp followers —

brothel-keepers, drug-peddlers, smugglers, blackmailers, and swindlers. Toyama helped the Japanese government to control such pests. He went to Shanghai with Inukai (afterwards Prime Minister), and at Inukai's request he distributed money to those " bad soshi." " I did not threaten them, but perhaps they were afraid of my followers," said Toyama. Anyhow, they disappeared and relieved the Japanese government of their embarrassing presence.

When the Chinese revolution broke out at Hankow in 1911, the Japanese government was at first disposed to support the Manchu dynasty. This was not to the liking of Toyama and other patriots and they founded a " Union of Friends of the Chinese Revolution." The support Inukai and Toyama gave the Chinese revolutionists was not entirely to the advantage of the latter; it had been thrust upon them by the Japanese, who had other motives than the reform of China. That ambitious warrior Yuan Shih-kai accused the Japanese " Friends of the Chinese Revolution " of plotting to seize Manchuria. The republicans agreed and the break-up of China into warring camps was avoided for a time.

When Sun Yat-sen's second revolt failed, he fled to Japan, and Toyama was of some use to him. The Japanese government at first refused to allow Sun to land. Toyama went to Inukai, and Inukai saw the Prime Minister and told him (according to Inukai's own account) that Toyama was prepared to protect Sun Yat-sen by drastic action if necessary. Every Japanese understands what that means, adds Mr. Inukai, and Sun was allowed to enter Japan under the wing of his formidable protector.

Much was expected in return for Toyama's hospitality. The editor of the Tokyo *Asahi* claims that Sun Yat-sen admitted that China could not survive without Japan's " unchanging co-operation." This suggestive admission was " the fruition of the sympathy and assistance Toyama ungrudgingly gave to the Chinese revolutionary cause." Toyama also extended some kindness to Chiang Kai-shek when he visited Japan. Toyama believes that Chiang in his resistance to Japan was misled by others. He is " unable to believe that Chiang in his true heart could be false to Japan." So writes the chief editor of Japan's greatest newspaper. One can but record the sentiment and add that it was written in 1940, when the " China incident " was in its third year.

Toyama, now nearing ninety, has been a venerated and innocuous figure for many years. He takes a daily walk to the Meiji shrine — the memorial of that Emperor whose restoration opened a career to Toyama as to many other millions of Japanese subjects. He sometimes favors a really important patriotic gathering with his presence, and the part invariably allotted to him is that of calling for three cheers for the Emperor. He never sees Japanese reporters; the Japanese newspapers never seek his opinions on the news of the day. A few American visitors have obtained interviews, in which the old gentleman has confined himself to commonplaces. He then remembers that he has always been on the side of the people whether they wanted votes or war. When he is gathered to the ancestors he will have a funeral such as Tokyo has seldom seen. The Cabinet will attend in a body and burn incense before his ashes. For as Premier Hirota said, " There is no such powerful civilian in other countries."

His thoughts on world peace have been translated by the *Japan Times:*

" Each state has the right to display its national glory and splendor and work out its own destiny. Each state must therefore have the armaments necessary for the realization of this supreme object. . . . No power can check the westward march of our civilization. China and Japan must be like brothers. . . . What Japan needs China must give before it is asked."

There is internal evidence that this was written even before the first China war in 1894. Its simple central idea has become familiar to every reader of Japanese newspapers since the movement of expansion by force began: Japan by reason of her superior power is the leader and overlord of East Asia. What she needs must be granted to her. If her wishes are freely granted there will be no war. Those who oppose Japan's demands are the war-mongers.

Chapter XIV

LEADERS AND GANGS

The typical, or pure-bred, patriotic society consists of a leader and a gang. In times of political excitement and consequent patriotic prosperity, funds are easily raised and then the societies may acquire secretaries and offices. In quiet periods the superfluous flesh melts away and leaves only a skeleton — the boss and his personal henchmen. Records hardly exist; the absence of business-like procedure is as truly a characteristic of the movement as the lack of a tail is a characteristic of a Manx cat. A member of one society may be and usually is a member of a dozen. Members move from one association to another; new societies are always being formed and the old ones, like old soldiers, never die, they only fade away.

Admission to that queer world is sometimes supposed to be effected in thrilling ways. The patriotic society best known abroad is the Kokuryukai, or Black Dragon Society. While I was writing this chapter a copy of the Edinburgh *Scotsman* was sent to me. The *Scotsman* is a sober, conservative newspaper with a reputation for accurate reporting, and it is supposed to be difficult to pull a Scottish leg when it is firmly planted on its native heath. The issue of April 18, 1942 contained an article in which an Indian free-lance writer, Ganga

Jamutri, successfully performed the feat. He professed to be
a member of the Black Dragon Society and he described his
initiation.

He told how he had been blindfolded and taken to a Shinto
temple in the hills around Tokyo. He was ushered into a
room where silent men dressed in white ("the Shinto color
of death") awaited him, in their midst the dreaded chief,
Mitsuru Toyama himself. After answering questions, the
candidate was led out to a yard where an executioner, a dripping sword in his hand and a decapitated corpse at his feet,
warned him that such was the fate of traitors. Then he was
"washed in blood from head to foot," which, as he observes,
was disgusting, but the blood was washed off with spring
water and he was massaged with "choice ointments" like a
foreign lady laying a foundation for her complexion. The
committee of masked men voted on his candidacy, the ayes
signifying their pleasure by pointing their long swords to the
ground while the noes pointed the short swords. He was
elected and took an oath that he would work for the expulsion of the whites from Asia. Chief Mitsuru Toyama drew
his sword and pricked himself in the arm, letting three drops
of blood fall into a bowl of rice. The new member followed
suit, they exchanged bowls and ate the bloody rice, and the
initiation was complete.

The narrative is a pure Limehouse Nights Entertainment.
If its writer, or anybody else, had wished to join the Black
Dragon Society he had only to send his name to the secretary
with a modest contribution. But he might have had some
difficulty in finding the secretary, since, at the time of this
imaginative report, the society, though not formally liqui-
dated, had been in a state of coma for some years.

The accident of a romantic name has made the Black

Dragon Society a symbol to Western readers of Oriental intrigue, mystery, and murder and a peg on which to hang
high-colored hokum like the example quoted. Such stuff is
dangerous, not because it is pro-Japanese but because it is pro-
bunk. It gives us a false idea of the people we are fighting. It
was not an army of mountebanks that drove the British out of
Malaya and the Americans out of the Philippines.

The " accident of a romantic name " is simply explained.
To the Japanese the society is known as the Amur River Society. It was founded in 1901 to make propaganda for the
war with Russia which came in 1904 and to advocate a Japanese advance to the Amur River, then the frontier between
Siberia and Manchuria. The name " Amur " is a Manchu
word which the Russians have taken over. The Chinese name
for the river is Heilung-chiang, or Black Dragon River. The
Japanese use the same characters as the Chinese but pronounce them differently. *"Koku"* (black) and *"ryu"*
(dragon) are the Japanese pronunciation of the ideographs
which the Chinese pronounce *"hei"* and *lung.*" *"Kai"* is
Japanese for society or association. The Kokuryu-kai is the
Amur Society, or you can also call it the Black Dragon Society, just as, if romantically inclined, you can call the Mississippi the Father of Waters.

The implication of the title was always clear to every Japanese: Japan's frontier was to be advanced to the Amur. The
war of 1904–5 was not an undiluted success for Japan and the
goal was not reached. But in 1931 the Japanese army seized
Manchuria, and the Black Dragon River, flowing through
Chinese territory for a thousand miles, became the continental boundary of Japan. The celebrated Mitsuru Toyama is
often supposed to have been the founder and president of
the Black Dragon Society; he was neither one nor the other,

but it was formed in 1901 by his principal disciple, Ryohei Uchida, and Toyama always had it at his beck and call.

It was not the first; the patriotic-society movement cannot be traced back to any single spring; it flowed out of the lake of discontent left by the restoration-revolution of 1868. Another society, the Genyosha, founded by Toyama in his native place, can be conveniently taken as the starting-point of the movement, but the Genyosha was an amalgamation of several earlier groups. It became the parent of the Black Dragon Society and many more and it established the type.

Toyama was essentially a gang boss. He did not write or make speeches. He had found that the fear of assassination was as potent a weapon as assassination itself, and as the leader of a trustworthy gang, bound to himself by personal ties, he knew what he could do. His ablest disciple, Ryohei Uchida, had felt the influence of the Western ideas then sweeping over Japan. He was less of a gang leader and more of a politician. He loved to interview statesmen, write articles, organize political campaigns.

He founded the Black Dragon Society from members of the Genyosha and a few fellow travelers. Its object was to agitate for war with Russia. The first meeting of promoters was held at his house on January 14, 1901, and there were only fourteen people present. A public inaugural meeting held on February 3, 1901, in a restaurant in Tokyo, was attended by fifty-nine. Funds were provided by sources undisclosed working for war, and a month later the Black Dragons were publishing a magazine devoted to the embitterment of Russo-Japanese relations. Its second number was suppressed; it reappeared under another title and was again suppressed. Uchida then published maps showing Russian encroachments on Manchuria. Next he wrote a book, *Russia*

Going to Ruin, which was suppressed, and established a seminary to train young members in the Russian language. War came, and the Black Dragons had nothing to do till it was over, when they took a leading part in opposing the terms of peace and many members were arrested for rioting. Toyama, however, had found special employment for some deserving retainers with the army during the campaign. The activities of the " deaf and dumb interpreters " were told in Chapter XIII.

Uchida had been observed by the government, and when Prince Ito went to Korea as Resident General after the war, he gave him an income and a vague post. As part of his duties in Korea Uchida organized an agitation for annexation to Japan. He obtained a million signatures (from illiterate Koreans) praying the Emperor of Korea to ask Japan to annex his country. But Uchida lacked the suppleness needed to make good his foothold in the official service. Ito seems to have used him only once, when the Chinese government requested that Sun Yat-sen be deported from Japan, where he had fled after an abortive revolutionary attempt. Uchida claims that he served both governments by persuading Sun to go to Singapore.

Meanwhile the Black Dragon Society slumbered and a meeting held in December 1906 to discuss the outlook was attended by only a dozen people. Nothing remained of the membership but a handful of the faithful who could not fit into any orthodox party or movement. Its name still had power, and when a young Turk, of whom nothing has been preserved in the Japanese account but his name, Ibrahim, visited Japan, he called on Uchida, who duly recorded the incident as a sign that the patriots of Turkey were getting ready to co-operate with those of Japan. The latter have always conceived that part of their mission is to emancipate backward races everywhere from white oppression.

When Mussolini made war on Abyssinia, the Black Dragon Society held a meeting in Tokyo to protest against that fresh example of white imperialism. The meeting turned out to be an error of judgment, for Italy joined the Axis and Mussolini's conquests were thereby sanctified. I had incurred the attention of the Black Dragons by writing critically about some of their propaganda, but to be noticed unfavorably was better than not to be noticed at all and they invited me to the dinner that preceded the meeting. It was held in the Seiyoken Hotel in Ueno Park, a rambling structure in a romantic setting. The name means Western-style Restaurant; the patriots liked foreign food; and besides, a *pukka* Japanese dinner with geisha girls would have cost too much. So we had fourth-rate foreign food, which is at least better than fourth-rate Japanese food.

Why the Black Dragon should be concerned about Haile Selassie was something of a mystery, but the explanation was visible in the form of an autographed portrait which Haile Selassie had sent to Toyama. I was given to understand that the venerable gang leader's fame had reached Addis Ababa but how and why remained unexplained. Subsequently little clues came out one after another until, as in a detective novel, one could say: " Now you have all the facts; you have only to put them together properly to know what happened." The story is so descriptive of the fantastic element in Japanese affairs that it is worth telling.

Other events besides Mussolini's new Roman Empire were about that time bringing Abyssinia into the Japanese picture. Reports were being published of a Japanese concession of 250,000 acres said to have been obtained there. Sometimes it was cotton and sometimes opium that the Japanese were to grow in this fabulous concession. For fabulous it was. Its foundation was a story, itself very hard to trace, of some Japanese who had tried to peddle a concession he said he had obtained in Ethiopia. He produced no evidence and found no buyers.

The Japanese press was not interested in the peddler — there were too many of his kind — but it took a lively interest in the later story of the Ethiopian Prince and the Japanese Viscount's daughter. It appeared that a young nobleman of Ethiopia desired to ally himself in holy matrimony with a daughter of the rising sun. He had never seen one, but Japan's fame was spreading and the marriage was to symbolize the friendship that was to develop between the descendants of the Queen of Sheba and those of the Sun Goddess.

The young Prince's alleged agent in the matter was a Tokyo lawyer, a shyster of uncommon gifts. He got off on a wave of publicity when he told his story to the press, and presently he was able to announce that the daughter of Viscount —— of Tokyo had signified her readiness to wed the black but presumably comely Prince in Abyssinia. (Names suppressed; the peer and his daughter were innocent stooges.) Reporters flocked to the Viscount's house. He was the son of one of the new peers created in shoals about half a century ago. He had inherited nothing except an empty title and he did not deny that his poverty and not his will had consented to the union. The lady was shy with reporters but dutifully said that exile to a strange country was a sacrifice she was prepared to lay on the altar of Japanese and Ethiopian friendship. The lawyer became an important man in the eyes of the large circle of those who did not know him.

The Prince was to come and fetch his bride, but he did not appear. The newspapers and even the pullulating pulp magazines at last gave up hopes. The poor bride and the penniless peer sank back into their genteel poverty and the lawyer returned to the twilight where his tribe lurks.

Did the bogus concessionaire get the portrait when he was in Addis Ababa? Did the shyster lawyer organize the wedding fable as a publicity stunt to help along with the peddling? Did one or the other give the portrait to the head of the Black Dragon Society? If all the parties could be assembled in the presence of Sherlock Holmes the answer would appear, neatly and convincingly. Here the questions can only be asked and the reader assured that if he assumes a connection between the bogus concessionaire, the shyster lawyer, the Black Dragon Society, and the portrait of which Toyama was so proud he will at least have constructed a plausible hypothesis.

That meeting about Abyssinia seems to have been the last gathering of the Black Dragons in their corporate capacity. A glance at the members was enough to show that the society was no longer formidable. Toyama, beaming behind his spectacles, was the picture of contented old age; Uchida's hair was white; and the Black Dragons seemed more likely to boast to their grandchildren of what they had done in the good old days with dagger and pistol than to take up pistol or bomb today.

I stayed with them for two or three hours and then went home, having an absurd prejudice against verbosity. The rest of the evening was vinous. As the night lengthened and the fumes of the saké rose, the Dragons became militant and one passionate gentleman, who wore his hair long in imitation of Lloyd George, was expelled. Toyama, always smiling and always speechless, went home early. Later a group of merry patriots, dispensing with the formality of lacing their shoes, rolled noisily towards the elevated railroad and the street-cars.

Soon afterwards Mussolini joined the Anti-Comintern Pact, and the Black Dragons realized that their enthusiasm for the freedom of the colored races against the white oppressors had been in this instance a mistake.

After the Russian war and the annexation of Korea, Japanese jingoism was temporarily satiated and the Black Dragon Society sank into a lethargic state. The break-up of China in revolution and civil war revived it, and members were sent over to fish in troubled waters. Among them was Ikki Kita, who afterwards became an evangelist of revolution, converting the young officers to national socialism. Kita was a socialist, and though the Japanese authorities were hanging socialists in Korea they made use of one among the Chinese revolutionaries.

Uchida, president of the Black Dragons, wrote a book, *How to Reform China,* and was for a time employed by Sun Yat-sen in Nanking as adviser. Sun Yat-sen did not accept his advice. Fearing Japanese aggression more than Chinese militarism, he joined forces with Marshal Yuan Shih-kai, the Chinese war lord, and China, for a moment, was united. Uchida returned to Japan and wrote another book demanding expansion of armaments. The Black Dragon Society promoted mass meetings demanding the dispatch of troops to China to avenge some insult to the Japanese flag. The jingoes in Japan were enraged by the lukewarmness of the government's China policy and on September 5, 1913 Mr. Abe, director of the Political Affairs Bureau of the Foreign Office, was murdered. Suspicion fell on the Kokuryu-kai, and its offices were raided, but nothing was found.

The Black Dragon Society was in the main an association of patriotic busybodies, led by an arch-busybody who would have been a successful politician if there had not been some stubborn ingredient in his character which inhibited him from being a good subordinate. There were few assassinations during the Kokuryu-kai's active years. Its own record boasts of only one affair of violence; six stalwart members waylaid and beat the president of the *Asahi* newspaper, which they disliked because of its moderation. Uchida spent eighteen months in jail on suspicion of instigating a youth to murder the Prime Minister, Count Kato, but was not tried. He continued to pour out pamphlets, magazine articles, and books. When an elderly banker was murdered, the Kokuryu-kai surreptitiously circulated a document the assassin had written to justify the crime.

When an unknown man committed suicide in front of the American Embassy as a protest against the immigration law, the Kokuryu-kai gave him a funeral. The flag stolen from the American Embassy during a riotous demonstration against the immigration law was found in a cheap lodging-house operated by the Kokuryu-kai as a hostel for poor patriots.

The Kokuryu-kai approved of the disgraceful massacre of Koreans conducted by hysterical vigilance committees after the great earthquake of 1923. It published a fictional *Report on Atrocities Committed by Koreans and Socialists,* and petitioned for an amnesty for the murderers of Koreans. At times of public tumult its members have been arrested for rioting, but when the rice riots in 1918 endangered a conservative Cabinet headed by Field-Marshal Terauchi somebody unknown hired them to attack the rioters. Latterly the Kokuryu-kai had become a mere shrill voice, too familiar to be heeded, and in 1930 Uchida and his intimate collaborators launched a new society, Dai Nippon Seisanto, calculated to make a better appeal to the changing age.

Dai Nippon Seisanto (Great Japan Production Party) was a native Japanese vehicle for Nazi ideas. It claimed 100,000 members. At its inaugural meeting at Osaka, June 28, 1931, Ryohei Uchida described it as a labor party based on Japanism, and not one formed on foreign models. The description is as good as any that could be offered. Japanism is what all the patriotic parties professed to stand for. It is broad enough and vague enough to connote imperialism, loyalty to the throne, the continental policy, the Imperial Way, and the other slogans which, when translated into practice, mean reaction at home and aggression abroad.

The approach to labor showed that the old-fashioned patriotic groups were losing their power to attract. They had to broaden their appeal. A new generation was rising; the doctrines of Marx were taking hold. The industrial proletariat in the cities was forming trade unions and there were two models to imitate — the British, American, German, and French unions which believed in social democracy and were internationalist and pacific, and the Communists with their new cry of dictatorship of the proletariat. A third school was rising in Europe under Hitler's leadership which was to provide just what Japanese patriotism was groping for — an omnipotent centralized state devoted to armed aggression — but it was as yet hardly known in Japan.

The Japanese super-patriots were crying for the abolition of the political parties and the " restoration " of Imperial rule, a slogan which showed that some of the keener intellects had perceived that centralized authoritarian socialism was no enemy to aggressive nationalism. Ikki Kita had successfully propagated the idea among the young officers; he conceived the Japanese army to be the proper instrument of revolution and the natural ruler of a totalitarian " national defense state," devoting the entire productive power of the nation to armaments and national aggrandizement. The function of labor in such a state is production; the new party was therefore called the Great Japan Production Party. Uchida hoped to combine the fascists, the nationalists, and the socialists into a national party on which he could climb into power. The spokesman of a rival gang, the Imperial Flag Society, described his aims with a mixture of sarcasm and envy: " Capitalism will be overthrown and state socialism established and the great patriots of the Seisanto will become the government. Happy Japan, where only the economics of Marxism will be realized and not its hateful democracy! "

The object of the new party was defined as " administration of the state on the basis of Great Japanism." Its platform consisted of three articles: (1) unity of ruler and ruled; (2) abolition or reform of institutions which did not accord with the national policy (or abolition of parliament) ; (3) put the nation on a self-supporting basis (or acquisition of the resources needed for a powerful " national defense state ") . To this platform the society appended some minor reforms, including: no more peers to be created outside of the Imperial family; only legal heads of families to have the vote; taxation of men exempted from conscription, the funds so raised to be used for the support of soldiers' families and the maintenance of young men's training institutes; a foreign policy devoted to fulfilling the mission of Japan; restriction of hereditary property; redistribution of great estates; a house for every citizen; abolition of the metric system; industrial companies to become the common property of shareholders, managers, and workers and the profits to be divided among them;

state control of the money market; reduction of debts and interest and compulsory mediation between debtors and creditors. The Seisanto's governing committee included a number of socialists who had been converted to nationalism. It was in fact a National Socialist Society; it repudiated all connection with " proletarian " bodies, and boasted that its " executive power " was very strong — a way of saying that it controlled more bullies than any other society.

Uchida had dreamed rightly but too late. Less than a year after he founded the Great Japan Production Party, the Prime Minister was murdered by officers of the army and navy. When the fighting forces took over the principles and practices of the patriotic societies the latter became superfluous. Eclipsed by the rise of a greater light, the Seisanto has been but a claque for the stronger forces that have taken charge. But its aspirations have been more than realized. All its old enemies — the communists, the liberals, the weak-kneed diplomats, the political parties, the free press — have disappeared. China has been " chastised " and the navy and army, esteeming their power even more highly than the patriots ventured to do, have attacked and invaded every foreign power in the Pacific Ocean and embarked on the construction of a new order of Greater East Asia extending from the Amur (the old original Black Dragon) to the Bay of Bengal and the coasts of Australia. The patriotic societies could be but supers in this vast drama.

The newest of the large patriotic societies is the Jimmu-kai. Jimmu, the first human Emperor of Japan according to orthodox history, as I have said, led the tribal warriors who, about the beginning of the Christian era, invaded and conquered the main island of Japan. A phrase attributed to him: *" Hakko Ichiu "* (eight corners under one roof), was often quoted when the Japanese army began the war which was to bring China under the Japanese Imperial ceiling. The name of the first Emperor became a symbol signifying the expansion of Japanese dominion. The Black Dragon Society had expressed the agitation for the expulsion of Russia from the Far East and the extension of Japan's frontiers to the Amur. The Jimmu-kai capitalized the demand for expansion all round — the new order of Greater East Asia.

Its founder, Dr. Shumei Okawa, was a doctor of law, and, in formal education and scholarship, a whale among the patriotic minnows. When he stood in the dock beside the conspirators of the Blood Brotherhood the contrast was striking. His long, narrow-eyed intellectual features of the pure Mongolian type, which is rare in Japan, might have been those of a diplomat. He dressed immaculately in foreign style, and in manners and demeanor was always the aristocrat. When an aristocrat strays into the revolutionary camp he is dangerous, and Okawa was well hated by his social equals.

The Jimmu-kai was the third society he had promoted. He began, as was natural, in the intellectual circles of Tokyo Imperial University. After Germany's defeat in 1918, democratic ideas came into favor. Politicians boasted of their liberalism; demands for manhood suffrage were growing and were not frowned on by the authorities. The universities were stimulated by the vision of a world made safe for democracy, and " new thoughts," called by various names, humanistic, democratic, even socialistic, became the subjects of essays and debates. The Imperial University had a group of liberal-minded professors, and many of the students proposed to enter the public services in a world where the liberal nations had won a victory. A " New Men's Society " among the students and professors was the outcome of this mood. Its hue was hardly pink; its heroes were Lloyd George and Woodrow Wilson, and its spiritual father was John Stuart Mill " On Liberty." Liberalism was fashionable, and as some always like to be ultra-fashionable, there appeared the comic " Marx-boy," red outside and empty inside.

Those phenomena did not differ essentially from the superficial emotions which inspired the youth of Oxford to declare that on no account would they fight for king and country. But it seemed to old-fashioned, narrow-minded Japanese that the flood gates were opening to communism and the end of all things. A conservative professor, Shinkichi Uesugi, whose reasoned views hardly differed from old Toyama's instinctive prejudices, mobilized the academic gladiators of the right in opposition to the New Men's Society. He was assisted by a university lecturer called Kanokogi, who had once been a socialist but had been violently converted by the horrors of the Russian Revolution. He founded a society of patriotic students and it did not lack supporters.

The university, both faculty and students, was torn by faction. The liberal wave was too feeble to make headway. It ebbed and finally disappeared under the flood of nationalism set in motion by the army. Before it disappeared it had evoked a counter-movement among nationalists more modern-minded than the Black Dragons. One of these was Dr. Shumei Okawa, whose mind could accommodate simultaneously nationalism and Marxism. Kanokogi, the converted socialist intellectual, joined Okawa and a few others in an effort to establish a new society of socialist nationalists. Their first attempt, called the Yusonsha, had too many leaders and it fell asunder. The second, called the Kochisha, was scrapped by Dr. Okawa on second thoughts and replaced by the Jimmu-kai, designed as a union of patriots and militarists. Some retired generals and younger officers on the active list were connected with it at the outset. After the murder of the Prime Minister, Okawa was arrested and tried and the Jimmu-kai lapsed into inactivity. Its principal contribution to history was the book already described, *A Reconstruction Program for Japan*, written by Ikki Kita at the instigation of Dr. Okawa.

The Jimmu-kai's manifesto opened with a preamble which gathered together the poverty of the farmers and workers, the oppression of the white races, and the selfishness of the plutocracy and the party politicians. It proclaimed as the governing principle of the society: " emancipation of the non-white races and moral unification of the world." Its program pledged it to " destroy the abuses of the political parties and work for an Imperial political and economic organization." The only practical steps suggested were restoration of the gold standard and a moratorium for farm villages. The former was utterly impracticable. The moratorium catered not only to the farmers but to the army officers who were disturbed lest rural depression should affect with unrest the farm boys who furnished eighty per cent of the conscripts.

It can hardly be said that Jimmu-kai imitated the Nazis, for they were not then well known in Japan. Traveling by native roads it had arrived at the same goal — belief in a state which should be aggressively nationalist and at the same time socialistic.

The three societies just described, bearing the impressive names of Amur River, Production, and Jimmu, the first Emperor, were shoots of the same luxuriant tree. They were the church militant, so to speak, of the powerful and popular creed which in Japan calls itself patriotism. It is difficult for any sober-minded person to study their principles and objects and take them seriously. It is impossible, however, to observe the development of Japanese policy and deny the correctness of their intuitions. They were flies on the wheel, but they knew their wheel. They were no Canutes on the shore; they were part of the flowing tide.

The liberals, the Japanese who knew the world and not Japan only, the diplomats, scholars, and business men who were Japan's contact-men with America and England, these were the Canutes. They believed that new Japan would become a progressive commercial power something like America and England. They have been powerless to prevent her becoming an Oriental edition of Nazi Germany. The three societies just named mark the successive stages of the journey — first, foreign conquest; second, totalitarian economy; third a fusion of both into national policy.

Two other major societies of similar complexion should be mentioned to complete the picture, since both of them figured conspicuously in the news of the period when the present policy was developing and both possessed large memberships. One was eminently respectable, and one conspicuously disreputable.

The Kokuhonsha, or National Foundation Society, was headed during its heyday by Baron Hiranuma, a celibate old lawyer of narrow nationalist views, who has been Chief Procurator, President of the Privy Council, Prime Minister, and finally Home Minister in the last Cabinet that opposed war with America. Its original nucleus was a society of students of the Imperial University of Tokyo who got together in opposition to the New Men's Society.

A foolish student had fired at the Crown Prince as he was passing through the streets to the opening of parliament in 1924. An attempt on the life of the sacred Emperor-to-be was unprecedented and had been supposed to be unthinkable. It stirred the loyalty of his subjects to the depths, and an imposing group of Japanese leaders, horrified by the spectacle of young intellectuals taking to direct action, took hold of the student society and expanded it into a powerful, or at least a large and imposing, organ for the propagation of correct thought among the young.

Its president was Hiranuma and the governing board glittered with admirals, generals, statesmen, and capitalists. It attained a membership of 140,000, and its size if not its power helped Baron Hiranuma to become Premier. Many people supposed that he intended to use it as his political machine, but they were mistaken. Hiranuma was a sincere unbeliever in political parties. Anyhow, it was always an inert body — the kind of thing that right-thinking men of conservative views will join but which asks no effort from them except the payment of an annual subscription.

It lived on in its vegetative way till 1936, when it was quietly disbanded by vote of its directors for the ostensible reason that its president had become President of the Privy Council. They probably realized that it was only an imposing shell, lacking the low but vigorous form of life that distinguished the real patriotic societies. Its *raison d'être* had disappeared; the country was in the grip of a movement which had already carried it far to the right of the position originally held by the statesmen and officials who associated themselves with it. Its officials said the ideas of the public had so changed that the society's basic purpose of " consolidating the national foundations and making manifest the essence of the national principles " had been largely accomplished. The time for propaganda of ideas is past, it was explained, and the time of direct political action had come.

The Kokuhonsha could alarm nobody, but another large

professedly patriotic society scared all peaceful citizens. It was called the Dai Nippon Kokusui-kai, or Great Japan National Spirit Society. It had a few respectable politicians among its titular leaders and advisers as well as Mitsuru Toyama, the venerable gang leader. The politicians doubtless were conscious of the voting power of the members it claimed and not less aware of their propensity for breaking up meetings and beating up opponents. Its platform declared the spirit of chivalry to be its guiding principle; its members rallied round the Imperial throne and offered themselves to the state in times of need; and they pledged themselves to abide by the old Japanese customs and standards of morality.

The key to this collection of platitudes is the word " chivalry." It has already been explained that in old Japan groups of " chivalrous men " professed to protect the downtrodden against oppression and arrogance. Some who bore that name also " protected " the brothels and gambling-houses, and their name was as unsavory as that of racketeer today. When the feudal system was abolished the " chivalrous men " found their occupation gone, and the army of coolies, their recruits, were no longer needed to carry the palanquins of the feudal lords in their yearly pilgrimages to and from Yedo. The coolies became unskilled laborers employed mostly by building contractors, and the " chivalrous men " become labor contractors who furnished strong-armed men to builders and others. This mass of unskilled labor, with its bosses and their obnoxious traditions, made up the bulk of the 170,000 members of the Kokusui-kai, and the society was patronized with an eye to their votes by Kei Hara, the first party Prime Minister. It retained its political character for a number of years. In 1926 another society, called the Kenkoku-kai, or Empire Society, broke off from the Kokusui-kai with a fascist platform which advocated personal government by the Emperor, abolition of parliamentary politics, and extermination of communism and all forms of socialism. Both societies have been a reservoir of the kind of men from whom killers are recruited; beyond that it does not appear that they accomplished anything.

A round-up of gamblers conducted by the Tokyo police brought in, among others, Tsurukichi Umetsu, described by the official news agency as one of the Tokyo leaders of the Dai Nippon Kokusui-kai. He specialized in racecourse blackmail and, according to the police, had extorted over 50,000 yen from the Tokyo Race Club and over 40,000 yen from the Negishi (Yokohama) Race Club. That will serve as a typical example of the close connection that has often existed in Japan between patriotism and blackmail.

Chapter XV

THE PRAYER–MEETING PLOT

A writer of detective fiction would hesitate to use the story of the Shimpeitai, or God-sent Troop, or the Prayer-meeting Plot. It is too fantastic. It lacks the air of plausibility that a good detective story should have. Like many things in Japan, when rendered into English, it seems too crazy to be credible. It is crazy, it is incredible, and it happened. The story is told here as the outstanding example of the close relationship of patriotism and crime in Japan. It exhibits the types of men the patriotic societies recruit; it shows them at work in their natural way. And besides it is a queer story.

Patriotism — or what passes for patriotism — blackmail, fraud, embezzlement, and ordinary rascality were mixed in the case. It differed from other " patriotic " crimes mainly in that the proportion of plain rascality to false patriotism was something like ninety-nine per cent. Among the actors, besides the ordinary gangster-patriots and their nitwit followers, were a big business man trying to engineer a stock-exchange bear market, a retired colonel acting as go-between and handling large funds, and a Tokyo barrister who had acquired great publicity in a patriotic *cause célèbre*.

It began with a prayer meeting. The shrine and park consecrated to the spirit of the Emperor Meiji (1852–1912) is one of the sacred sights of Tokyo. Country people from all

213

parts of Japan go there to worship and admire. If they are in luck they may see a new Prime Minister or a promoted general come to announce his appointment to the Imperial spirit, or they may see that great patriot Mitsuru Toyama, patron saint of the Black Dragon Society, taking his morning walk.

A hostel has been built near the shrine to give a night's shelter to tourist pilgrims. In summer the country people are busy in the rice fields, and when, on the night of Monday, July 11, 1933, the hostel suddenly filled up with late visitors, the policeman at the corner was curious. He found that forty-nine members of patriotic societies had come from the country to attend a prayer meeting next morning at the shrine. The Japanese people were at that moment acutely conscious of patriotic societies. The Prime Minister, the Minister of Finance, and Japan's best-known capitalist had been murdered and the trial of the murderers had filled the newspapers with sensation. The policeman went to his box and telephoned. Metropolitan Police sent two wagons and the forty-nine spent the rest of the night at headquarters answering questions. No third degree was needed. They produced invitations issued by Zenichi Suzuki, chief of the Youth Section of the Great Japan Production Party (Dai Nippon Seisanto). The invitation said:

" In 1936 the London naval treaty has to be revised. Japan must recover its naval strength, which was impaired by that treaty, and then restore the nation's defensive power to its former level. A meeting for prayer to this end will be held at the Meiji shrine."

The circular explained that it had been intended to hold the prayer meeting on May 15, the anniversary of the Prime Minister's assassination, but the police had forbidden it.

At three a.m. a bus from the provincial city of Mito drove

up to the hostel with seventeen members of the Native-Land-Loving School. The principal of the school and several of his colleagues and students were then awaiting trial for attempting to bomb the power stations which supply Tokyo's electric light. The police, now in possession of the lodging-house, sent them back in the bus they had come on. Eleven more members of the same seminary for instruction in patriotism and agriculture were routed out of an inn and placed on the morning train for their homes. All asserted that they had come in answer to the invitation and had but one purpose, to pray as ordered. It was also found that Suzuki had provided traveling expenses on a liberal scale, sending 300 yen ($150) to each branch which sent delegates to Tokyo.

The police visited the local branch of the Great Production Society, situated near the shrine, and found a collection of objects not strictly relevant to devotion. There were eighteen cans of gasoline, a number of automatic cigarette-lighters, four Japanese swords, banners with fiery slogans — " Restore the Imperial Way," " Abolish Plutocratic Government," " Strengthen National Defense," " Eradicate Communists " — written on them, and a number of Japanese towels such as warriors tied round their heads to absorb perspiration and signify a readiness for desperate deeds. Those latter properties bore the crest of Kusunoki, a loyalist of the fourteenth century, whose example is much quoted by protagonists of a new restoration.

There were also handouts prepared in advance. One declared that " The Metropolitan Police Board is completely . . ." (The police suppressed the end of the sentence.) Another circular set forth that, having accomplished certain actions, the actors were about to surrender themselves. Some appealed to the army; some to the citizens of Tokyo; some contained general principles for a reform of the Empire. They were signed " God's Soldiers of Japan."

The police got to work with alacrity, aided by inside information. The next find was forty-one Japanese swords collected by a local dealer at the order of a member of the band and said to be wanted for a campaign against bandits in Manchuria. Next came the discovery of fifty-three more swords packed in a basket in the shop of a Tokyo lacquer dealer, brother-in-law of a member of the Patriotic Labor Party. Three members of the Patriotic Labor Party were taken at a hot spring and put through the mill.

It was found that 15,000 yen ($7,500) had been distributed as traveling money. Such lavishness told the police that far larger amounts had reached the perpetually hard-up patriots who had organized the prayer meeting. It must have been a very fine orange that had so much squeeze left for private patriots after passing through the hands of their leaders. Ostensibly the money came from two persons, the secretary of the Seisanto, already named, and Torao Maeda, president of the Imperial Farmers' League, who was also the moving spirit of the Patriotic Labor Party. It should be explained that those titles do not indicate any connection with farmers or laborers. The name of a Japanese patriotic society is selected for sound, not for descriptive accuracy. A league, association, or brotherhood may be accommodated under one man's hat. But the possession of funds on such a scale indicated that someone in the background possessed not only high " sincerity " but an overflowing purse.

In a week the police had arrested 118 persons and seized 108 swords, the last 11 of which were found in the headquarters of a rural group calling itself " Soldiers Sent by the Divine Wind." Members of this gang had come up to Tokyo on the favoring breeze of a free trip, but they escaped the police raid and went home.

Without the cash the affair would have looked like ordinary patriotic melodrama. As it was, the Seisanto took alarm and announced that it had nothing to do with the prayer meeting and regretted that some younger members had got out of control. But it asserted that, in view of the circumstances of the time, the government could not avoid responsibility:

" The corruption of the parties has now reached an extreme point and no one can deny that if the existing conditions are allowed to continue, the future of our nation will be dark. This unprecedented national crisis has given rise to a cry for a government of one sovereign and millions of subjects in conformity with our national structure. . . ."

The phrase " one sovereign and millions of subjects " is a classic way of demanding the abolition of parliament. To hold a government responsible for a plot to murder its own members is orthodox patriotic reasoning.

The Japanese sword was a great weapon in its day, but modern patriots recognize the superior utility of the automatic, and the police were looking for pistols. A porter at a suburban station found on the platform a bundle some passenger had forgotten. It contained a gold-plated pistol and six cartridges. Two hours later an elderly man claimed it and was taken to the police station. He said he had been sent by the brother of a man who published a woolen trade magazine, the *Koerimono Shimpo*. It is an innocent-looking and respectable-looking occupation and many Japanese patriots publish trade journals. The printer's bill is insignificant, the circulation is a secret, and soliciting expensive advertisements from capitalists who will pay to be left alone is no crime.

The police went to the publisher's house and found a

Mauser, forty-six rounds of ammunition, and another sword. The publisher said he was keeping them for a friend who happened to be a member of the Production Party. The friend had thought it well to be out of the way while the police were searching, so he left home. He spent the first night in a geisha house to indemnify himself against a possible period of enforced continence and then stayed for a week with the publisher. He left when another member " squealed."

The police net had so far caught only small fry, but one by one the patriot-gangsters told their stories, and a series of domiciliary searches led to bigger fish. Lieutenant Colonel Tetsutaro Yasuda (reserve) confessed that he had given 25,-000 yen ($12,500) to the promoters of the prayer meeting. It appeared that the colonel augmented his pension by raising funds for the Seisanto and the Patriotic Labor Party. The discrepancy between the 25,000 yen Colonel Yasuda handed over and the 15,000 yen the Seisanto disbursed did not need explanation. As the orange travels on its way, each one who handles it is entitled to a squeeze. The original donor turned out to be a prominent business man, Hikoichi Naito, managing director of Matsuya, one of the largest department stores in Japan. He kept discreetly in the background. He gave the money to his private secretary, who gave it to a friend, who gave it to the colonel, who gave it to Suzuki, who distributed it to the prayerful patriots.

The trail that led to the business man also led to the lawyer. In Chapter III the story is told of Priest Nissho Inouye, who organized the two preliminary murders of the first young-officer conspiracy. When the prayer meeting was being arranged the priest was being tried; he was defended by a Tokyo barrister called Tatsuto Amano, also a patriot, loud-mouthed, insolent, audacious, and yellow. The lawyer mixed with a group of strange sinister figures living by their wits on the narrow borderland between patriotism and crime. They were go-betweens and they had contacts with the patriotic societies in Japan, with the Japanese army in Manchuria, and with some big corporations in Tokyo.

In pursuit of contributions Colonel Yasuda went to Lawyer Amano. The lawyer went over to Manchuria, then being rapidly built into Japan's New Order. The police raided his office, and next day the newspapers published the names of large steel, oil, and mining companies with which they alleged the colonel had established relations on the strength of his influence with officers in Manchuria. The puppet empire of Manchukuo had just been created and its primary object was exploitation by Japan; hence the interest shown by these corporations. Amano was arrested in Harbin and brought back to Tokyo.

A night's questioning in a police office " opened the flood gates of information," as Tokyo newspapers put it. The lawyer's comrades expected that he would talk and as a precaution they had attempted to poison him while he was hiding in Harbin. One night in the waterfront police station in Tokyo was enough. Next day the lawyer was transferred to prison to await trial, a sure signal that he had told all. Shortly afterwards the Department of Justice issued a statement outlining the results of the judicial preliminary inquiry.

From this statement the public learned of the arrest of Commander Saburo Yamaguchi, a naval air officer. He had been assigned the role of bombing the Prime Minister's official residence from the air while the Cabinet was meeting within.

Commander Yamaguchi was the brother of Priest Nissho Inouye. The difference in the names of the two brothers is a common thing in Japan and is explained by the prevalence of adoption. Either the priest or his brother had entered another family and taken its name. The naval officer had once commanded an air " corps " (the Japanese word does not show its size). When his arrest was revealed he was described as a reserve officer, but an officer who gets into trouble is often placed on the reserve list before he is tried. Yamaguchi died in custody before being tried or even indicted. Nothing came out to show whether he was a sincere fanatic like his brother, or one part patriot and three parts scoundrel like the others. It is not easy to believe that a man who had brains enough to become a commander in the navy was stupid enough to believe in the plot he associated himself with. On the other hand nothing has come to light which would indicate that there is any limit to the credulity of the patriotic mind in Japan.

Actually there was a plot within a plot. The plot for which sixty-two persons were tried was a melodrama of blood and thunder, murder, revolution, and dying for the country, but it was only a stage setting for the real play, the money-maker.

The Department of Justice gravely recounted the confessions. The prisoners said they had reached a conviction that " the spirit of Japan was in danger of collapsing because of the influx of materialistic ideas from the West." They had thought the murders of two statesmen and a capitalist a year earlier would " bring the privileged classes to their senses," but had been disappointed. An unprecedented national crisis was coming on due to the forthcoming naval conference, and national prestige had been endangered. They decided therefore to " do away with the Cabinet, establish a new political organ, revise the Constitution, and establish the Emperor's administration in the true sense of the term."

The Prayer-Meeting Plot

With these lofty motives they organized the God-sent soldiers. The "troop" was to assemble at the shrine. Commander Yamaguchi was to take the air and bomb the Cabinet and Metropolitan Police headquarters. This was to give the signal for squads headed by the president of the Imperial Farmers' League to conduct raids in which Cabinet ministers and many notables were to be murdered. The offices of the political parties were to be set on fire and the God-sent Troop was to continue in action till martial law was proclaimed, when it would hand over the revolution to the army.

So ran Amano's confession. He professed to have been inspired by a desire to carry on the work that Priest Inouye had started. He confided his intentions to the president of the Imperial Farmers' League, which, it may be as well to repeat, was not an organization of farmers but a name used by a notorious professional patriot for his gang. The lawyer was unable to finance the enterprise, so he consulted his intimate friend the money-raising colonel already mentioned. And then the plot within the plot took shape.

The colonel heard that Naito, the department-store director, had lost heavily on the stock exchange. It was common talk, and not new. A few big financial and insurance houses knew it to be true, for they had advanced over three million yen to Naito on promissory notes. A man who can borrow three millions is able to take a few knocks in the stock market, and Naito's standing was not outwardly affected. Some of the colonel's and the lawyer's shady friends heard that Naito had also been raising loans from money-lenders in an effort to recoup his losses by further speculation. Three of the men who were subsequently tried devised a plan and communicated it to a fourth who was acquainted with Naito's confidential secretary. The friend brought the colonel and the secretary to-

221

gether at a small private spree in one of the simple but luxurious geisha houses in the theater district. (" Geisha house " is not the literal translation of the Japanese name, but it describes the nature of these establishments. They are called " *machiai,*" literally " waiting houses," and the verb " to wait " is used in various of its values. The client waits until the geisha girl [or girls] arrives from her home near by; the geisha, singular or plural, waits on the client and his friends at the subsequent feast, and they can all wait till morning if the girls like them and the cash runs to it.)

But Colonel Yasuda had grave matters to open with the millionaire's secretary, and the geisha girls were excused from further ministration as soon as they had served the rice and tea which close a Japanese feast. He told the secretary that Naito, the embarrassed capitalist, need not go to moneylenders since he could obtain advance information which would enable him to effect a " killing " in the stock market on the grandest scale. The secretary sniffed the bait and agreed that advance information was always worth a price. The " sales talk " was easy. He did not have to be told of the unsettlement created by the discovery of revolutionary sentiment in the army. The alliance of young officers and a patriotic death band had already resulted in a bloody outbreak. A sequence of sensational trials, all fully reported, had evoked a wave of mass sympathy with the conspirators. The market was jittery already and would react quickly to bad news.

Colonel Yasuda told the secretary that another uprising would soon occur; air officers would participate; the statesmen who obstructed reform would be killed *en masse;* the army would take charge and a new government would be formed. Later, when the bait had been swallowed, Naito was told that Yasuda, as the man behind the scenes, could get him appointed Minister of Commerce and Industry in the new administration. But that night, as the three sat close together on the mats behind the paper windows of the demure Japanese house by the waterside, it was enough to point out that the occurrence of another and bigger "incident" would spread panic in the stock exchange and all prices would crash. The price Yasuda asked for disclosing infallibly the date of the outbreak was one hundred thousand yen.

And so home, amid cries of "*Sayonara*" and "*Irrashai*" ("Please come again") from madam and her attendants, the colonel to think he was about to raise the biggest contribution he had ever handled, the secretary to reflect that the information he had been offered might dig his master and himself out of a deeper hole than anybody but themselves knew. It came out at the trial that Naito had not only borrowed 3,600,000 yen from banks and insurance companies; he had forged 22,000 stock certificates of his company and posted them as security for a further 1,200,000 yen. Worse still, it was alleged that he had caused the seal of the Tokyo District Court to be copied and had used it on a document.

More meetings followed. Naito was ready to pay for information, not, of course, 100,000 yen, but half of it. The secretary brought 10,000 in cash to Yasuda, and later a promissory note for 40,000 yen. As the colonel preferred cash, the note was bought back for 39,000. Naito re-entered the market as a bear in 64,000 shares of Tokyo Stock Exchange New, the favorite speculative counter of that speculative establishment. The original orange being thus 49,000 yen, the colonel gave 25,000 to the organizers of the prayer meeting and they gave 15,000 to their followers.

The preparations that had been made — cans of gasoline, cigarette-lighters to set them aflame, and Japanese swords —

have an air of melodrama rather than of murder and revolution. Only excessively simple patriots will believe that the chief of the Youth Section of the Production Party and the president of the Imperial Farmers' League, had any intention of risking their necks. It was said that they intended to distribute the swords at the shrine and march their followers a mile and a half through the streets, banners waving, handbills flying. They would hardly have got past the second police-box. Waverers, however, were to be told that the leaders had formed themselves into a death band and would commit harakiri if they failed. Suicide would be a noble gesture; it is impossible for a patriot to refuse to follow a leader who is ready to perform it; it would propitiate the authorities, who might then deal leniently with the rank and file.

The smart night policeman on duty near the hostel spoiled the plan. He had probably been told to expect something; there is a smear of "information received" over the whole police story. There was a sensation in the newspapers, but no panic of any account on the stock exchange. The fantastic web was not fully unraveled for several months. The police worked in darkness and it was not until two years later that the Department of Justice announced that fifty-eight persons had been committed for trial before the High Court. Of these fifty-three were charged with treason, four with conspiracy to commit murder, and one with violation of the Explosives Law. Commander Yamaguchi and Naito died in prison.

The trial of the others did not begin until November 1937, and it dragged tediously through ninety-nine hearings until the end of 1940. By that time the country was engaged in the China war. There had been another military outbreak of a far graver kind. The revolution for which the young officers and the patriots had clamored was well on the way to success.

Public interest in the God-sent farceurs had evaporated, and the number of prisoners in the dock at the final hearing had dwindled to seventeen. The seventeen had become extraordinarily insolent, and they were encouraged by the presiding judge. They refused to listen to the closing address of the procurator on the ground that his views on national polity were unsound. Lawyer Amano addressed the court at great length on the position of the Emperor in the Japanese state. He informed the judge that the accused disagreed with the procurator's views on that point and would immediately leave the court by way of protest.

The judge warned them that they would be contravening the law if they did so. The accused dramatically put themselves in the posture of praying and walked out of the court. The procurator protested. " It is an extremely inauspicious event that there should be a breach of order in the Supreme Court," he said. " Connivance by the presiding judge at the incident which has just occurred will seriously affect the system of procurators. As head of the prosecution I demand that the judge use his authority." The judge took till afternoon to think it over and ruled that the procurator could address the court in the absence of the accused.

They were sentenced to short terms of imprisonment. It is unlikely that they served their sentences.

Chapter XVI

PATRIOTISM AND CRIME

Patriotism that runs to assassination is an ugly thing, but it is not new and it can be understood. In Japan, however, professional patriotism and professional crime drew together and blended in a way that made patriotism a stink in the nostrils. The big patriotic societies were only the one third of the iceberg that shows above water; below, in the depths, a whole underworld of criminals hunted their prey under a mask of patriotism just as Dick Turpin robbed the highways wearing a mask of crepe.

There was a moral infection somewhere in Japanese ideas about their country. It could be traced in other symptoms, as when a soldier, the embodiment of Japanese chivalry (*bushido*, the code of the warrior), slapped an American woman's face in the streets of Peiping, or other soldiers, under orders, stripped British women in Tientsin while picketing the British section of that city. A step further led to that most unsoldierlike atrocity of Hongkong, the bayoneting in cold blood of enemies who had surrendered in battle. If a thing was " patriotic " it was right; the thieves had found out that grand axiom and they acted upon it.

Trying to understand this peculiar affinity between patriotism and crime, I collected cases, some of which are given below. In the end the explanation came not from a study of cases but from the stage. The kink in morality started from the perversion of an ideal.

In a feudal society loyalty to one's lord is the highest virtue, for without it the clan would not hold together; and in Japan loyalty has been morbidly exalted until it excuses any cruelty, any crime. The classic example is the dramatized vendetta of the forty-seven ronin. (A ronin, literally waveman, as said before, was a samurai who had lost his master and become a vagrant soldier without rice or regiment.) Seldom in the literature of any nation has revenge been so exalted and loyalty pursued over such dubious paths. The forty-seven had become masterless men because their lord had been compelled to commit hara-kiri for attacking with drawn sword another nobleman doing duty in the Shogun's palace. The offense was unpardonable, but the offender had been goaded beyond endurance by the mean behavior of the peer he attacked. The forty-seven swore revenge. After many adventures that require a whole series of plays for the telling they succeeded, and at daybreak on a snowy morning in 1702 they marched ceremoniously across Yedo carrying the bloody head of their enemy to lay on their master's grave.

The story is the most famous of all Japanese dramas. It was first staged in 1748. Ever since then Japanese playgoers have wept with the ronin and incidentally learned to regard almost any morally revolting action committed in loyalty's name — for example, the selling of a daughter into prostitution to provide the sinews of war — as a regrettable but shining deed.

The affair appealed intensely to the loyalty fixation of the Japanese, and the government of the day hesitated for two years before it sentenced the ronin to commit hara-kiri. From their graves in a Tokyo temple yard the smoke of incense never ceases to rise. On the anniversary of their suicide-execution the schoolchildren are led to the graveyard to pay tribute to their memories and swell the Vesuvius of incense. The play is performed every year. The time is usually the spring, when the parks and even some of the streets are a pink haze of cherry blossoms. At this season the people from old times have been accustomed to give themselves up for a spell to the pleasures of nature and mild liquor. When the army was fairly launched as collective führer it got the Home Office, which controls the police, to prohibit the wearing of fancy dress by cherry-viewing citizens and order discontinuance of the picnics, masquerades, and communal drunks enjoyed by the proletariat.

The theme of the play, and of almost all old Japanese plays, is loyalty. The revenge it commemorates is popularly considered one of the grandest examples of that virtue, and successive playwrights have strengthened the action with incidents they believe appropriate. One such incident is a scene in which a ronin sells his dearly loved daughter to a brothel-keeper because in no other way can funds be raised to keep the gang together until the revenge is accomplished.

There are few dry eyes in the audience as the scene snivels to its degrading climax. Every woman in the theater is weeping into a damp wisp of handkerchief, and the strange thing is that the tears are not for the girl, they are a tribute to the man. What heroism, what courage, to sell his own daughter to a pimp! How great his loyalty, how superior to common human feelings!

Another incident pointing the same moral was entrusted to the hero of the play, Oishi by name. In an effective and pathetic scene he turns his wife and children out of the house and takes in a prostitute from the Yoshiwara. To give a wife the air was a small matter by the code of old Japan, but a man's children were dearer than himself and Oishi's action was the meanest conceivable. The motive for a proceeding which struck everyone in the audience with horror was nothing more serious than a desire to put the enemy off his guard by suggesting that the hero was sunk in debauchery. There is loyalty for you (said the drama to the audience), loyalty so rare that it will commit the lowest of actions for even a hypothetical advantage.

The same well of emotion gushed high at the trials of the young officers. The hard outline of their crime was lost in a cloud of false sentiment about their pure intentions. How deeply they must feel for the country, how serious the condition of the country must be, when they risk their lives to kill a Prime Minister! Popular emotion about such crimes expresses itself in extravagant hero-worship. When the ringleaders of the 1936 mutiny were shot, strict orders had to be issued prohibiting pilgrimages to their graves, the erection of shrines to their memory, and glorification of the affair on screen or stage. Even the judges submit to this sentiment, as may be seen by comparing the mild sentences imposed on criminals who plead patriotic motives with those meted out to labor agitators or communist students.

When the moral sense of a community is so warped that it excuses any enormity committed in the name of its obsessional virtue, the vermin who prey on society will exploit its weakness. The nationalist societies, like the Black Dragon, practice patriotism by gangster methods and they have plenty of imitators who practice gangsterism by patriotic methods. The police know them well enough. In a series of raids in 1935 the police arrested 31,000 crooks and thugs associated with real or bogus patriotic societies, and 6,000 of them were indicted and tried for specific crimes. When the police were criticized for their previous laxity they replied that the criminals of the Right enjoyed protection. Powerful persons and interests had a use for them, and the respectable elements of Japanese society were rabbits.

The incidents narrated below are a selection of *faits divers* strung together to illustrate the affinity of patriotism with crime in Japan. The foolish and evil persons who pass rapidly before the reader are men of no importance, but by glancing at them and noting their characteristics he may get something of the impression he would receive if he could be transported for half an hour to a busy street in the slums of Tokyo. He will have a composite picture of a national type, the gangster-patriot.

Dr. Yoshio Imamaki, a thirty-seven-year-old Tokyo physician, was made a director of the Jimmu-kai patriotic society. Taking his duties seriously, he hired a thug to murder Viscount Saito, the Premier. The physician, in spite of his learning, which impressed the thug, was a sucker; the friend who encouraged his ideas and found the killer for him in a Tokyo dance hall was a fool; and the thug and his impresario turned round and blackmailed their patron.

The abortive plot was conceived while the public was stunned and patriots mightily exalted by the May 15 affair in which young officers of the army and navy had openly associated themselves with political assassination. The doctor shared the excitement and went frequently to the Jimmu-kai headquarters. There he met, among other believers, a young man of twenty-four, Obayashi, employed in a brokerage office, and an older man of forty-five, called Makino, described as a teacher of the Japanese harp; he had also been a pimp.

The three talked of the May 15 affair and the doctor expressed the view that the new Prime Minister was as ripe for killing as the old. He said in court: " I had no concrete idea. I merely thought it would be better to get rid of the Premier, believing his murder was necessary for the permanent development of the nation." The youth Obayashi " felt greatly honored " by receiving the doctor's confidence in such a high matter. The doctor and the stockbroker's assistant were mere dilettantes. Makino was a realist, living in the borderland where patriotism and crime act so much alike that by the pragmatic test they are indistinguishable. He had a mistress who kept a restaurant of such a kind that she needed a bully as bodyguard. The bully was a young man called Shimane, a hanger-on of Makino. The stockbroker's clerk met Shimane at a dance hall; a few weeks later he was introduced to the doctor as a strong-armed patriot ready to kill the Prime Minister.

The four of them continued to meet at the Jimmu-kai headquarters and talk of the plot. A definite plan was concocted at a meeting in a restaurant on the Jimmu-kai's premises. Shimane was to do the killing; the physician was to provide 100 yen ($50) to " pay for the preparations." An agreement was signed by which the doctor bound himself to pay the thug, Shimane, 100 yen and Shimane undertook to kill the Prime Minister. The pimp, Makino, signed as witness. Two days later the doctor handed over the cash.

Shimane's preparations took the form of a trip to Kyoto, ostensibly to bid farewell to his sweetheart, who practiced an ancient profession in a brothel of the licensed quarter. He stayed as a paying guest in the establishment where his mistress lived and labored. Unfortunately just then the police made one of their customary sweeps through the brothels in search of a wanted criminal, and Shimane was held in jail for a week. The doctor and the clerk learned of the arrest and were scared. Shimane, however, was no novice; he knew the police were not looking for him, kept cool, and was released.

But the doctor had had enough. He rebuked Shimane for his trip to Kyoto and told him that the conspiracy was off and his services no longer required. That development had been foreseen and was countered by a threat to expose the plot unless 1,000 yen were handed over. The amateur conspirators were not furnished with 1,000 yen in cash, but they made a beginning and 380 yen had been paid over when the police got wind of the plot and arrested all four. The physician and the stockbroker were given suspended sentences of eighteen months each and released. Makino got eighteen months and Shimane twelve months for blackmail. If they had got up on a soapbox and spouted communism they would have been liable to death and would very likely have received a life sentence.

The Mafia of Sicily was an organization of thugs who lived by extortion and terrorism. Its services could be hired and its judgments were not questioned because resistance meant assassination. Not long after the general election of 1928 a triple murder in the busy town of Wakayama revealed one of the big patriotic societies of Japan — the Kokusui-kai, or National Spirit Preservation Society — in the role of the Mafia.

During the election a local lawyer who supported the anti-government candidate was arrested on a charge of violating the election law. The election over, he was released. He alleged that he had been maltreated while in custody, and instead of letting bygones be bygones and waiting for his revenge until his party should be the government party, he commenced legal proceedings against the local chief of police. The case became notorious, and the opposition party threatened to move a vote of censure on the Home Minister in the approaching session of parliament.

Someone in the background who desired to prevent a public trial or a debate in the House aproached Kyukichi Sakai, the local head of the National Spirit Preservation Society, and asked him to " mediate." He advised the aggrieved lawyer-politician to withdraw the action and " arrange " the affair, but his recommendation was rejected. Attended by five stout henchmen, all armed with daggers, he went to the house of the lawyer in a " final effort to have mediation accepted." The politician was in conference with his attorney and several colleagues when they arrived. He refused to withdraw his action and there were high words. The leader of the gang flew into a rage, said he had been insulted by the refusal to accept his mediation, and ordered his gang to attack. There were eight persons in the room besides the patriots; three were killed and the others badly wounded. The killers marched to the local police station and gave themselves up. By their code they had committed a good deed and need not fear the consequences.

Many Americans still remember Baron Takashi Masuda, an able and amiable Japanese who for many years was managing director of the great Mitsui firm. He lived to be about ninety. After his retirement Baron Masuda built a house near the sea and he interested himself in embellishing it with old Japanese art. His entrance gate had once been part of an old farmhouse. Its iron hinges were ornamented with a design resembling the chrysanthemum of the Imperial crest. Subjects are strictly forbidden to copy or use the crest. A patriot passing by with his camera took note of the ornaments and photographed them.

233

He gave prints to three fellow patriots living by their wits and they blackmailed the old Baron with threats that they would lodge an accusation of *lèse-majesté*. There is nothing a Japanese dreads more than a charge that he has failed in respect to the Emperor, and Baron Masuda knew only too well that unpleasant publicity would follow the publication of such a charge. He paid 18,000 yen, and said nothing, and the police heard of the affair in the course of the third-degree examination of a suspect in another case.

All three of the blackmailers had interesting records. The one who confessed had organized a chimney-sitting exploit which caused a noise at the time. At the corner of the street of Tokyo in which Prince and Princess Chichibu have their mansion, a prosperous and locally famous Japanese pastry-cook has his establishment, called the Tiger House. The baker rebuilt his premises in a modern imitation of Japanese classical style, which he deemed appropriate to the locality, near the vast grounds of Aoyama and Akasaka palaces. Like other bakers he used an oven, and the oven required a chimney.

One morning the pastry-cook found a Japanese youth sitting on the top of his chimney. It was a time of chimney-sitting exploits, inaugurated by a printer's apprentice who climbed a factory smokestack during a strike and announced that he would stay there until the strikers received justice. The youth who had climbed the baker's chimney announced that he was making a protest against the *lèse-majesté* the baker had committed in erecting a chimney higher than the Imperial residence which it overlooked.

The charge was a plausible one, for by old Japanese ideas it is disrespectful to look down on royalty. When the Emperor drives through the streets of Tokyo all blinds on up-stair windows must be drawn. When the Metropolitan Police Building was erected in Tokyo a few years ago, the architect proposed to embellish it with a dome. The iron framework of the dome was erected and then taken down again. The new police headquarters stood near the moat and outer walls of the Imperial Palace and some busybody had pointed out that the projected dome would overlook the gardens in which the Emperor might stroll. The architect sacrificed his dome — architecturally it was no great loss — on the altar of loyal propriety, and a superfluous tower, on which the dome was to have rested, is all that remains. One of the three who blackmailed Masuda with threats of *lèse-majesté* was the instigator and paymaster of the youth who had sat atop the pastry-cook's chimney, a grimy living sacrifice to patriotic bunk.

Another of the trio had been in his youth an anarchist — anarchism was the color of the cloak he covered his crimes with — but when the Manchurian war turned the whole country patriotic, he became a loud patriot. The third had always been a Japanese patriot. He was the man, admired by many at the time, who presented Japan's chief naval delegate to the London naval conference with a dagger — a hint that the situation called for a suicide.

When the God-sent Troop was on the run, one of the fugitive leaders found refuge with the publisher of a weekly journal called the *Woolen and Textile Trade Review*. It may seem odd that the publisher of an organ so devoid of sex or any other appeal should be the friend of thugs. Such innocent-looking sheets are one of the main instruments of extortion used by Japanese blackmailers. They can be produced almost without capital. Job printers are numerous in

Japan and the cost of setting up and running off a few hundred copies is small. Even that expense is not absolutely indispensable. The instrument of extortion may be a mimeographed rag called commercial information and circulated by hand among business firms. The information consists of innocuous items copied from the commercial pages of the daily newspapers, among which a few paragraphs carefully aimed at certain firms or individuals are inserted.

Sometimes foreign traders are the victims, though generally the Japanese provide easier game, and the blackmailer seldom has sufficient knowledge of English to feel at ease in stalking a foreign quarry. The *Japan Chronicle* reported a case in which a representative of a foreign firm was repeatedly mentioned in a commercial-information sheet. It was insinuated that his firm was in difficulties and might not be able to meet its obligations. When he complained, his protests were blandly smiled aside and he was asked why he did not advertise. He banged the table and threatened to expose the game. But when his bank told him that the rumors were injuring his credit he capitulated. He gave the sheet an advertisement, paid his regular monthly blackmail, the slanders ceased, and he had no more trouble.

The great round-up of 1935 caught with some 1,400 smaller fry one Sinkichi Minoura, president of a newspaper and head of a patriotic party called the Taishu Kokusui Renmei (National Spirit Mass Party or League). He operated his racket in the profitable field of the suburban transportation of Osaka. He proposed that his newspaper become the organ of one electric railroad company for a payment of 2,000 yen down. When this was rejected he started a campaign for lower fares and was given 500 to discontinue it. By similar operations he netted some 50,000 yen from various railway and tramway companies, a bank, and a drug company. His ventures grew, and the latest of them before his arrest was the launching of another newspaper and a patriotic party of which it was to be the organ. The patriotic party was his gang of strong-arm solicitors.

Mysterious relations between the army and the gangsters are sometimes inadvertently revealed. The War Office in February 1934 found it necessary to issue an official statement explaining why a Tokyo business man, kidnapped in the street near his home by two patriots, had been taken to the headquarters of the gendarmerie. The military explanation did not satisfy parliament, and a member declared that the connection of the gendarmerie with the gangsters had been established. The War Minister spoiled his official denial by adding an expression of regret that many people suspected the gendarmerie of acting in collusion with rightist organizations.

The business man concerned was an auditor of a Tokyo company. He was going home one winter night when two men lurking in a quiet part of the street seized him and bundled him into a waiting automobile. He was taken to gendarmerie headquarters and one of the men stayed with him outside while the other went in. The man who went in remained there for a long time, and, feeling cold, the victim persuaded his captor to take him in. The doorman asked him to sign the visitors' book, and then the kidnappers discovered that they had taken the wrong man.

According to their own story, they had been lying in wait for a former member of parliament, the proprietor of a magazine called the *Business World* and other journals whose policy they patriotically disliked. When the mistake was discovered they apologized to their victim, who went home. They were handed over to the police. What the public wanted to know, and never did know, was why two kidnappers and presumptive extortionists should have taken their victim to the gendarmerie headquarters. Had they an accomplice inside who was prepared to "arrange a compromise"? Or, if they had caught the "unpatriotic" publisher-politician, would he have been kept in the cells and given a lesson with a rubber truncheon?

In the fall of 1932 the police discovered another plot organized by some of the people concerned in the May 15 affair and evidently intended to complete the massacre of statesmen begun by the young naval and military men. Some of the persons arrested were members of the Independent Youths' Society. Yoshio Kodama, leader of the Independent Youth, escaped, and when trapped by a friend, who happened also to be a friend of the police, he shot himself. He died a few days later and was given a magnificent funeral, conducted by Shinto priests and attended by nearly a thousand members of patriotic and political societies.

Kodama had been a practicing patriot from the age of seventeen. Labor politicians were his favorite enemies. He organized a movement to fight the Labor-Farmer Party and served six months in prison for attempting to present a petition on the matter to the Emperor as he drove through Tokyo. Another exploit which gained him publicity was his appearance at a May Day labor procession with a bucket of ordure which he flung on the processionists. He got a ticket of admission to the gallery of the Imperial Diet and scattered handbills in the House calling on the masses to rise and overthrow parliament. He sent Finance Minister Inouye a dagger and did five months' imprisonment for that. On release he toured Manchuria, and then, at the moment of the May 15 murders, he formed the Independent Youths' Association to follow the example of the young officers.

The plot proposed to conduct a battue of the Emperor's advisers when they were in attendance at the autumn military maneuvers at Kyoto. Its manifesto denounced the Prime Minister, Viscount Saito, and " certain corrupt and wicked high subjects waiting on the Emperor " whose names were concealed by the police. The author and signer of the manifesto was Rihei Okada, the man who gained notoriety in 1924 by stealing the flag of the American Embassy. Another of the gang was Masao Chiba, who showered the Lytton Commission with handbills as they left Tokyo station. At the headquarters of the Independent Youth the police found bombs of high explosive power and too elaborate to have been home-made. As the police report cautiously puts it, they had evidently been obtained from " certain quarters " having access to stores of special weapons.

In 1935 the craze for electing a beautiful girl struck Japan, and a popular beauty was chosen as Miss Nippon. Shortly afterwards she received a box purporting to contain a gift. When she opened it a snake uncoiled itself. Police inquiries revealed that a wealthy business man, her patron, had received a visit from two members of a " right thoughts " society who tried to extort money by threatening to reveal that Miss Nippon was " not a miss."

At eleven o'clock in the morning of March 31, 1932 the Salvation Army's headquarters in a busy street near central Tokyo was invaded by eight men who beat up the staff and smashed forty panes of glass. The police succeeded in arresting three, and one of them, who professed to be the leader, said the attack was made because the Salvation Army had secured the release of several girls from the licensed prostitution quarters.

The press of July 3, 1935 reported the arrest of one Shinji Abe, formerly head of a Japan Rescue Mission, on charges of blackmail. He was arrested in a general drive against toughs and gangsters which the police were then making. It was said that Abe had posed as a Christian and claimed, when soliciting contributions to his mission, to have rescued seven hundred girls. In March 1933 he traded his mission against 11,000 yen from the Osaka Licensed Quarters Association, and thereafter utilized his special knowledge by blackmailing brothel-keepers.

Feuds between "building contractors" and their respective battalions of coolie labor are common. Two contractors quarreled over their respective spheres of influence. A conference to seek an arrangement was held in a restaurant, and as one of the contractors was leaving, mellow with saké, three Japanese swords swung out of the darkness and he fell dead. Six months later the head of the rival concern was parboiling himself in a public bathhouse at a quiet morning hour when a couple of youths carrying long swords walked in and attacked him. One of them aimed a blow at his shoulder; he dodged and received only a slight wound. The other got behind him and ran half a foot of steel into his back. Morikawa, president of the Morikawa Building Company (such was his formal designation), lashed out, naked and unarmed as he was, and as he tried to kick his assailant, another flashing blow of the two-handed sword sliced off his foot. He was stabbed several times more as he lay on the wet floor, and when they were certain that he was dead, the two youths sheathed their swords, wrapped them up in cloth, and left the place.

The gangsters operate on their own account and can also be hired. There was a case in which two bullies were hired by a man to get back the funds he had embezzled to give to his geisha girl. They got 3,000 yen from her at the dagger's point before the arrest of the man gave the game away.

Money-leaders use gangsters to collect their debts, and their methods are often effective. A Tokyo gangster bearing the famous name of Chikamatsu, the " Japanese Shakespeare," got 4,500 yen back from a man who had defaulted in his payments to a money-lender. The man was decoyed into a house and Chikamatsu trussed him naked to the hook of the mosquito net and persuaded him to pay with a red-hot poker.

The patriotic gangs make it their pleasure to break up meetings that displease them. In 1933 a body called the Association of Friends of Peace in the Far East attempted to hold an inaugural public meeting. A group organized for the occasion under the title of " Association for the Study of Measures to meet the situation that will arise subsequent to 1936 " staged a rowdy demonstration outside the hall and then trooped in while the meeting was in progress, yelling imprecations and hurling stones. One of the speakers at the meeting was Captain Kokohu Mizuno, of the Japanese navy, a cultivated man and a sincere Christian. The gang sent representatives to the Metropolitan Police and the Tokyo gendarmerie to complain of Mizuno's alleged pacifism, and published leaflets declaring that an officer who " supports the peace theory is a radical defeatist and should be banished from society." Captain Mizuno replied that his profession as a naval officer did not prevent him from supporting any movement intended to bring peace in the world. He is now a member of the Emperor's staff.

Yukio Ozaki, the oldest and, as is sometimes said, the only liberal statesman in Japan, visited America and England at the time of the Manchurian incident. He wrote an article in which he supported disarmament and, apropos of Manchuria, declared that small countries might legitimately ask international intervention for their protection. A patriotic society intimated that he would not be permitted to return to Japan. Mr. Ozaki wrote a letter to his son in which he said: "Assassination is now much in vogue in Japan and any patriotic expression of opinion may expose me to danger. . . . One of the instructions I received from my mother when a child was that one should die with a smile. Many men of sterling worth have been assassinated, others have been attacked though they did not lose their lives, others have met an untimely end in riots and civil wars. . . . For a public man the best form of death is to fall victim to the cold hand of an assassin. Mr. Inukai [the Prime Minister], my old friend, was killed in his official residence. I could not help envying him; it was a death befitting a statesman."

When an eminent statesman who has never been accused by his worst enemies of venal conduct declares that a public man in Japan must regard assassination as the best death, he has illuminated with a flash of lightning the conditions in which Japanese statesmen live.

Threatening letters are common and comparatively unheeded weapons in the armory of patriotic terrorism. A few are quoted here as samples. In 1933 Baron Hiranuma, a na-

tionalist himself, received from the Imperial Banner Die-
hard Society a letter signed in blood. It declared that the nation should " do a certain act upon the person of " the Prime
Minister, Viscount Saito, who had " smeared and muddied
the glorious name of the Emperor of Japan, whose name
shines over all the world and who is saving the world from its
present crisis. The world and all human beings under the sun
should be subject to the divine Emperor of Japan."

While the trial of naval and military officers for murdering
the Prime Minister was in progress, Count Makino, Keeper
of the Imperial Seal, received a letter from the National Policy Protection Association calling on him to repent and resign.
" If you remain in office a serious situation will be created.
We trust you will resign and thus prevent any untoward
event." Count Makino, now eighty years old and in retirement, is perhaps the world's best example of the adage:
" Threatened men live long." His life has been attempted by
bomb, by army rifle, and by dagger. His father, one of the most
eminent of the restoration leaders, perished by an assassin.
But in Makino's frail body there is the heart of a lion.

In 1934 Japan negotiated a trade treaty with India. When
the chief Japanese delegate, Setsuzo Sawada, afterwards Ambassador to Brazil, was on his way back to Japan, the Aikoku
Roheitai (Patriotic Worker-Soldiers) started an agitation denouncing the treaty and instigating popular action to prevent
Mr. Sawada from landing. The police " opened negotiations "
with the gang to have them call off the campaign. The gang
also " opened negotiations " with Japanese firms trading with
India, evidently expecting to cash in on the agitation.

The son of a millionaire cotton-spinner was the victim, to
the tune of 60,000 yen, of a thoroughly characteristic black-

mail. Masajiro Tanaka, head of a self-styled patriotic party, learned that the cook in a Tokyo café claimed to be the natural son of the millionaire's deceased father. Tanaka persuaded the cook to register himself as the son, forging the necessary documents and the family seal. Thus equipped, the cook presented himself at the family mansion and requested a suitable allowance. When his demand was rejected he enlisted his friend, the leader of the patriotic party, as his representative. Japanese swords were produced, and the family parted with 60,000 yen. The cook received 10,000, the remainder was divided among the " party," and the story came out when Tanaka was arrested in a general raid on gangsters.

" Sincerity " is a word greatly in vogue in the Orient. One of its many uses was illustrated by the action of a Tokyo gang trying to extort money from a former boss. Two of the group chopped off three of their little fingers and sent them to the victim, who became frightened at such unmistakable proof of " sincerity " and parted with 2,000 yen.

The entire transaction, and especially the formula employed to give moral tone to the episode of the little fingers, is illuminating. The victim was a building contractor, a term which usually means a man who can furnish coolies for rough work or questionable enterprises. For considerations undisclosed, he had employed five men to wreck the temple of a Buddhist sect in the course of a dispute over the authenticity of a Buddhist image. They were caught and served eighteen months in prison. On coming out they demanded to be compensated for the time they spent in prison. The contractor employed an attorney to deal with them, but showed no sign that he intended to pay. Thereupon one of the men who had been acting as go-between chopped off his little finger as an apology to his comrades for his failure. Struck by such " sincerity," his fellow go-between chopped off both his little fingers. The three fingers were put in a jar and delivered to the erring contractor, who gave the men a thousand yen apiece. When they spent it and tried to obtain more, the contractor appealed to the police.

The little finger may be of comparatively little use while attached to the hand, but when amputated and pickled in alcohol it is one of the most effective stage properties of the extortionist. A large printing firm in Tokyo went bankrupt and its president was prosecuted for incurring fraudulent debts amounting to about a million yen. The plant was attached by an insurance company for unpaid loans. The proprietor of an obscure newspaper and two other men attempted to extort money from the printing company by threatening to reveal that the insurance company had been favored to the detriment of small creditors. A director of the printing concern was menaced: in desperation he cut off his little finger and gave it to the blackmailers, pleading that they leave him alone. The finger was then sent to directors of the insurance company, a silent but potent threat of what might befall them. They paid 20,000 yen before deciding to take the police into the affair.

Dissolute lads who fail to make good are the stuff of which patriotic gangsters are made. Toyotaka Yoshida's parents in rural Saitama were too poor to send him to any of the recognized universities, but they managed to support him in Tokyo while he spent a few years at some small private institution calling itself a college. After graduating he made lecture tours advocating " social justice." He joined a patriotic society, but left it and organized his own. One of his converts was a sub-lieutenant on the reserve list who had heard him lecture. Another was an infantry private. Two others were students of a private university. Country members were enlisted among the youth of Yoshida's home town.

They prepared elaborate paper plans for a wholesale slaughter of politicians, after which they were all to assemble before the Imperial Palace in Tokyo and solemnly rip their bellies open. There were also schemes for raiding banks preliminary to " inaugurating a reign of terror in Tokyo."

Their plan for the public murder of Dr. K. Suzuki, leader of the Seiyukai Party, was worthy of a dime novel. Suzuki was about to address a party rally at Kawagoe. A member of the gang who while in the army had won a prize for marksmanship was to secret himself in the gallery with a hunting rifle and shoot Suzuki while he was orating. A group of youths, each with a dagger concealed in his clothes, was to be seated close to the stage, ready to spring in case the marksman missed his aim. Men armed with swords were to guard the entrance and hold back the police. Before this pretty plot could be carried out the police swooped down on the gang. Only one member fought to defend himself.

Those youths had lived for half a year in an empty house which had been lent to them. They cooked some of their food, which they brought from their homes, and ate some meals at restaurants, paying with money obtained from their supporters. Admiring friends, after they were in jail, subscribed to present them with complete formal Japanese outfits so that they might make a dignified appearance at the trial.

Hajime Suwidate, aged twenty-eight, president of a reactionary society called Kokumeiso walked into the office of the Soviet trade representative in the heart of Tokyo's business and banking district. Brandishing a sword, he scared the Japanese clerks, then began to smash windows and furniture. Having done all the damage he could, he re-entered his waiting taxicab and drove to the office of his society. He surrendered to the police when they arrived and stated that he had been moved to indignation by press reports that Soviet police had killed three Japanese fishermen on the Russian fishing grounds in Kamchatka.

Sato, a patriotic thug who shot and nearly killed the Soviet trade representative, was not punished. He appealed the District Court's sentence of three years. The Appeal Court reduced it to eighteen months and granted a long stay of execution. He served none of his sentence.

When the Far Eastern Olympic Games were held at Manila in 1934, the Kobe Patriotic Young Men's Federation were offended by the thought of a Japanese team appearing in an American dependency. Their method of opposition was effective in causing many resignations from the Japanese team. They sent gangs of bullies out to the quiet roads near the training grounds. As the youths returned to their quarters in the dusk they were ambushed and beaten about the body and legs with clubs. Families were alarmed and many of the prospective competitors resigned. The secretary of the Physical Culture Association issued a statement urging members of the team not to be scared. " We shall certainly go to Manila," he said, " provided the team is not weakened too much and the government does not prohibit our leaving." The government encouraged them to go and sent 60,000 yen to pay their expenses. Lieutenant General Nobutaka Shioten, managing director of the Imperial Aviation Association, started an agitation against the games on the ground that

" the Far Eastern Olympics are a puppet of Freemasons and Jews who utilize sport to achieve their aims." As a footnote to that statement it may be added that the only Freemasons in Japan were three or four small lodges composed of foreign residents who met inconspicuously and the only Jews were a new foreign business men. It is hard to guess what the general was afraid of. He had evidently been reading Fascist literature.

Political assassination — or the organization of gangs and a profession of readiness to attempt it — became a way of living. In August 1934 the Patriotic Iron and Blood Brotherhood was established in Fukuoka. Its founder was Toshinori Wakasaki, aged twenty-seven, of no regular occupation but at one time the registered publisher of a magazine called the *Great Sacred War*. The other members, so far as they became known to the police, were a group of young coal-miners between twenty and twenty-three, some unemployed youths, and a girl of nineteen, daughter of a miner.

As required by the press law, Wakasaki had lodged 250 yen with the police as security for his magazine. He stopped publication, drew his 250 yen, and departed with two members of his society. The police keep a routine check on publishers, and when the proprietor of the *Great Sacred War* withdrew his deposit and left town, they looked through the belongings he had left behind. They found a letter declaring he intended to sacrifice his life for his country and expressing a belief that future historians would approve of what he was going to do.

The police inferred that he had gone to Tokyo and would be found in patriotic circles. He had and he was. He confessed that on an earlier visit to the capital he had been inspired with a faith that violence was necessary to bring about better conditions in the country. He returned to the country and his friends among the young miners. They supplied him with dynamite which he brought back to Tokyo. But though the power to obtain dynamite was doubtless a useful recommendation in the eyes of the patriotic leaders in Tokyo, it was not the best weapon for the assassination of Prince Saionji, Count Makino, Mr. K. Takahashi, the Finance Minister, Baron T. Mitsui, of the Mitsui firm, and Baron K. Iwasaki, of the Mitsubishi firm, whom the Volunteer Union of Empire (Kokoku Giyuta), successor to the Patriotic Iron and Blood Brotherhood, had undertaken to kill as they returned from the Imperial chrysanthemum garden party.

The trio came to Tokyo to commit the murders and one of their number was sent over to Manchuria to obtain pistols and ammunition. Though Japanese officers in Manchuria had on other occasions furnished automatics and hand grenades to equip political murderers, the volunteer who made the trip failed to obtain any, if he tried. He rejoined his friends in Tokyo. They had printed a thousand copies of a patriotic declaration and mailed them before doing anything else. They returned to Fukuoka and obtained more dynamite from their girl colleague, the miner's nineteen-year-old daughter. A conference was called, but Wakasaki, the leader, failed to appear. The other two, believing or affecting to believe that he had been arrested, bolted to Tokyo. Their money was running short, and they went to Yawata, where they found their leader and quarreled with him. Some months later, his funds also being exhausted, he returned to Tokyo and was arrested while trying to raise funds for a new society.

One of the flamboyant scoundrels of that hectic era was Hanni Ito the Great, Savior of Asia. His real name was Masanao Matsuo, and he had others. He first burst on the public in a big way when he bought a Tokyo newspaper, the *Kokumin,* and announced that he would rest content with the colossal fortune he had acquired by speculation and devote the rest of his life and his genius to the new Far Eastern principle. He called himself " the genius of speculation "; the publishing venture was the outcome of operations on Osaka Stock Exchange in which, according to Ito, he had made 10,000,000 yen. There is a certain amount of drudgery in journalism: it cannot all be done by talking, and there was no money to be made by acquiring the debts of a third-rate newspaper. Ito's presidency of the *Kokumin* was short, but new horizons were opening in Manchukuo, which the Japanese army was developing with all the enthusiasm of inexperience as a new kind of military socialist state. Ito raised a campaign fund in Japan " through the co-operation of advocates of the Far Eastern principle " and went over to the mainland to organize " the New Far Eastern Unit," for which he afterwards claimed 1,500,000 members.

Manchukuo did not come up to expectations. Hanni returned to Japan and undertook a lecture tour. Thousands of people flocked to see and hear " the genius of speculation." After the lecture he would discourse familiarly with the wealthier residents of the towns he visited, and many of them were allowed to invest in his projects. He was next heard of as president of a 10,000,000-yen trust company in Shanghai which proposed to drive Western influence from the Far East. " He specializes in speculative bargaining, at which he is a genius. All the vast sums of money needed for his movements are obtained from his winnings. Shanghai is his favorite sphere of action. He has established the Shanghai Trust Company, of which he is director-general. It is his aim ultimately to direct the financing of London from Shanghai as an example of the New Orientalism. By dethroning London from its position as monetary center of the East, Hanni intends not only to put Shanghai in London's place but to enrich China and Japan "; so wrote one of his disciples. When Japan went off the gold standard in December 1931 and the stock exchange had to close for three days, Ito claimed that his colossal operations, resulting in a profit of 10,000,000 yen, was the cause.

Anticipating and exceeding the Californian "ham and eggs" party, Ito proclaimed that one of his aims was to give every man and woman all the money they needed:

" Currency is as much a necessity of human existence as anything else. Currency is a wonderful instrument in that it brings joy to and drives away sorrow from man. I shall see that all Orientals get a larger share of currency. Why should the Orient continue to trade with the Occident? If the harmful trade with the West is eliminated, the Orient will be able to adjust its commodity prices and free industry will be reborn."

The newspapers told a curious story about Ito's first successes in the Osaka stock market. He found that many of the dealers were members of a Buddhist sect and were in the habit of basing their speculations on " God's words " as revealed by the chief priest. It was a simple matter for Ito to fleece such simple gamblers, and he is reported to have made hundreds of thousands of yen and thus laid the foundation of his fortune.

IV. *Seeking for a Soul*

Chapter XVII

THE "SOUL OF JAPAN"

The years when Japan was drifting to war were a time of spiritual restlessness. The nation was turning away disillusioned from the ideals it had embraced half a century before and many were searching for something of Japan's own, something Japanese and unique, which would furnish a better philosophy of the state than the nation had developed from its nineteenth-century borrowings. So there began a debate on the soul of Japan, the national spirit; and philosophers, patriots, the army, and the government took part in it. It arose from a belief or a hope that in their native ideas the Japanese could find a rule of life that they needed as a nation and there was also, in the earlier stages, an undertone of longing that foreign nations should understand the Japanese soul and a painful conviction that neither the Japanese publicists nor any of their interpreters had put that soul across.

The Japanese at home are pleasant people to live with. Their desire to be better understood was natural and I sympathized with it. And like another inquirer into matters beyond his grasp

I heard great argument
About it and about, but ever more
Came out by the same door where in I went,

defeated by the discovery that neither the philosophers nor the men of action were able to put into plain, intelligible, translatable words what they meant by the Japanese national spirit.

Lafcadio Hearn wrote a book on the soul of Japan. It is true that Hearn idealized everything he touched, but he was a great artist and his pictures of the Japanese people have a spiritual verisimilitude that no one who has lived long among them would deny. But Hearn was about as non-political as an intelligent human being can be; he described the human soul of the people, what we call the heart to distinguish it from the head; and what all Japan was debating in these years was the national spirit, a something emanating from and pertaining to the Japanese state. Hearn saw the Japanese as persons; they were seeing themselves as a national entity and were sure that they had a national soul peculiarly their own, peculiarly Japanese. In the end it appeared that what they meant by the Japanese soul was the Japanese mission in the world, and that mission was defined by those members of the national family who commanded the power and incarnated the ambitions of the state.

The achievements of the modern Japanese empire, in evil and in good, have been so considerable that an effort to get into the Japanese mind is worth making. Let us sit down with them and listen to what they have to say.

Masa-atsu Yasuoka, a patriotic philosopher, author of *Oriental Political Philosophy,* a man of means and a man of culture, founded a school in Tokyo for the study of the Japanese national spirit, and he wrote on the subject in periodicals published in Japan for foreign readers.

He introduces himself in terms that at once win the reader's attention: " I am a Japanese and consequently disposed to revere what I conceive to be the spirit of my people; but I have also studied with interest and intense admiration the cultural adventure of the Western world." He proposes that we drop the false idea of cultural homogeneity and try to compose our differences by understanding them rather than by ignoring them. Western philosophy, he says, is analytical, conceptual, and logical; Japanese philosophy is intuitive. Western learning is inspired by a passion for analysis; Japanese learning by a passion for synthesis. " The West draws a distinction between the things that are Cæsar's and the things that are God's; in the East Cæsar and God are blended harmoniously."

Yasuoka illustrates the difference between Western and Japanese ideas by a comparison of clothes. Clothing in the West, he says, is sharply individualized; not so in Japan, where the traditional dress of men and women, restrained by rigid conventions in line, color, and form, is a kind of uniform. " The idea of clothes as an expression of personality, which a casual glance at a fashion journal would suggest is a very important one to Western people, is unknown to us."

The " differends " Mr. Yasuoka describes are more interesting to the student of philosophy than to the general reader, but his comment on the practical applications of the Japanese spirit are politically important. It explains the hive mentality which is so pronounced a feature of Japanese political concepts: " The Japanese spirit fits the Japanese for a self-abnegation and a greater social solidarity than can ever be possible in the individualistic, classifying West. It develops relationships between master and servant, protector and protégé, which are so much the product of our culture that it is impossible to conceive of the one side resenting or the other abusing them. They make for a certain dependence and absence of self-reliance. *The essence of the Japanese spirit is eagerness on the part of the individual to find a person worthy to be served with unremitting devotion."* (The italics are mine.)

And so he comes to the question of death and gives us an explanation of the Japanese army's suicide squads which at least is less degrading than some others: " A differentiating, individualistic culture tends, quite apart from religious dogma, to stress the sanctity of human life. To those trained by a culture which is forever seeking to grasp and serve a large entity the individual life is relatively unimportant. For a Japanese death is not awful in the true meaning of that word, nor is it important except in relation to the purpose it serves. It is not even a sacrifice any more than the life of devotion is a sacrifice. It is simply the last act of that life of devotion, and that alone gives it its importance. We must know how to die well, we must be assured that our death will serve effectively the purpose which has animated our life. Death for us is a gesture, like life, and consequently we seek to make it an effective one. Thus, even in life and death, there is no differentiation."

A Christian philosopher might have written that passage. The only comment to be made is that Mr. Yasuoka is thinking of the eternal spirit of man, and that is not what his compatriots mean when they speak of the Japanese national spirit.

He describes a Japanese committee meeting to show us the difference between the Japanese and ourselves. The Japanese, he says, marshal all the reasons pro and con as keenly as does the West, and then they reach a unanimous decision by a process of " emotional attunement." But any decision of any committee calls for reason and right as well as emotional at-

tunement among those who make it. Recalling his remark
that " the essence of the Japanese spirit is eagerness to find a
person worthy to be served," one wonders if emotional attunement does not mean simply submission to the strong.
Cæsar and God have been synthesized in Japan, he says. And
so they have; it is one of the most illuminating remarks ever
written; in Japan Cæsar is God demanding not only his due
but body and mind as well.

In the last passage I shall quote, Mr. Yasuoka shows us himself: " Brought up on the traditional Japanese culture, I
graduated, like so many of us, into cold light still shed and
reflected in the Occident from the Attic plains. It blinded me
at first, it fascinated me thereafter, it left me dissatisfied and
confused in the end. I returned to my native learning and
slowly and with a sensation of infinite appeasement it ' teased
me out of thought as doth eternity.' And as I meet our young
men who glibly handle the counters of Occidental culture, I
am moved to wonder first how much they have grasped of the
realistics behind, and second how coherent are their spiritual
processes, derived from two such different sources. Sometimes
I speak to such young men of the value of attunement in the
approach to truth, of the culture that is theirs by right, to
bring them comfort and at the same time a rich and inspiring
field to explore. Using their language, I sometimes murmur:
' *Il faut cultiver son jardin,*' with a slight emphasis on the
' *son.*' And mostly they take no notice of me at all."

It is charming. And does it not show us the deep inner
malady of the modern Japanese, wandering between two
worlds, no longer spiritually at home in the crude paganism
of the official state-worship and unable to break with it without profound suffering? The " infinite appeasement " Mr.
Yasuoka found, was it not his submission to the doctrine that

the strong shall rule? That also is a philosophy, but if it is to be ours we need never have left the jungle.

It is sad to have to add that the school Mr. Yasuoka founded in Tokyo became the resort of fanatics and murderers — to wit, Priest Nissho and the young thugs who killed Finance Minister Inouye and Baron Takuma Dan.

Even in the army thoughtful persons were disturbed by the absence of a scientific explanation of the ideas they believed. An effort to meet the want was made in a pamphlet written by a member of the Investigation Bureau of the War Office and published by the Reservists' Association on April 23, 1935. One hundred and fifty thousand copies were distributed.

The anonymous writer regarded the issue as fundamentally one of faith and not of science. " The ultimate object of this study," he says, " is not a theoretical conclusion but a religious belief." But, he adds, " the intelligence of the nation has so much advanced in modern times that to force the people to believe in mysteries may in some cases only brew doubt. Some people may say: ' the polity should be believed. To study it theoretically is blasphemy.' But let us be magnanimous because magnanimity is a great characteristic of the Japanese spirit. We should spare no effort to remove those doubts."

Such language was new. Foreign readers turned to the pamphlet with the hope that they would find at last a rational account of what the Japanese believe. They found an evidently honest comparison of Japanese and Western political ideas, but instead of a scientific and comprehensible exposition of the Japanese idea, there were only sounding phrases and mystical dogmas. The writer insisted that the Japanese system was unique, peculiar to Japan and therefore not to be judged by Western standards; yet he declared that it was as universal as a law of nature and furnished a model which all nations might copy.

The Japanese and Western ideas of government, he said, are fundamentally different. The "great principle" of the Japanese Constitution is "Imperial government with national assistance." The error of constitutional scholars is that they regard the sovereign power as belonging to the state, a juridical entity based upon social conscience. But social conscience is only public opinion. "This theory may be harmless in Western countries where the national polity is often reconstructed, but in Japan we can accept no theory that would impair the eternity of our polity. Ever since the foundation of the country the nation has believed that the Emperor is the ruler of Japan. We are governed by the Emperor, not by a juridical entity. This belief must be regarded as our 'social conscience.' "

The military author thinks that Japanese jurists tacitly admitted a fear that some Emperor might use his power for his personal benefit. His answer was that those who fear the Emperor might misuse his power "have not understood the essence of the Imperial government."

The author may have felt that elaboration of the last point was too delicate a task for public discussion. Taken in conjunction with the constitutional practice by which the Emperor acts only on the advice of his ministers in civil affairs and on that of the chiefs of the Army and Navy General Staffs in military affairs, the "essence of the Imperial government" is that the ruler has no real power. He is clothed with supreme power as with a uniform, but he does not govern; he is a dictator who does not dictate but can only register the decrees of others. It was made unmistakably clear in the disputes of those years that the army regarded itself as the sole authority to advise the Emperor on everything connected with defense, and that defense was interpreted in the broadest sense to cover foreign policy, finance, and national economy.

The military philosopher made a comparison between Japanese and Western fundamental ideas of government. First, Western constitutions respect the interests of individuals. They regard the state as an organ to promote the welfare of the individuals. Japan, on the other hand, " views the nation as an organic substance forming a happy whole with the Emperor as the nucleus, a living body which grows and develops eternally." Second, Western nations cannot abandon the idea that the interests of the people and the ruler may conflict. In Japan there can be no question of opposition between ruler and ruled. " The Emperor is the center of national life and the core of national growth, and the nation united in a common body grows and advances towards a common object. It is the duty of subjects to assist the Emperor in the great task of accomplishing the ideal of the country." Third, Western nations, for both theoretical and historical reasons, cannot find the center of government in a human being. They therefore make law the center of their systems. But in Japan " the Emperor is the center of national life. Why should we imitate the West? "

Thus the military pamphleteer who began so promisingly ends with question-begging phrases. " The nation is a happy whole with the Emperor as its nucleus. . . . The Emperor . . . is the core of national growth . . . the duty of subjects to assist the Emperor." Nothing tangible, nothing defined, only vague shibboleths. For all its scholarship and good intent, the pamphlet again shows that ideas which the Japanese consider profound, and which have a lofty sound, when written in Japanese, dissolve into froth when they are translated into the language of "the analytical West."

The soldier-author was himself to get a taste of the quality of patriotic bigotry in Japan. In one of his more rhetorical passages he had exclaimed: "The prosperity or decline of the Imperial house is the prosperity or decline of the nation." A few days later a "certain person of a certain organization," identifiable as Mitsuru Toyama, the veteran leader of patriotic gangs, called on the War Minister and pointed out that even to speak of the possibility of the decline of the Imperial house was sacrilege. The War Office received the rebuke with humility and passed the buck to the Home Office, which had sanctioned publication. The Home Office said the matter would be arranged. The eminent patriot having been thus appeased, no more was heard of it.

If the Japanese find satisfaction in thinking that the "Emperor is the center of every phase of the national life" and that the nation is "an organic substance forming a happy whole with the Emperor as its nucleus," there is no reason why any Western critic should disagree. When it comes to practical affairs, the "organic substance forming a happy whole with the Emperor" has to use political, judicial, and administrative machinery just as do nations which have adopted the soulless concept of the juridical state. Our interest does not lie in the divinity claimed for the Japanese Emperor nor in his long descent, but in the manner in which Japan is governed. We have a supreme interest in knowing whether policy is directed by a government representing the general body of the nation with all its diversified interests, or by a figurehead manipulated by the powerful groups who can enforce the right to "assist" him.

The claim, so often made, that the Japanese Constitution

is different from that of other countries because it was bestowed by the ruler and not extorted from him like Magna Charta is as pointless as the dispute whether the hen or the egg came first. The Constitution, with its two Houses, its ballot boxes, its popular suffrage, and its millions of voters, was the method ordained by the Emperor for providing that "national assistance" which he needed. But the exponents of Japanism were united in their dislike of all those things, and none disliked the democratic features of the Constitution more than did the army.

Another phase of the debate found that the difference between the Japanese system and the systems of the West was that the former was "Emperor-centric" and the latter were "parliament-centric." A lengthy communication sent to me privately by a Japanese scholar compared the Japanese system with the British constitutional monarchy and the Constitution of the United States. I had put the question: If there should be a difference of opinion between the Diet, as constitutional organ for assisting the Emperor, and the ruler, who is to decide? The Japanese scholar answered that if such a difference arose, the nation would at once accept the view of the Emperor.

It was evidently impossible for him as a Japanese to admit that there might be a bad emperor, or one with bad counsellors. He did not face the possibility that the military power would again take control. He did not see that the system in which he believed left the Emperor without means of overruling the military power whenever it chose to assert itself. He did not realize that the Emperor-centric system is just the old system by which the Emperor is a dignified and powerless figure, an autocrat in theory only, powerless against the military element whenever it kicks over the traces.

His argument and attitude showed that the restoration of 1868 was but a half-finished revolution. And if he was correct, the Japanese are satisfied to have it so, satisfied with a continuance of their traditional system, by which the strongest member of the national family takes the governing power with the nominal sanction of the Emperor, who is in effect an absentee sovereign. It does not seem that the revolution will be soon completed since in the minds of the Japanese people, with all their quickness and capacity for seizing foreign ideas, there is no conception of the idea of government of and by the people.

In the spring of 1938 the Department of Justice in Tokyo issued one of the most remarkable documents ever produced by a government office. The occasion was the refusal of the Chinese leaders to submit after the fall of Nanking. Japan then realized that a long war was inevitable. The statement excused the miscalculation with which the war had been begun, rationalized a policy of aggression by representing it as a historic national mission, and appealed for united exertions. It was propaganda in the ordinary modern sense of that word, but as propaganda addressed solely to the Japanese people by their highest judicial authority it threw light on the Japanese governing mind.

The war had been begun, it said, with the idea of giving the Chinese a punishing blow so that they would " realize the disastrous consequences of anti-Japanism." But even after the fall of Nanking the Chinese leaders " persisted in their blindness," so Japan was compelled to abandon hopes of settlement and " strive for the construction of a moral order in East Asia." The statement explained that this was a task bequeathed to Japan by the first Emperor in accordance with his ideal of the whole world as one family. It went on to expound the Japanese conception of the state: " To the Japanese mind there has been no conception of the individual as opposed to the state. All members of the nation have conceived themselves as parts of the state. . . . Underlying Western types of ideas exists an individualistic view of life which regards individuals as absolute, independent entities . . . the standard of all values and themselves the highest of all values."

But that Western way of thinking is called a basic error. " All human beings, while having their independent life and existence, depend in a deeper sense upon the whole and live in co-ordinated relationship with each other. They are born from the state, sustained by the state and brought up in the history and traditions of the state. Individuals can only exist as links in an infinite and vast chain of life called the state; they are links through whom the inheritance of ancestors is handed down to posterity, making possible continued growth and development in the future. . . . Individuals participate in the highest and greatest value when they serve the state as parts of it. The highest life for the Japanese subject is to offer himself in perfect loyalty to the Imperial throne so that he may participate in its glorious life."

This statement is, in form, more German than Japanese. It is a summary of the Hegelian doctrine of the state, the philosophy on which National Socialism is founded. From Hegel came the teaching that man's chief end (to use the old Calvinistic phraseology) is membership of the state and promotion of its greatness; that the state has the right to subordinate the liberty and the happiness of individuals to its own purposes; that the supreme virtue of war is the completeness of the discipline it imposes and the sacrifice it exacts for the state; that the aims of the national state are more important than international morality. The philosophy of the Japanese "new order" is the philosophy of Nazism; it is the latest of Japan's long list of borrowings. Yet it must be said that Japan brought a mind made ready by history and tradition to absorb it. The Japanese soul was a vessel well adapted to receive and retain Hegel's heady philosophy of the state. Nature abhors a vacuum; Japan's meager political inheritance, Shinto and ancestor-worship, was a void into which the wine of National Socialism rushed irresistibly.

The Japanese have been great borrowers throughout their history. Their ideological debt to Nazi Germany is as plain today as was the earlier debt of the modern Japanese Empire to England and America. In the beginning they borrowed almost everything from China. As they were growing into national self-consciousness they saw the civilization and might of the Central Flowery Kingdom dominating the whole Far East and drawing to itself the lesser peoples around its far-flung borders, and they too felt its magnetic power.

Perhaps because of their insular security, the Japanese were different from the Koreans, the Burmese, the Annamites, the Tibetans. Their strong sense of nationality impelled them to resist absorption and they Japanized the ideas they borrowed. The history and the metaphysics of Japan's political philosophy are beyond the scope of this chapter or my purpose; I am only trying to describe Japanese political ideas, but a glance at origins and evolution helps us to understand the Japanese mind today.

"Kodo," the Imperial Way, is, we are told, Japan's guiding principle and its extension is the object of the present wars. "Kodo" is the Japanese version of the Chinese ideographs "Wang-tao," meaning Enlightened Rule. It came from China to Japan, together with the Confucian morality which, despite all that has been said about Japan's uniqueness, is still the ethical basis of Japanese life. All that the Japanese inherited of their own was Shinto, or the Way of the Gods. It originated as a primitive animism and it was combined with a primitive fear of ghosts and worship of the dead ancestors whose spirits had to be appeased if their heirs and successors were to have peace. According to Imperial Shinto, the Japanese throne was handed down by the Imperial ancestors, the first of whom had received his mandate to conquer and occupy the country from the grandson of the Sun Goddess. In a book called *The Genealogy of the Divine Emperor,* written about 1340, the national faith which the young officers profess today was stated in the words they still employ: " Japan is the land of the gods. Its foundations were laid by the divine ancestors who transmitted the succession to the Emperor forever. This exists only in our country."

This invincible native idea was not supplanted by the powerful ideas imported from China in the Buddhist religion and the Confucian precepts. Another Japanese scholar reconciled the two by identifying Kodo, the Way of the Emperor, with Shinto, the Way of the Gods. The national passion for synthesis was gratified. Japanese scholars, who had been teaching Chinese philosophy in opposition to Shinto, accepted the amalgamation of Confucianism with Shinto, and the philosophy of modern Japan was born. The land of the gods was also the land of the divine emperors. The movement which culminated in the restoration-revolution of 1868 came at first in the form of an agitation for the revival of pure Shinto. " The Kodo spirit was the main motive power of the restoration," writes Professor W. J. Whitehouse. Its victorious slogan was " Restore the Emperor and expel the foreigners." Its exponents, however, were divided about practical policy. One school favored a continuance of national seclusion; another wanted to carry the Imperial Way overseas, annexing Saghalien, Korea, Manchuria, and the Loochoo islands. The edicts of the new restoration government were full of Kodo doctrine and explained Kodo as " the system of administration which shall unite the whole nation and combine religion and political administration." The identical phrase was used by General Senjuro Hayashi to describe the policy of the Cabinet he formed in 1933. It was no secret that his statement was written by a scholar of the old school, but the general adopted his language, thinking to placate the army.

The Kodo spirit of 1868 was submerged by constitutionalism in the great flood of modernization which subsequently swept Japan. The leaders of the new nation were more concerned to make Japan strong than to engage in premature military adventures and they were under the sway of Western ideas. With the Manchurian adventure in 1931 it revived, and Dr. Tetsujiro Inouye, of Tokyo Imperial University, recently observed: " Many army men now speak of Kodo and state that it means unity of religion and political administration and a return to the policy of the Kodo party in 1868." The " Kodo party " was the chauvinistic group which raised a rebellion in order to compel the new government to invade Korea.

By " unity of religion and politics " is meant the rule of the divine Emperor unobstructed by foreign innovations like parliament. The precept of the first Emperor was an order to extend the Imperial rule. The restoration of Imperial rule by the army today gets rid of free enterprise and representative government, and provides the warriors with the authority and the resources they need to extend the Imperial Way over regions which have not yet known its benefits.

Chapter XVIII

THE SUPPRESSION OF A SCHOLAR

On the afternoon of April 25, 1935, one hundred and fifty rural reservists assembled on the flat roof of the Military Club in Tokyo and with wooden faces watched the burning of three books: *Essentials of Constitutional Law, A Course in the Constitution of Japan Article by Article,* and *Fundamental Doctrines of the Japanese Constitution.* The books had been discussed in parliament, and the Prime Minister, Admiral Okada, had said the House of Representatives was not a suitable forum nor its members suitable persons to discuss legal theory. For himself, he said, he had tried to read the books but was unable to understand them.

The rural reservists had no doubt of their capacity to be judge and executioner. They had prepared themselves for the auto-da-fé by worshipping at the two great national shrines of Tokyo. They followed it by attending a feast given in their honor at which members of both Houses were present. Such demonstrations are seldom spontaneous in Japan. The visit to Tokyo was paid for by persons who knew what they were about better than did a group of farmers.

The burning of the books was part of a controversy which had raged for six months. The stake and the faggots were not the only features in which it resembled the religious quarrels of bygone centuries. It turned ostensibly on a point of doctrine as obscure as any of the questions of dogma which had set the fires of bigotry blazing in the past. Correspondents could not even comprehend what the believers believed. It was a political dispute conducted in the spirit and terms of medieval theology. Yet a practical purpose was pursued behind mystical rhetoric, and the Minobe affair, as it was called, was full of instruction on the real nature of Japanese government.

The author of the books, Dr. Tatsukichi Minobe, was a member of the House of Peers by Imperial nomination and the attack was opened in the House of Peers. Dr. Minobe had been Professor of Constitutional and Administrative Law in the Imperial University since 1902. He was considered the foremost living authority on the Japanese Constitution. He had received from the Emperor the highest decorations that can be conferred on a civilian, and he had lectured in the Palace by command.

Thirty years of professordom and the exceptional honors his abilities had earned had given Dr. Minobe his full share of scholastic pride. When a back-bench peer, Baron Takeo Kikuchi, made a speech in the upper House declaring Minobe's teachings to be disloyal, the public did not at first take him seriously and Dr. Minobe did not conceal his contempt. The press learned, however, that the army was interested. General Mazaki, Vice-Chief of the General Staff, issued instructions to divisional commanders on the subject, and General Hayashi, the Minister for War, gave the Prime Minister an " advice " and told reporters that he was ready to give another if necessary.

Dr. Minobe's contempt was excused by the palpable fact that his critics did not understand his theory and had not the qualifications needed to judge it or amend it. They were convinced that Minobe was a heretic of the worst kind, yet they were unable to formulate an intelligible theory to take the place of his. The positions were irreconcilable; Minobe was arguing law and they were asserting mystical dogma.

Minobe was accused of teaching that the throne was an organ, or institution, of the state. The offending passage read: " The state is the possessor of the governing rights, and the Emperor exercises and controls those rights as the head of the state, or its highest organ." Minobe's critics said that this definition made the Emperor of Japan nothing more than a European constitutional king or a republican president. Most of his assailants found it sufficient to vociferate that the " Emperor-organ " theory was incompatible with the sacred and unique position of the descendant of the Sun Goddess. More serious criticism was offered by Professor Kyoki Minoda, professor in an institution called the Kokushikan (National Spirit) College. Minobe's heresy, according to Minoda, was this: From Minobe's theory of the throne as an organ of the state it follows that the state is a juridical person, and the Emperor is its representative. The Emperor therefore does not possess the governing powers but is entrusted with them. " An ' organ ' is an instrument or a means. Now," continues Minoda, " a means serves an object. If the means no longer serves the object we can change the instrument. This is pure Chinese or Western revolutionism, which holds that the sovereign can be expelled for the benefit of the people. Minobe is theoretically a materialistic individualist and morally an anarchist."

Minobe replied to his parliamentary critics from the rostrum of the House of Peers. He explained that his teachings dealt with legal theory. In law, he said, right connotes interest. If the sovereignty of the state is the Emperor's personal right it follows that it could be used for his personal interests — an interpretation " quite incompatible with the peerless national polity of Japan. The Emperor's sovereignty is to be regarded as power, not as right in the legal sense, and it is to be exercised under the provisions of the Constitution, not as absolute and unlimited power. The state is a permanent living body; the Emperor is its head and exercises sovereignty as its representative. He is the embodiment of the state."

The defense might have gone down well enough in a gathering of jurists. The House of Peers, though its benches were crowded with his former students, received it so coldly that the learned professor was abashed and made no further effort to teach the legislature constitutional law. He realized that constitutional law was a lost cause.

Minobe had trained practically the whole active generation of Japanese administrators, judges, and diplomats. It is a pleasing trait of the Japanese that they have a deep reverence for their teachers. "*Sensei*" (teacher, or master) is one of the most honorable titles by which in Japan one human being can address another. Dr. Minobe had been " sensei " to countless Japanese who occupied important positions. Not one of them said a word in his defense when his books were suppressed and his loyalty impugned. Some may have felt that honoring the " sensei " was all very well when the master was in no trouble but quite another thing when loyalty involved some risk or at least unpopularity. The majority were terrified to show even by a gesture that they could sympathize with a man whose view of the Imperial function was questioned by those fierce guardians of orthodoxy, the soldiers and the chieftains of the patriotic societies.

Major General Genkuro Eto, a retired officer who had entered politics, went to Tokyo District Court and filed a change of *lèse-majesté* against Dr. Minobe. The alleged *lèse-majesté* consisted in a statement found in the books, that the people had a constitutional right to criticize decrees issued by the Emperor. The charge was investigated. Minobe was not arrested but he was questioned for sixteen hours. Six weeks later the procurators announced that the charge could not be sustained as the books contained many passages dwelling on the sanctity and prestige of the Imperial house, but they were not satisfied that the author might not be guilty of an offense against the Press and Publications Law passed in August of the previous year. The legal inquiry continued for eight months longer. The report explained in an apologetic tone the reasons why the idea of prosecution had been finally dropped. The procurators found that Minobe's constitutional theory which regarded the Emperor as an institution or organ of the state was "deemed to produce undesirable effects in the present social conditions." His books might be regarded as "disturbing peace and order" and he was therefore liable to punishment. But as the books had been published twelve years earlier and had evoked no criticism, it was considered that it would be too harsh to inflict punishment now, especially as the author had shown himself repentant and had promised to exercise greater care in future.

Dr. Minobe announced that he had never dreamed that his books would be found to have violated any law, but that he had determined to abide by the decision of the procurators. He resigned from the House of Peers, ceased lecturing and writing, gave up his house near the Imperial University, moved out to a new suburb, and effaced himself. The Cabinet had already yielded to army pressure and ordered the three books to be suppressed.

The Suppression of a Scholar

Minobe's retirement did not protect him. Just a year after the attack in the House of Peers, a murderous attack was made on him in his home. He had a guard of three policemen, but by the simple device of a false visiting card the assailant got past the guards. He asked Minobe if his views on the theory of the Constitution had changed. Minobe said: "You have not read my books, have you?" His assailant shouted: "No," and began shooting. His aim was bad and he only inflicted a wound on the leg. He professed to have been since early youth a member of a patriotic organization which advocated the principle that the Imperial house is superior to all else in the world, spiritual or material. His career was like that of many shiftless youths who adopt patriotism as a camouflage for idleness. He had aspired to become an attorney but failed and he drifted about until a patriotic school gave him a job as superintendent of its dormitory. The headmaster lent him the revolver. His trial produced no noteworthy feature except his confession that he had once plotted to kill T. V. Soong, at the time Finance Minister of China, but had failed because Soong did not leave his steamer. He was sentenced to a term of imprisonment.

The Minobe affair passed out of sight in a curious twin agitation that arose demanding something called "clarification of national polity." It was conducted with irrational heat and passion. Correspondents were bothered; it is impossible to explain a thing you don't understand; news editors at home, wanting to give their readers news and not mysticism, dealt with it summarily. Sometimes a cable error or a wrathful desk-man would change "polity" into "policy" and give the stuff a false air of intelligibility. Intelligible or not, it was a serious affair in Japan. The powerful reservists' association, controlled by the army, published a manifesto on the subject which the government would not allow to be broadcast. One of the senior generals made clarification his condition for entering the Cabinet as War Minister. The effort to clarify clarification leads us into some peculiar by-ways of Japanese political thinking.

If American senators, congressmen, military and naval officers, writers, and professors had clamored for something that seemed on the face of it unintelligible, all the intellectual machinery of the United States would have been turned on the problem. As it only affected the Japanese, we muttered " Bats in the belfry " and turned to something we could understand.

In Japan successive governments issued statements, learned men wrote articles and addressed meetings. All were agreed that Japan's national polity was unique and sublime, but the sublimity was still unclear and the agitation went on. There was never any indication that the public understood the demand. When it eventually died away there were no postmortems in the press. Looking back, it can now be seen that something did happen. A War Minister resigned, overthrowing a Cabinet, and the new administration gave a pledge to the army that it would create a new political structure on totalitarian lines suited for war. Now the word which is translated " national polity " includes " national structure " as well as many other things. The " national polity " of the agitators was in fact the political structure, the body of institutions and laws which make up the Japanese system. In the result the structure was clarified by a purge; the political parties were induced, more by menace than by persuasion, to dissolve themselves; the capitalists by similar means merged their enterprises into a national whole, and complete blueprints for a new totalitarian structure were adopted. The national polity had been clarified by being remade.

In the West, where words have a recognized relationship to things, we would say after such an event that the people who knew what they wanted had got what they wanted and the honest fools who thought " clarification " meant making clear had got what they deserved.

But we have to remember the vagueness of the Japanese language, which reflects a corresponding vagueness of thought. "Vagueness" is our word; the Japanese would say the condition reflects and expresses an Oriental consciousness of the essential unity of things. The following example is sometimes given: the two-stroke character called *hito* means a man; it also means a person, a life, human, popular. Are these different meanings? Is the unity not greater than the difference?

The Japanese word translated "polity" was "*Kokutai.*" It is untranslatable by any English word. Like so many Japanese words, it includes many things which, to the analytical mind of the West, do not belong together.

"Kokutai" means the Constitution and the body of laws and customs which make up the Japanese system of government, but it also means the traditions of the race, its genius, its way of life, its national spirit. These, the army held, could be more clearly expressed in totalitarian than in liberal institutions; to set up a fascist-like state organization was therefore a clarification of the national polity, structure, essence, spirit and genius. So said the clarifiers, and arguments which are unconvincing when rendered in the finical language of the West, sound plausible in the many-meaninged tongue of Japan. The clarifiers were the strongest, and a learned Minister of Justice declared: " The Japanese spirit is nothing but what can be translated into action as occasion may require."

" Kokutai " is written with the characters meaning " country " and " substance." It is what we mean when we say " Americanism " or " the American way of life." The American Constitution is part of the country's " Americanism." So are the laws of the country, even when they differ from one state to another; prohibition and the repeal of prohibition were " Americanism." But to make the intangible essence called " Americanism " into a football of politics would not be common sense. As one reads those Japanese arguments the conviction grows that the clarification most urgently required is a clarification of mind, of thought, and of language.

" Kokutai " is untranslatable because it includes many separate things. It includes the Emperor and a whole system of mythology; it includes the Constitution and the laws; it includes the country and the genius of the people. All are gathered together into one majestic combination of ideographs, and a verbal entity is created which is at once sacred and unreal. The fundamental confusion is the assumption that the nation and the state are the same thing. The nation, its way of life, its cultural inheritance, is sacred and eternal; it lives on though institutions change; it commands the loyalty of all its nationals irrespective of religious and political differences. The state, the institutions of government and the men who administer them, is changeable. When the army in Japan, like the National Socialist Party in Germany and the Fascist Party in Italy, declares that the state and the nation are one, it is defending its own usurpation of power. It is stealing for a section something that belongs to the whole.

When the Constitution of Japan was being drafted its architect, Prince Ito, explained that the new political machinery embodied the experience of other countries. The question arose whether those changes would not affect Japan's cherished and immutable " Kokutai." A state councillor of the old school was perturbed and went to Kaneko (afterwards Count) , an American-educated secretary, to ask if anything was known in Europe or America about Kokutai. Kaneko replied that the Japanese word had no equivalent in English or French or German. It was unique, and he defined it: " The Emperor of a line unbroken through the ages, holding the three sacred treasures and ruling over the people, is the basis on which our country is founded, the Imperial throne for this reason being eternal and the Kokutai august." Foreigners, added Kaneko, are utterly unable to understand " Kokutai." If national organization or governmental system were meant, the word used should be " seitai." (The difference in literal meaning is hard to convey but might be indicated by saying that " seitai " means government, or administration-substance, while " Kokutai " means " nation-substance.")

Prince Ito differed from Kaneko and said: " Kokutai has always been written with the characters meaning ' country ' and ' substance.' The mountains, rivers, plants, people, language, clothing, food, and civilization — these are Kokutai. When you build a railway between Yokohama and Tokyo, you cut away mountains and fill in the sea. Isn't this a change in Kokutai? When you change the government by opening a parliament, don't you change the Kokutai in the same way? You wear foreign clothes. They're very different from the old kimona. When foreigners come to live everywhere in Japan, the people will change too."

Ito afterwards said that he knew that forms of government might change, but " Kokutai " never. But the difference between his two statements was simply the difference in the meanings of the word " Kokutai." He said in one: " laws may change, but the spirit of Japan never." In the other he said: " different laws will bring a different spirit." " Kokutai " could include both.

This passion for impossible syntheses, for imposing a unity where reality makes a difference, is peculiarly Japanese. It sometimes seems that the fundamental trouble of the Japanese is a lack of belief in their institutions. It expresses itself in passionate asseverations to the contrary. " The imperishability of the Japanese state is the faith of the Japanese people," writes Professor Shin-ichi Fuji, in his book *The Essentials of Japanese Constitutional Law,* published in 1940. He continues: " The Japanese have stood firm and unmoved in their faith in spite of the scientific advance, international turmoil, revolutions abroad, and changes in human thought witnessed throughout ancient, medieval, and modern times. . . . The Japanese race will last as long as the world, united in their faith under the virtuous Emperor, who is the head of this Grand Family." In the professor's discussion of the origins of the Japanese state he makes no distinction between myth and history. Japanese political practice today leans heavily on myth. The first action of a new minister of state or a new army commander is to visit the national shrine and report his appointment to the Sun Goddess. Dr. Izutaro Suehiro, Professor of Civil Law in Tokyo Imperial University, wrote:

" The most important political function in Japan, at least so far as forms are concerned, is paying homage to the Imperial ancestors. . . . Public functions begin with worship to the spirits of the Imperial ancestors, to whose spirits must be reported as a matter of cult all important affairs of state."

But excessive insistence on outworn forms is a symptom of inner decay. The living faith is going out of them. The Japanese cannot escape the age they live in. They have been eager absorbers of Western thought. They are told that their way of life, their Japanism, is bound up with " the Emperor of a line unbroken through ages eternal, holding the three sacred treasures, the throne for this reason being eternal." But how much longer can even literate peasants at this time of day believe in the Sun Goddess? The Japanese revulsion from Western liberalism expresses a fear, so deep that with the majority it lies in the subconscious, that this cherished Japanism they revere cannot live in contact with a world which values freedom more than tradition.

A political motive inspired and used the agitation for clarification. It came into the open at a congress of the reservists' association in 1935. From then on it became clear that the fighting services were the power behind the movement, and that its primary cause was the navy's fury at the London naval agreement of 1930, signed by the government in defiance of the Chief of the Naval General Staff. The government had overruled the fighting services in a matter directly concerned with defense. A precedent had been set which would make party cabinets the real government of Japan.

To the fighting men, with their itch for supremacy, it was an intolerable prospect. Slowly, inexorably, all the historical machinery of revolt came into action — conspiracy, assassination, agitation, and finally mutiny. The demand for clarification of the national polity was the legal-political phase of this movement. A naval writer who concealed his name wrote: " Administrative reforms will follow if the national polity is once more seen in its pristine light. What the reservists object to is the view that the state is a juridical body. This interpretation may be valid in foreign countries but not in Japan, which is a sort of family. There is no need for a state which is a juridical body in dealing with treaties with other nations."

In the discussion over the naval agreement the Prime Minister had consulted Dr. Minobe, the highest authority on Japanese constitutional law. Minobe had ruled that the state is an entity with a central government whose decision is supreme. When high authorities, in this case the Prime Minister and the Chief of the Naval General Staff, differed, the opinion and advice of the Prime Minister, as head of the government, should prevail, according to Minobe. But according to the fighting services, the government is not an entity; it is a group of power-holders whose sole focus is the Emperor. In questions of civil administration the Prime Minister is the last authority; in matters of defense the final authority is the army and navy, each in its sphere.

The demand for clarification of the national structure was therefore a demand for partial abolition of the central government which the restoration had set up. The " pristine light " which was to be restored was the light of feudalism, in which the Japanese state was a congeries of clans, each exercising sovereignty in its own domain, and united only by common loyalty to a powerless High-Priest Emperor. Such a system is really a kind of anarchism in which the units are groups instead of individuals. It is unworkable in a developed society. Japan had a shogun, or generalissimo, who exercised power over the clans. This form of state survived in Japan for 230 years. It collapsed, and the Imperial power was restored when the Japanese realized that only a centralized government would enable the nation to retain its independence under foreign pressure. The clans were abolished and central government established. Beginning as a clan government, it was developing under the Constitution into representative government. The fighting services were usually able to get their way, and so long as the central government yielded to them in matters they regarded as their own, they accepted the Constitution. When a Prime Minister arose who said that in questions of international policy, even when they concerned fleets and armies, the central government must have the last word, the fighting men revolted. The demand for " clarification of the national polity " was in essence and substance a demand that a Chief of the General Staff should not again be overruled by the head of the civil government. Japan did not need " a state which is a juridical body " if such a state could make treaties on arms limitation without the consent of the soldiers and sailors.

When the " Kokutai " agitation had succeeded in driving out the constitutional theory of the Japanese state, an archaic phrase: " Hakko Ichiu," became the slogan in which the advancing wave of imperialism expressed itself. It was was taken from the famous but mythical instructions issued by the first Emperor, which have been found so useful as a justification of aggression. He said: " We believe it good for us to place the four directions and the four corners of the world under one roof." He was at the time engaged in establishing his capital in central Japan after six years of successful invasion. The slogan figured in the refrain of a popular song about the China war, and its meaning was the subject of discussions in the House and in the press. Japanese armies were advancing into China, and the significance of " four corners under one roof " seemed clear enough. Fluent young men writing in the English language for readers abroad audaciously said it meant " universal brotherhood." The Minister of Education admitted that when the first Emperor used it he was bidding his followers conquer all Japan, and said that if it were applied to modern problems it must mean the whole world. But, he said, it does not mean aggression. " We are constructing a new order in Asia. We must not forget that Japan does not exist alone in the world. Mutual friendship and co-operation are needed with adjacent countries, thereby making them neighbors worthy of the name." Thus to send armies into China to bring China under the Japanese roof is, according to the Minister of Education, a sort of good-neighbor policy.

Lieutenant Colonel Okubo, a member of the War Office staff renowned for his gift of exposition, wrote an article to explain the hard-worked phrase. Its meaning is very lofty, he said, and " those affected by the materialism of America and Europe cannot understand it easily." It means " the boundlessly great spirit of the first Emperor. He pacified Japan and founded the Empire. Even if he used force it was for pacification of the unruly, not for territorial aggression. Before starting his campaign he advised them to surrender. It was only when they did not heed his advice that he took action. Japan is determined to make China cast off its mistaken notions and then co-operate with us for the construction of a new order. . . . It is not right to call it a war."

The appropriate comment comes from Professor Shoji Kimura: " It is not merely by chance that the Japanese are deeply interested in modern German philosophy."

Chapter XIX

THE IMPERIAL MYTHUS

The *National History for Primary Schools,* used by order
of the Ministry of Education in all Japanese schools, begins
with an account of the origins of the state. The child naturally
accepts it as true and it gives him his first indelible consciousness of his own country.

It opens brightly with the story of a quarrel among the
gods in heaven, the upshot of which is that the brother of the
Sun Goddess is sent down in disgrace to Japan, the country
the gods had made. He found the population there " extremely afflicted " and he and his son " put things in order,"
but many of the people were still " very rebellious " and the
Sun Goddess next sent her grandson down, bidding him " go
and rule." The narrative continues: " The foundations of our
government, like heaven and earth unchangeable through all
the centuries, were really laid then." The next item is a genea-
logical tree showing a short and straight line of descent
from the Sun Goddess to Jimmu Tenno, the first " human
Emperor."

The teachers who use the *History* are aided with a commentary officially supplied. It tells them: " We subjects who
live under such an illustrious Imperial family are for the most
part descendants of the gods." This flattering announcement

leads up to a passage in which national conceit is expressed with unsurpassable naïveté:

> It is clear that the foundation of our state has been superior from ancient times to that of other countries. . . . If we consider the history of other countries we see that the existence of the people comes first and that subsequently the rulers were chosen. That is why so many revolutions occurred among those nations and hardly one of them has kept its original structure. Considering this, we shall understand why our national structure is superior to that of all other nations.

The *Handbook of Ethics* used in the schools goes to the same fountain to find reasons why Japanese boys and girls should become good men and women and to show them the kind of goodness expected of them:

> From the year Jimmu Tenno ascended the throne 2,600 years have passed. . . . There are many countries in the world but there is not one that, like our great Japanese Empire, has one Emperor of the same dynasty through the course of the ages. We who have been born in such an exalted country have to become excellent Japanese and do our best for our government.

Thus are plastic minds stamped with the idea that they, the Japanese, are a special race with an Emperor-god, a unique government, and a superior destiny.

If the Sun Goddess were not part of the theory of Imperial divinity and if Imperial divinity were not part of the hocus with which the Japanese people are self-hypnotized, the mythology would have only an anthropological interest. It is not originally Japanese but a mixture of Polynesian and

Chinese myths of creation. Other primitive tribes have believed that their lands were created by gods and donated to a chosen people. The legend that a god and goddess married and gave birth to the islands of Japan is not unique, nor is there anything abnormal in the claims of early historians that the rulers for whom they wrote were the heirs and successors of these gods. The abnormality is the elevation of this crude mythology in modern times into the political religion of a heavily armed Empire.

The dogma that has drugged the consciences and intoxicated the imaginations of the Japanese people is the belief in national uniqueness leading to a great destiny. The human desire to possess their neighbor's property is thus synthesized with their duty to their Emperor, their gods, and their country. The proof that Japan is called to an unparalleled destiny, the outward and visible evidence of uniqueness, is the singular duration of the Imperial house, " unbroken for ages eternal" and "coeval with heaven and earth." The histories attest it, the government documents solemnly recite it, and the schoolbooks proclaim it to be historical fact that Japan alone among the nations of the world has preserved her form of government under her divine emperors since 600 years before the birth of Christ.

Aside from claims of divine descent and continuous rulership, the continuity of one family for two thousand years is a remarkable social phenomenon. But as soon as we examine the records we find that the appearance of unparalleled age is achieved by unparalleled flexibility in the rules of descent and succession. The new Emperor in any reign was not necessarily the son of his predecessor; he might be the descendant of a former Emperor. As there were sometimes two, three, or four emperors alive at the same time, plenty of room existed for intrigue and substitution. A forty-second cousin could be put in the same position as a son. Legitimacy as we understand it was unknown. No marriage certificate was needed to place the son of a pretty court lady on the throne of the Sun Goddess. Many of the emperors were the sons of concubines.

Now, the Merry Monarch did not lack descendants got on the wrong side of the blanket, but they were not heirs to the crown of England. The Japanese succession has continued unbroken because any son, legitimate or illegitimate, could be chosen as heir, and in default of a male scion in the direct line, a youth could be adopted from relatives. All such measures were legal and to the Japanese they seemed rational. The Tokugawas, who ruled Japan until 1868, were accustomed to select the "heir to the throne" from the male children of three related families. The present Emperor and Crown Prince are "legitimate" in the sense that they are sons of empresses. But the last Emperor, Hirohito's father, was the son of a court lady, Madam Aiko Yanagiwara. When she died a few years ago, the newspapers announced without evasion or glossing over that she had been the unmarried mother of an Emperor.

There was no question of legitimacy in the Western sense. The question does not exist. The Imperial House Law which regulates the succession to the throne is quite clear. It provides that "the Imperial throne of Japan shall be succeeded to by male descendants in the male line of Imperial ancestors . . . an Imperial descendant of full blood shall have precedence over descendants of half blood." That is the Japanese system. Whether it is better or worse than our own does not matter. The point is that the uniqueness and unparalleled continuity of the Japanese dynasty disappear when reason is substituted for mystical dogmatism.

In a country where the laws and customs pertaining to succession are so flexible it would be expected that other families besides the Emperor's would have long pedigrees. And they have. The Matsudairas, the Konoyes, and many other families could claim as long descent as the Emperor if they cared or dared. Some could also claim divine ancestry. The chronicles which record the Imperial family's descent from the Sun Goddess also tell of the god Ama-no-hohi, " Heavenly Burning Sun," who, says the historian, " is the ancestor of the grandees of Omi and the Governor of Idzumo and the Chief of the Clayworkers' Corporation. The amiable historian was not intentionally recording folk-tales; he was providing genealogies to support title deeds.

The twin to the legend of unsurpassed antiquity is that of continuity in government. The political history of the Japanese dynasty is in reality not different from that of other dynasties in other lands. The Japanese Imperial house has had its full share of misfortunes. Emperors have been assassinated and deposed. Rival emperors have waged war on each other. Crown princes have been murdered as callously as the two little Princes in the Tower of London and for the same reason — to get them out of the way. Actually the most conspicuous feature of Japanese history is the relegation of the Imperial line to obscurity for a thousand years (670 to 1868) while the country was governed by successive dynasties of hereditary administrators or warrior chiefs. The *de facto* rulers were not all of the same family; the period was marked by bloody feudal wars as one powerful leader after another arose and ousted the possessor of power. But in all that time there was no period in which Imperial rule flourished. There were on the contrary many periods during which the descendant of the Sun Goddess lived in poverty. In 1500 the Emperor Tsuchi II lay unburied for six weeks until his son borrowed money from Buddhist priests to pay the funeral expenses. One of the shoguns, Yoshimitsu Ashikagi, obtained the title of King of Japan from the Emperor of China and paid a thousand ounces of gold for it, a modest price, the equivalent today of about $35,000.

The Japanese nation has but to read its own history to realize that its past differs in no essential from that of other peoples who have made the long journey from primitive to modern society. The divinity and uniqueness of the emperors is but a myth revived and reconsecrated by its modern rulers.

It would be going too far to say that the Constitution-makers deliberately intended to create a figurehead for a military government. They exalted the young Emperor whom they had called out of obscurity as a unifying force to rally the nation behind the new government. They took nineteenth-century Germany as their model and, like Germany of that day, they paid half-hearted tribute to the rising force of democracy. The Japanese people, like the German people, believed they had obtained representative government and, like the German people, they discovered that the army, which was also their Nazi Party, was the strongest thing in the country and that national socialism in the hands of those who think in terms of tanks, planes, and tommy-guns is more terrible than any medieval despotism.

The myth of the god-king has been dragged from the earliest age to the latest to give aggression an air of destiny. Correction of this imposture — or delusion, for in many cases it is a delusion of immature minds — is a task for the Japanese; they alone can debunk themselves. The only instrument required is freedom for Japanese scholarship to use modern standards in dealing with history. Many Japanese historians are able to take a scientific view of national relics without doing them the smallest irreverence. Japanese historical scholarship was beginning to discharge its duty honestly and cautiously. In 1916 Professor Katsuro Hara, of the Imperial University of Kyoto, published an admirable *Introduction to the History of Japan,* which opened with a conspicuous omission. He commenced his narrative in the sixth century after Christ, when written records in Japan began, and ignored the " age of the gods " and the fables of Imperial divine descent. Had he written twenty years later his silence would have been found treasonable and irreligious, patriots would have laid accusations of *lèse-majesté,* and the historian would have been lucky if disgrace and dismissal had been his only punishment. The enemies against whom the army and the patriotic societies sent their thugs were the intellectuals who believed Japan had nothing to fear from truth and the statesmen who thought the central government could overrule the military departments.

Readers of Arthur Waley's rendering of *The Tale of Genji* will remember how the charming narrator, Lady Murasaki, never saw a farmer or a carpenter, or even a cook, in her gallery of portraits. The only people she was conscious of were lords and ladies with their perfumes, their amours, and their seventeen-syllable poems. The Japanese historians in favor today are so engrossed with gods, emperors, and warriors that they have lost sight of the people. They have banished universal standards. A thing is right or wrong, false or true, as it helps or hinders the state. It was wrong for the

Americans and British to help China, but right for Japan to help Germany. What the Japanese soldiers did in China was right because Japanese did it. As Dr. Ley said, " Right is what the Führer does." But the Japanese state was no mystical abstraction with the sanction of unparalleled ages behind it; it was a group of men whose ambitions had run amok.

V. *Imperial Figurehead*

Chapter XX

THE EMPEROR OF JAPAN: AS MAN

The Emperor of Japan is a man, a god, a high priest, a symbol, and a ruler. This combination of functions was common in the early ages of human society and Japan has performed the remarkable feat of revitalizing it for modern uses.

As the religion of a totalitarian state, in which the first freedom to be tabooed is freedom of thought and inquiry, Emperor-worship has shown certain advantages over other efforts along the same line. By the divinity function it releases the religious impulse instead of damming it up and channels it into the service of the state. The high-priest function is ornamental, dignified, and venerable. It expresses immemorial continuity and gratifies religious sentiment without wasting on religion the emotional responses which are reserved for the more important secular demands. The symbol function conceals the real nature of the Moloch state. Using the oldest of political stage tricks, it sets up a symbol of the state so powerful in its mass appeal that the men who run the state and who are the state are lost to sight under its magnetic beam. The ruler function is a method of conferring on policies the sanctions democratic governments draw from the vote of the majority. It is the equivalent of the Nazi glorification of Der Führer.

Within these veils is a man of flesh and bone who was born in the lying-in chamber of Aoyama Palace, Tokyo, at ten minutes past ten on the evening of April 29, 1901.

Imperial divinity inhabits an ordinary human dwelling. In his forty-second year the Emperor is a man of average height among Japanese and a short man among white men. He is growing stout; all his uniforms are tight and his too well-covered features tend to puffiness. Shyness once made him awkward and uncomfortable in the presence of strangers. At formal court functions his father would appraise the diplomatic ladies with a roving eye, but Hirohito was embarrassed and could not hide it from the ladies who curtsied before him. No trace of that nervousness remains. His last public appearance in the presence of foreigners was at a gathering in front of the Imperial Palace on February 11, 1940, commemorating the legendary 2,600th anniversary of the dynasty and the Empire. He addressed the 50,000 people present with ease and confidence, and was heard without the aid of a microphone by all except the deaf in that elderly assemblage. Few of his Cabinet ministers could have done so well, though Prince Konoye has an informal man-to-man style which goes very well over the air. The Emperor's speaking voice is one of the best in Japan and he knows how to use it.

Five minutes earlier as the American Ambassador, Joseph Clark Grew, read the address of the diplomatic corps, the Emperor had been seen to nod vigorously at a passage in which the Ambassador hoped that the rest of his reign might enjoy peace and prosperity. The Emperor does not speak English, but he had a translation of Mr. Grew's speech in front of him.

The Emperor's demeanor on that occasion suggested that he could have played the part of a constitutional sovereign better than that of theocrat imposed upon him. He was educated for a modern throne and in earlier days found modern ways congenial. But Japan does not want a human ruler; she wants a deified figurehead, a god made in her own image, and the man who, when he inherited the throne, chose the name Enlightened Peace for his reign has become the figurehead of a vast aggression hardly equaled since Genghis Khan. He could not help himself; the ruler cult of Japan is the religion of a ruthless militarism.

Japanese ladies sometimes excuse the aberrations of the men by saying that in Japan it is the old men who sow wild oats. Married off early to a bride chosen by the family, the men hardly have a chance to look around them until middle life. The Emperor of Japan is now over forty and his eldest child, a girl of seventeen, is about to be married. Whether the later years of his life will display colors that it has hitherto lacked remains to be seen; power is a poison few characters can resist, but Hirohito's virtues are of that tough bourgeois fiber mistakenly called commonplace. As he grows older he becomes more abstemious and more conventional. It can hardly be said that he presides over a puritan court, for a court in the European sense, meaning a glittering circle at the summit of society, does not exist; but he presides over a model family.

In the days of his grandfather the official gazette used to print the names of the twelve court ladies to whom the Emperor Meiji might throw a handkerchief when he was so disposed, but no such list sheds a purple patch on those dull pages now, and gossip has never suggested that the Imperial fancy has strayed. When Prince and Princess Chichibu visited London for the coronation of George VI the thing they enjoyed most was a long ride on top of a London General bus, but there are no Haroun-al-Raschid escapades in the Emperor's life.

He was the kind of youth that mothers adore; he always did the correct thing and liked it. He is at the moment a correct and conventional Japanese Emperor, signing what he has to sign and saying what he has to say, and setting his subjects an example of war thrift to the extent of having his underwear mended. But bearing in mind that Japanese penchant for asserting oneself late in life, there is still room for speculation as to what may come. The dutiful but perhaps not wholly willing figurehead of the militarists may live to be the figurehead of the reaction that will follow defeat.

If Hirohito had been a little boy in America during the green decades he would have liked spinach after he had been told it was good for him. This is a legitimate deduction from the story of a Cabinet minister who when lunching with the Emperor allowed curiosity to overcome his sense of awe. Mr. Chuji Machida, Minister of Agriculture, accompanied the Emperor on a country tour and was asked to lunch in the Imperial coach. The Governor of the prefecture was the other guest. They were given the usual two small boxes in which Japanese informal lunches are packed, one containing cold rice, the other cold vegetables, pickles, and fish. The Minister observed that there were two kinds of rice in his box: white, which the Japanese like, and brown, which they don't like in spite of the doctors and beriberi, while the host had brown rice only. He asked the Emperor if he always ate brown rice, and the Emperor said he did because it was better for his health.

Governor Shirane (in frock coat and high hat) accompanied the Emperor's party on a picnic up Mount Amagi. The lunch served consisted of six small balls of brown rice mixed with barley, a few slices of meat, and some pickles. Vice-Admiral Idemitsu, former aide-de-camp, was once asked to lunch with the Emperor alone. The menu was spinach boiled in soy sauce, dried fish with grated radish sprinkled on it, meat and onions boiled together, soup, pickles, and brown rice. If the public knew how simply the Emperor lives, observed the admiral, the controversy over brown or white rice would cease. It was easy for the Emperor, when the war with China dragged on, to cut out foreign cigarettes and order that no more foreign wine be served in the Palace.

This admirable appreciation of the unexciting pervades the private life of the Son of Heaven. Here it may be explained that that superhuman designation is no flight of fancy or survival from the past. It is the orthodox title officially promulgated six years ago. Until then Hirohito, like his predecessors, had been called Nippon Koku Kotei — Emperor of the Nation of Japan. As from June 1, 1936, his title is Dai Nippon Teikoku Tenno — Great Japan Imperial Son of Heaven, or, as the Bureau of Decorations translated it, watering down the literal meaning: " God-sent Ruler of the Great Japanese Empire." At the same time the name of his residence in Tokyo was changed from Teikyu — Imperial Palace — to Kyujo — Imperial Castle.

The Imperial Castle is a disappointment to tourists. They rush from the hotel expecting an Oriental Versailles, vast, symmetrical, splendid, crammed with the treasures of two thousand years. All that they see is a great moat defended on the steep inner side by walls of massive, unmortared, irregular stones. It is probably the only royal residence in the world completely hidden from outside eyes. In fact, there is little to see. Those cyclopean walls are the only architectural feature for which a kind of rude majesty can be claimed. Like modern Japan, the rest seems improvised, impermanent, a village growing round a few temples.

The state apartments are temple-like structures, something like magnificent barns, whose green copper roofs can be glimpsed through the thin winter foliage. Many smaller houses that have been built at different times cluster around them in a haphazard way. These are of the usual Japanese type, mostly one story high; they are surrounded by verandas and connected by broad corridors. Here is a terrace or a courtyard; there a broad sunny space faces a venerable hall. All these buildings huddle close to one another; they are a single edifice, yet a hundred.

Within this private village is a dwelling in no way different from the other buildings. A porte-cochere under which cars and carriages draw up shelters its entrance. It looks out on a simple garden; no fountains, no statues, only undulating greensward and a few flowering bushes. In this structure the Emperor and Empress live.

The rooms are Japanese, comfortably but plainly modified to suit modern tastes. The roofs are coffered, the floors carpeted; an occasional dwarf pine or gold screen relieves the austerity. The living-room is a comfortable square room, not very large, with a fine ceiling and a floor of hardwood covered by a carpet. A few pictures — personal favorites, not show pieces — hang on the walls.

In summer the Emperor rises at six, in winter at seven. Having no taste for luxurious personal service, he shaves himself. He worships his ancestors in the customary manner, closing his eyes, clasping his hands, and bowing to a miniature shrine that has been constructed in the private apartments. At the same moment a chamberlain visits the three official shrines in the Palace compound and formally worships the ancestors on behalf of the Emperor. Breakfast is in " foreign " style, this mild luxury being advised by physicians who say that a Japanese diet needs vitamin reinforcement by at least one foreign meal daily. It is simple enough — fruit, cereal, coffee, toast, and, in peace time, bacon and eggs. The Empress usually joins him, and the little princesses may come in before setting out for the Peeresses' School. Then the Emperor glances through the Tokyo papers which are laid out on his study table. They are not clipped. He questions his secretaries about any item that attracts his attention. Before the China war he used to go to his office in the next room at ten o'clock; now he goes in at nine. He sits at his desk, receiving officials, reading documents and commenting on them, transacting the business of an Emperor, till half past twelve, when he takes an hour off for lunch. In peaceful days he used to spend another hour in the private grounds, playing golf one day, riding another, or walking in the garden. Now he goes right back to his office and stays there till half past six.

When he receives members of the government or high officials, he does so in the presence of his own senior staff, whose duty it is to see that the Emperor is fully informed and that all the bearings of the matter under advisement are made clear. It is their business to make sure that the Emperor does not decide any question or sanction any proposal without knowing all sides of it. The rule is strictly enforced. Some years ago a Prime Minister, General Tanaka, was in serious trouble, not for having refused to allow his Education Minister to resign, but for having opened the matter to the Emperor without the presence of the Lord Keeper or other competent political adviser. It is because of the moderating influence of those advisers and the opportunity they have of probing into policies that the young officers and the nationalists are always demanding the dismissal of the " statesmen close to the throne."

Imperial Figurehead

Throughout the present reign those statesmen have been, and in a lesser degree still are, men of wide experience and moderate views. If it is asked why they did not prevent the present war, the answer is that their first duty is to preserve the security of the throne and the unity of the nation. When the fighting services had made up their minds, when their preparations were complete, when every question had been asked and every objection exhausted, the Emperor had to agree with those all-powerful subjects and he would be so advised. It would be dramatizing things too much to say that a situation ever existed in which the Emperor's yes or no would have meant the difference between peace and war. When that stage was reached the answer was inevitable.

The Emperor is a methodical worker — so methodical that time is spent on system which would be better expended on thought. Everything in his office must be in its place, and every document of importance must be dealt with immediately. No accumulation of papers is permitted, and his secretaries are not allowed to hold anything over because it comes in after office hours. Everyone who has come in close contact with the Emperor of Japan is impressed by his absorption in details. He is annoyed if any secretary or aide should do something which he is accustomed to do himself, and routine never bores him. When the weather is bad he orders a chamberlain to ring up the weather bureau and ask how the farmers are affected. Like all his subjects he was impressed when the young officers used rural depression as an excuse for conspiracy.

In the old days the Emperor spent a quiet family evening after leaving his office. His hobby was using the microscope. The study of biology caught his youthful imagination, and in his earliest personal portrait he chose to be photographed in civilian clothes beside a table on which his microscope was placed. Mendelism and marine biology were his special branches, and his visits to the seaside and his walks in the Palace grounds yielded new specimens for his researches. After his third successive daughter was born, a Japanese newspaper hit off the disappointing situation unconsciously by remarking: " His Majesty then went out into the garden and gathered fungus."

This peaceful life has become a thing of the past. A tight khaki field-service uniform is the Emperor's daily wear, generals and admirals his most frequent visitors. No longer can returning ambassadors give lectures in the Palace by command on their success in making Japan better understood in America. Strategy and carnage are the daily occupation, willy-nilly, of the Emperor Enlightened Peace.

The anecdotage so useful for brightening a portrait clusters but sparsely around the Son of Heaven. Once when he was a boy at school, his teacher told him to sing a song the class was practicing, a song about a Japanese hero of eminent loyalty in a disloyal era. The young Prince rose and sang, and General Nogi, titular principal of the school, who was in the room, was so moved by the resemblance of the boy's voice to his grandfather's that he turned his worn face away to hide his emotion.

Another story tells that when the Emperor was spending some winter weeks in the country he went riding one morning with a few attendants. As they passed a farmer's house a boy of seven or eight ran out holding a toy balloon on a string. Surprised by the horsemen, the boy let go of his balloon and howled. The balloon passed close by the Emperor, who turned his horse and chased it. And now I quote the Japanese author who recorded the story: " The Emperor neared the balloon but missed it by a matter of a few inches, and the balloon went up unmolested. The Emperor for a time looked at the ascending balloon, but soon His Majesty gave a sad look at the boy. Under ordinary circumstances His Majesty would have easily caught the balloon, but the narrow road on which the Emperor was and the closeness between His Majesty and the crying child prevented His Majesty from extending a hand to the balloon in time. The boy had ceased crying. The Emperor for some time continued looking at the boy with a face full of love and sympathy."

It is a curious little story, and for all its triviality it turns a merciless flash on character. We see a sudden good-natured impulse end in failure; there is no attempt to recover, no spontaneous word or coin for the boy, no action at all except embarrassed looks which, though " full of love and kindness," were a feeble finish to a good intention.

When all Japanese were ordered to give their gold jewelry to the government, the Emperor sent in his gold spectacle frames and took to cheap ones of white metal. His wrist watch is chromium-cased, Japanese-made, and cost three dollars. His Majesty does not have an opportunity of slicing up envelopes and writing notes on the back, but he does not allow a sheet of paper to be wasted. The paper, pens, and pencils used in the Imperial office are of ordinary quality. It is customary for the Emperor to send gifts of "funeral money" to the families of ministers or public men after a death. Acting on the broadcast exhortations of the Treasury, he now sends war bonds in place of cash. (They all come from the government printing press anyhow.) Three or four years ago when the hoarding of oil by the fighting services for war purposes was drastically accelerated, the Emperor ordered a charcoal-burning automobile for himself and another for the Crown Prince. His shoes, socks, slippers, and underwear are such

Chapter XXI

THE EMPEROR OF JAPAN: AS GOD

When the Emperor Meiji, the first restored Emperor, lay dying in 1912, thousands of the citizens of Tokyo gathered nightly in front of the Palace and prayed for his recovery. Their prayers were directed to no other god than the divine ruler himself. I should not offer this statement on my own authority; mob emotion seems to me a better explanation than conscious belief in the godhood of a dying old man whose existence had been in no way remarkable, but it is the explanation given by Dr. Genji Kato, Professor of Comparative Religion at Tokyo Imperial University.

Imperial Shinto, or state-worship, the state being personified in the Emperor, was revived less than one lifetime ago by the leaders of the restoration-revolution, who needed some super-political sanction to foster political unity on the ruins of clan feudalism. Another eminent scholar, the late Basil Hall Chamberlain, wrote a pamphlet called *The Invention of a New Religion* describing the measures by which Imperial Shinto was set up side by side with the modern institutions the new Empire was then installing. Chamberlain, in effect, represented the leaders of new Japan as getting round a table and saying: " Let us invent a new religion, call it the ancient cult of Japan, and foist it upon the people so

307

that we may more easily control them." But Chamberlain was of Gibbon's opinion that all religions were considered by the people as equally true, by the philosopher as equally false, and by the government as equally useful. It is hard to reconcile his too rational explanation with the spectacle of those thousands of people praying in the snow. Even in Japan the government could not create a new religion in this self-conscious and fraudulent manner, and the idea of state-worship, of Japan as a unique and superior state with rulers of divine descent, had existed for many centuries. All that the government did was to turn this idea to its use, and it has grown to proportions which the Japanese statesmen of fifty years ago would not have believed had they been told.

Professor Kato claims for Shinto all the qualities of a major religion. The essence of any religion, he says, is " absolute trust in and complete self-surrender to the object of worship." The Japanese people, he continues, find this in Shinto because for them the Emperor is " God revealed in human form . . . occupying for the Japanese the place of the one whom the Jews called God." Dr. Kato places Shinto on the same plane as Buddhism and Christianity as a world religion. " If it is the boast of India that she produced the Buddha, and the boast of Judea that she counts among her sons Jesus the redeemer of the world, it is enough for Japan to boast that she has been from generation to generation under the sway of emperors who, in an unbroken line, ascended the throne of Imperial — that is to say, of divine — dignity."

He claims also that Shinto brings the world a supreme hope. The Jews, he says, cherished the hope of a political Messiah. When this hope failed it was transferred to the spiritual sphere and Christianity extended its moral dominion over many nations. If Buddha had been willing to accept political supremacy this might have been India's mission, but he too turned aside to spiritual leadership. Dr. Kato continues: " The great Messianic ideal which those ancient nations vainly longed for the Japanese possess, and thus we see, rising in the Eastern heavens, that great hope of humanity, Messiah the Ruler."

Dr. Kato is no patriotic or military windbag, nor is he a bigot. He is a scholar of high rank, and his work is well known to foreign scholars. His book *Waga Kokutai to Shinto (Our National Structure and Shinto)* closes with a touching appeal to Christians to come together with the Japanese " in the spirit of religious brotherhood in one assembly hall and, making no mention of Buddhism or Christianity or Shinto, clasp one another's hands." There is no greater authority on Japanese religion, and when Dr. Kato claims that Emperor-worship is a religion in the fullest sense of the word, and not merely a ceremonial manifestation of loyalty, as Japanese apologists have represented it, we must respect his opinion. Yet, as a layman, speaking only from long observation of Japanese life, I must record my own opinion that Dr. Kato's description is an overstatement.

It is not merely a question of the eternal difference between the devout and the indifferent. For every Japanese who prayed in the slush to the dying Emperor, ten thousand stayed at home. That proves nothing; we would have to say the same of many other religious communities. But there is a fundamental difference between the god the Japanese prays to and the God the Christian or the Jew prays to. Shinto began as nature-worship; it saw a god in every natural force and it worshipped the spirits of the woods, of the rice fields, of the tides, of fire, of water, of everything. Ancestor-worship was imported from China and incorporated. There is something to be said for the theory that the early rulers, claiming descent from the Sun Goddess, caused that deity to be set above the Food Goddess in order to strengthen their own position.

The conception of one God, who made and rules the universe and who alone is divine and worthy of worship, has no place in the Shinto scheme of things. To the Christian, the Jew, the Mohammedan, God is above and apart from the world that he made; to the Shintoist, as to all pantheists, godhood manifests itself in the world and is part of the world. The Emperor is the god of Japan; he is part of Japan; his father was a god before him, and his son will be a god after him. One need not be a theologian to see that when a Japanese says the Emperor is god, he means something different from the Christian.

But the Emperor is the only god he has. When children go to school on New Year's morning and see the portraits of the Emperor and Empress brought from their sanctuary with the reverence the Christian shows to the consecrated bread and wine, they are not worshipping an eternal father, their creator and redeemer; they are worshipping the Japanese Empire.

Dr. Kato is not a political philosopher or he would have seen that such a religion exalts and justifies unbounded aggression. Some newer forms of Shinto have taken the step which Dr. Kato did not see. Starting from the divinity of the Emperor, they claimed that Japan, by right of its unique and inherent qualities, should become the dominant power of the world, with the Imperial family as the new Messiah. An American missionary and scholar, the late Dr. Albertus Pieters, quoted the following utterance of one of the new nationalist Shinto sects:

" Japan is the parent nation of the world. He who is hostile to this nation opposes the will of God." And again: " The

The Emperor of Japan: as God

Imperial family of Japan is the parent not only of the Japanese race but of all the nations on earth. In the eyes of the Imperial family all races are the same. It is above all racial considerations. All human disputes therefore may be settled in accordance with its immaculate justice. The League of Nations can only attain its object by placing the Imperial family of Japan at its head, for, if it is to succeed, the League must have a strong punitive force of a super-racial and super-national character and this can only be found in the Imperial family of Japan."

In some of its manifestations the " divinity " of the Japanese Emperor seems to be the sign of an inferiority complex so morbid that it cannot bear the thought of Japan being governed or reigned over by a human being as other countries are. Count Yoshinori Futara (who had a modern education, including foreign travel) discussed the question whether loyalty to the Emperor had diminished or increased during the reign of Taisho (1912–26), Hirohito's immediate predecessor. He thought its essence still survived despite the skepticism of a modern age. Japan of our day, he wrote, began to regard the Emperor as simply a person and young men thought the emperors of the past were historical personages. They therefore respected the present Emperor at the beginning of his reign as an august person who ascended the throne by right of birth. But this, continues Count Futara, " is quite inconsistent with the racial ideal of Japan. The Emperor who should reign over us eternally from time immemorial to the endless future must not be regarded as merely an august personage, he should be venerated as a superhuman existence."

The national megalomania, of which worship of the Emperor was a symptom, was not taken seriously by other nations. Japan was far away on the rim of Asia and the white world undervalued it. The amiable Japanese who were Japan's contact-men with the West described Emperor-worship as a simple cult of loyalty wearing the garments of a quaint and ancient civilization. They did not say, because they did not see, that Japan's religion was a new paganism whose inherent barbarism would in no long time plunge Asia into bloody wars.

Chapter XXII

THE EMPEROR OF JAPAN: AS HIGH PRIEST

Hirohito, chief of a contemporary state, is also its high priest. In that little city within a city where the Emperor dwells is a massive temple-like structure called the Shinkaden. As dusk falls on the last Monday of November each year sacred fires of pine logs are lit in iron braziers around the courtyard. On the appointed date in 1940 the smoky light of the fires flickered on the handsome features of Prince Konoye as he crossed the courtyard and slowly climbed the steep old steps, preceded by a priest who showed him to his place. The hall was filled with the soft glow of paper lanterns. At the head of the hall facing the entrance a Shinto altar was dressed and ready. The court musicians sat on the floor, voluminously robed in scarlet cloaks and pointed headdresses, and fingered their archaic instruments. Ladies of the court in antique white costumes hovered near the altar. High dignitaries were silently marshaled to their places, the Emperor's youngest brother, Prince Mikasa, a brown, sturdy young soldier, at their head. Prince Saijo, an old man with an ascetic priestly face, stepped in front of the altar and intoned a Shinto prayer. No one understood a word of it; it had been composed perhaps a thousand years ago, perhaps more; the language was no longer intelligible; even the ideas could only have been understood by students of primitive beliefs.

313

When the Chief Ritualist had finished the prayer, the Emperor appeared. He was dressed in robes of heavy white silk and he carried in his right hand a small baton called a shaku, symbol of the priestly office. He shuffled forward on the straw matting to a lacquered chair or throne and seated himself. The musicians began a piece in which shrill discords dominated a broken, irregular theme. The ladies took offerings of new rice and rice wine from a table and placed them on the altar. The Emperor advanced to the altar, offered the wine and the rice to the gods, raising them high as the priest does in the Mass. He recited a prayer of thanksgiving and returned to his seat, and the Imperial Princes, the Prime Minister and other worshippers moved up to the altar one by one and worshipped.

In this ceremony the Emperor as high priest offered the thanks of Japan for the harvest its gods had bestowed. At eleven o'clock the same night he returned to the hall, escorted only by a few priests, and before the same altar performed another more elaborate ritual which lasted for two hours.

Thirteen times every year the Emperor of Japan officiates as high priest at major Shinto religious observances. Anthropologists would find the occasions familiar; they originated as nature festivals — harvest thanksgiving, spring and autumn equinoxes, the New Year; and Japanese ancestor-worship has added to them a number of the anniversaries of dead emperors.

Nature, the ancestors, and the Japanese Empire are the gods whom the Emperor worships. The first festival of the year, on January 3, is the Genshi Sai, or " Festival of the Sacrifice to the Origin." The Emperor, attended by princes of the blood and high officials, reads prayers and makes offerings in the three temples of the Imperial Palace at ten in the morning, and after he retires, princes, peers, and officials worship in the order of their rank. The " origin " which is commemorated is the origin of throne and Empire, and the ceremony is held at the beginning of the year to show gratitude and remembrance to the earliest Imperial ancestors before any other business of state is transacted.

The second festival, held on February 11, has been exalted in late years until it dwarfs all the others. It commemorates the foundation of the Empire and the dynasty; it is Empire Day and is celebrated now with a fervor which few Christian countries bring to the greatest anniversaries of their faith. All day long, processions march through the streets of Tokyo with bands and banners and uniforms, converging in the great space in front of the Palace walls where they perform the brief gestures of worship to the Emperor and the Empire. It is a singular and sad spectacle — millions of literate people worshipping and deifying the state. The more ignoble, greedy, and blood-drunk that state becomes, the more ferocious grows the adoration of its devotees. The greatest festival of Japanese Imperial Shinto is an orgy of national vainglory and chauvinism.

On a sunny winter day it was pleasant to walk in the great open space before the Palace and see the youths enjoy their parade. Splashes of the unexpected enlivened the crowded scene, as when one enthusiast led a troop of children dressed like ancient warriors. The chubby infants in Japanese helmets and armor looked grotesque, but the childish pleasure of the bystanders was innocent enough. Yet it was disquieting to watch so many passionate believers in a faith so loaded with menace to their lives, their future, and all the progress Japan had made.

The third festival, held on the day of the spring equinox, is the " spring sacrifice to the spirits of the Imperial ancestors." The fourth, held by the Emperor on the same day but at another shrine, is the " spring sacrifice to the gods." The fifth commemorates the death of the first Emperor. The sixth and seventh repeat at the autumnal equinox the sacrifices to the ancestors and to the gods which were offered in spring. In October the eighth festival, held in the Imperial Palace in Tokyo and at the Great Shrine at Ise, presents the first fruits of the year to the first Imperial ancestor; and the ninth (which has been described) offers the first of the new rice to the ancestors and the gods. The tenth, eleventh, twelfth, and thirteenth festivals are domestic; they commemorate the last four Emperors. A distinction is made in law between the Great and the Small Festivals. The Great Festivals are so named because the Emperor conducts them in person; he is then high priest as well as king; at the Small Festivals he is a worshipper and the service is performed by the Master of the Rituals.

Hirohito is never more truly Emperor of the Japanese than when he stands at the altar in priestly robes worshipping their gods. It is probably of greater interest to the Japanese people that he should perform those rites than that he should appoint or dismiss prime ministers. The combination of priest and king in the same person is a survival from the earliest ages of mankind. In primitive tribes and ancient societies the king offered sacrifices to the gods. A dual function which was universal at the dawn of society is now preserved in Japan alone.

Do the modern Japanese believe in the religion of their ancestral tribes? It is difficult to answer for seventy million people, but one cannot go about the country without seeing that every spring, every glen, every pine grove has its tiny shrine, from which offerings are never lacking. The simple people of the farms see their land as the home of spirits, and each place has its presiding divinity. They are mostly kindly spirits now, but early Shinto writers described evil deities who swarmed and buzzed like flies. " In Japan we have Christian doctrines and Buddhist creeds, both of them important spiritual roads, but not the main highway running from before the beginning of history to the present day, from the center of our life to its remotest fields. That highway is Shinto," writes Professor Noritaki Tsuda.

Chapter XXIII

THE EMPEROR OF JAPAN: AS SYMBOL

The human qualities of the Emperor are loyally admired, and doubtless his patched underwear will find a place in the schoolbooks of tomorrow among other examples of war-time virtue. But Japanese scholars jealously warn us not to suppose that the personal character of an emperor affects his position in any way. A Japanese historian wrote: " The Emperor of Japan does not occupy his position because of his virtue nor owing to his popularity, nor by military force. It is as the representative of the whole race, existing from time immemorial and enduring till the end of time, as the abstract figure converted into a concrete and manifest symbol, that he fills his place. Those who regard him as a monarch or an autocrat fail to perceive wherein his spiritual influence over the nation consists."

Professor Masanori Oshima, once vice-president of the World's Federation of Educational Associations, emphasizes the same idea. " The throne of Japan," he says, " is not open to a virtuous man," meaning that good personal character will not qualify a man to be emperor, nor will bad behavior disqualify him. Plato's philosopher king and the allied Chinese conception of the virtuous man as king are alike rejected by Professor Oshima. An emperor rules " not by virtue of character or mentality but by natural inheritance. No ability of mind qualifies an emperor for the throne; the only qualification is that he is heir to the Imperial line. Therefore the Japanese Emperor is the personification of the whole race, not an individual. . . . The Emperor holds the whole race together just as gravity holds us to the earth."

The Chinese doctrine that a wicked ruler forfeits the mandate of heaven and absolves his subjects from continuing to obey him is extremely repugnant to modern Japanese nationalism. There is a remarkable psychological resemblance between the Japanese assertion that the Emperor is divine and the Emperorship above all earthly vicissitudes and the German passion for a superman to lead them. One is tempted to say that something in the nature of the German and Japanese peoples demands a stability beyond human experience. Leaving such deep matters to philosopher-psychologists and keeping our feet on the political ground, I merely observe that this craving for a master is an instrument made to the hands of any powerful group that gets control of the machinery of state.

General Hata in his book on national defense already quoted pins his faith on the extreme antiquity of the Imperial family and writes: " In this respect — the country being ruled by unbroken Imperial lineage from time immemorial — the German leaders profoundly envy the Japanese system, but in the absence of one like it they have adopted what they consider the next best thing." Hitler, to wit; and the final results of Hitlerism to Germany will not greatly differ from the final results Japan will draw from the insensate nationalism of her Emperor-worship.

Yet this abject glorification of the Imperial figurehead is a modern invention. The title " Son of Heaven " only became official on June 1, 1936. It seems to have been first used officially of a living Emperor in the Constitution of 1890; before then it had been reserved for dead emperors. And before 1868 emperors living or dead had counted for little in government. The first treaties Japan ever made were made in the name of the Tycoon. The first document signed and issued in modern times by a Japanese monarch was an announcement by the Emperor Meiji on January 31, 1868, telling foreign diplomats that henceforth the title of Emperor was to be substituted for that of Tycoon in the treaties. One historian declares that that was the first occasion on which the name of an emperor had appeared during his lifetime.

The clan statesmen of the nineteenth century who made the Constitution deliberately surrounded the Imperial dynasty with the mystic emotional halos and sanctions that accompany divinity and divine origin. They did so to create unity in support of a regime they had established after a revolution. By identifying the ruling house with the gods they were using religious myth to prevent the growth of democratic ideas, then making headway. They achieved in the popular mind a complete fusion of political with religious and theocratical ideas. The fusion of religion and nationalism resulted in the hypertrophied ambition which is trying to subjugate Asia. It has elevated the power and prestige of the dynasty till human emperors are worshipped as gods, but all the benefit of this power and prestige has accrued to the fighting services and the bureaucrats who actually exercise it. The Emperor is god, high priest, symbol, figurehead; power is still "the prerogative of the high command."

Chapter XXIV

THE EMPEROR OF JAPAN: AS EMPEROR

Hirohito was not educated to be a deity but a constitutional monarch. He grew up in a liberal era in which his inherited divinity was explained as reverence for great men or men in great position. It was but a larger share of the divinity that dwells in all men. His priestly functions were treated as survivals of a past the nation held dear and were compared to some of the quaint ceremonies of the British court, preserved because they were charming and nobody wanted to abolish them.

His political duties were expected to grow more and more like those of a modern constitutional king. He would remain a fixed point in the state amid all changes, its permanent titular chief, accepted by all and placed above any conceivable rivalry. All responsibility rested on the executive heads of the administration and the army and navy. The single political function in which the Emperor had to exercise initiative was the selection of prime ministers, and that was performed for him by the Elder Statesmen. The last of the Elder Statesmen, Prince Saionji, believed that party government had come to stay, and that the selection of prime ministers would become automatic, since the holder of the office would always be the leader of the majority party.

Imperial Figurehead

The ideas of Prince Saionji and of all the Japanese liberals were profoundly mistaken. They did not realize that the Constitution had provided no balance wheel against the military power. The flaw that wrecked Japan's prospect of evolution into a liberal modern state was the independence of the fighting services from political control. But that independence was endorsed by the will of the people. The fundamental trouble was the inability of the Japanese people to operate representative government. Japanese liberals apologized for the feck-lessness of parliament by complaining that politicians were corrupt. The parliaments of England in the eighteenth century were also corrupt, but those country gentlemen had something the Japanese politicians never had — a firm conviction that they had been elected to govern the country. The Japanese were an Oriental people, only a day's march distant from feudalism. They had no notion of government by the people. To them power came from above, from the strong, from those who possessed it. They had never struck a blow for self-government and they did not know what it was.

The Emperor in his political role is invested with unbounded power. His absolute sovereignty is the fundamental principle of the Constitution. Its first article reads:

" The Empire of Japan shall be reigned over and governed by a line of emperors for ages eternal." Prince Ito, architect of the Constitution, amplifies this statement in his *Commentary:* " The Emperor on the throne combines in himself the sovereignty of the state and the government of the country and his subjects." The power of language is exhausted when his powers are described. Etsujiro Uyehara, lately Vice-Speaker of the House of Representatives, thus writes in a book which was originally a thesis for the London School of Economics:

The Emperor of Japan: as Emperor

" The Emperor is to the Japanese mind the supreme being in the cosmos of Japan as God is in the universe to the pantheistic philosopher. From him everything emanates; in him everything subsists; there is nothing on the soil of Japan existent independent of him. He is the sole owner of the Empire, the author of law, justice, privilege, and honor, and the symbol of the unity of the Japanese nation. He has no pope or archbishop to crown him at his accession. He is supreme in all temporal matters of state as well as in all spiritual matters; and he is the foundation of Japanese social and civil morality."

Under the Constitution he is head of the executive branch of the government and supreme commander of the army and navy. He makes war and peace and concludes treaties. In short, all power of the state is summed up in his person.

This all-embracing authority is not conferred by the Constitution. It is assumed as an article of faith that it is the Emperor's by right and has always been his. Yet nothing is more certain than that the Japanese Emperor reigns but does not govern. Combining in one impossible synthesis all the powers of heaven and earth, he is a grandly adorned figurehead. And he has about as much control over the forces that propel the ship.

The keystone of the Japanese political system is the Emperor, not the human chief of state whose industrious days have been described, but the built-up figure endowed with godlike attributes. The weakness of the system is its attempt to combine functions which are humanly incompatible. The Emperor is at once the nation's grand symbol of unity, its god, its high priest, and its chief executive. As symbol of unity he must not divide the nation by opposing policies on which its strongest members are determined, even although

323

as chief of state it may be his conviction that such policies should be vetoed. But the unlimited power which he is supposed to have inherited from the Sun Goddess and the ancestors is like the crown of a European monarch; he may wear it, but it is not his property.

The Japanese Emperor is not an autocrat; every act of state must be made on the advice and responsibility of an official person who takes full responsibility. Responsibility to whom? In theory, to the Emperor, who in turn is responsible to his ancestors. Such a system is merely a cover for irresponsibility. It is true that even in Japan governments cannot ignore public opinion, but public opinion has no influence over policies in the making. Its rudimentary organ of expression, the Diet, has been converted into a phonograph, and the channels through which opinion can make itself felt, the political parties, have been persuaded to commit hara-kiri. Japanese public opinion is like a dumb man who cannot speak though he will emit painful screams when he finds himself in deadly danger. The only thing the military leaders of Japan have to fear is failure; until the results of their policy cannot any longer be concealed from the peasants in the fields, they enjoy a free hand.

The Emperor is the great figurehead of the state who dutifully approves of policies after he has been dutifully advised that they are right and necessary in the opinion of those who have formulated them. He may not himself think that these policies are necessary for the security or progress of the Empire, but if his powerful servants so advise him, the Constitution absolves him of further responsibility. He is hardly richer in real power than his forefathers, the absentee emperors, pensioned and perfunctorily honored by the military chiefs. "In Japan," writes General Hata, already quoted,

" the Imperial family, the state, and the nation are one and the same." The Emperor, that is to say, being one with the state, will not refuse what it demands. The state today is the fighting services who have appointed themselves to exercise power in the Imperial name. The Emperor has hardly had time to forget that his grandfather was the son of a powerless absentee, living in a provincial city in a position different in no essential from that of Europe's exiled kings who moped away their empty days in Paris.

Why the glorious restoration of 1868 failed to change this is explained by the persistence of a military power under a constitutional form. The Constitution did not confer power on the military class, but it could not prevent that class from recovering the power its feudal predecessors had exercised. The restoration was but a half-finished revolution. It destroyed the old center of power and failed to establish a new one. The intoxicating enthusiasm with which Japan absorbed the culture of the West was the sign of an eager desire to rise to the heights that the West had gained, but the means were lacking. The dwarf-tree civilization, trained in soil borrowed from the static culture of China, could not alter the curves and contortions so laboriously cultivated in a feudal era prolonged three centuries beyond Europe's. The timorous experiment in democracy failed because the Japanese people are politically immature. When the enormous effort they had made to assimilate an alien civilization brought its inevitable reaction, they had no institution strong enough to take the shock. The past came rushing back; the warriors had changed their uniforms but not their minds.

VI. *Post-War*

Chapter XXV

WAR GUILT

In these pages some Japanese have depicted themselves by action and word. We have heard patriots proclaim from the dock the creed they practiced with pistol and bomb. We saw the nation grow hysterical in its admiration of those dubious heroes, and justice falter and lose countenance as if more than half convinced that right was in the dock and wrong on the bench. We saw patriotism not as the last refuge of a scoundrel, but the first. Not least astonishing in the twentieth century, we saw Japan go back to the superstitions of its infancy and deify its ruler.

The evidence consisted mainly of small things — people in the snow praying to a sick Emperor, the thoughts and intrigues of second lieutenants, the patriotic gangsters as they live, a bar association memorializing a court that assassination is not murder. These things are significant because they are native and spontaneous manifestations of the Japanese mind.

It need not be said that there is another side. There is a Japanese way of life which is easy and dignified and simple. The people in the mass are kindly and polite, and they have a natural social democracy of manner which makes them pleasant to live with. They are honest in the affairs of daily life; if you leave an umbrella or a coat in a train or a taxi you are almost certain to get it back. The country people — all the people — will take trouble to set a stranger on his way. The beauty and culture associated with old Japanese civilization cannot be the expression of a brutal or barbarous people. They testify to fine traditions and a character of a different kind from that exhibited in these pages. It is a country of strange and deep contrasts. As Sir Stafford Cripps said after his visit to Japan in 1940: " Fujiyama and the Imperial divinity typify the unity of Japan, but it is a unity of opposites." A Jekyll and Hyde country.

To balance the picture I should write some account of the cultured and Westernized Japanese whom foreigners know best and among whom I had many friends.

But when the tug of war came it was not the amiable graduates of American and British universities who counted; it was the chauvinists, the fanatics of empire, the vain and ignorant patriots who believed Japan to be a unique nation with a special mission, the self-supposed realists who fancied they saw soft foes in all the democracies which devoted their wealth to welfare instead of to armaments. The Rotary Club of Tokyo was a group of successful men of more than average ability; all of its members had traveled and lived in America and England. They were engaged in international trade; they knew the world and they wanted peace. But when the military gave the order, those millionaire bankers and shipowners folded up the Rotary Club and took their places in the host that was then closing its ranks for the attack on the United States. They are today working with all their might for the army and its ideology of conquest. We can count on the goodwill of this group in the future, but we cannot depend on its power or on its courage to stand against the militarists and the assassins. To be riddled with a tommy-gun is not, after all, much of an end for a man who has made his million. The peace we make must be one that we ourselves, the United Nations, can take care of.

Japan's spiritual malady is the same as Germany's — a false philosophy. It is a belief that the Japanese race and state are one and the same and that it has unique qualities that make it superior to its neighbors and give it a special mission to perform.

It was always difficult to know how much of this belief was honest national prejudice and how much was adopted as a way of rationalizing and justifying national predacity. Would the Japanese have been so sure of their national mission if they had not possessed the biggest army and fleet in Asia? Some of one's Japanese friends merely smiled and gently hinted that Japanism, like religion, was not a topic for social conversation. These were the agnostics, the men of the world, and their attitude was like that of the witty Frenchman when an indiscreet lady asked what his religion was. " Madame, my religion is the religion of all sensible men." " And what is that? " " Madame, sensible men never tell."

It was equally clear that many did believe it with the simple faith of those dangerous people, the passionate believers. There were others, notably in official and political circles, who adopted it for the reason that makes the small-town politician go regularly to church. The skeptics gave it lip service, the ambitious paraded it, the simple believed it, the fanatics practiced it. It was an effective belief; the doubters and the indifferent acted as if they believed it, and its emanations colored all national policies.

The idea of uniqueness was found in every statement of the Japanese nationalists. " It all goes back to the Sun Goddess," wrote Mr. Chigaku Tanaka, a philosophic exponent of Nipponism whose erudition was greater than his understanding. But the international scholar Dr. Kato, while ready to admit that the Sun Goddess and her story belong to mythology, tells us that this mythology is the vessel in which a great truth is conveyed. The Japanese Imperial line is to him the Messiah that will save the world.

If the Japanese believe that Hirohito is god it would be no business of ours so long as they kept it to themselves. But when a race gets a national mission into its head, it becomes a menace and a nuisance to its neighbors. That mission, when expressed in practice, is always found to be the aggrandizement of the state. Japan's self-assigned place in the new order is that of lord and master, guiding, exploiting, and guarding the lesser races around her. This false philosophy has been so sedulously inculcated and so eagerly swallowed that at last a policy of live and let live, a position of equality, and a willingness to compromise seem intolerable humiliations. The only position Japan will consider is that of overlord and protector of East Asia. But in what form has she revealed herself to the races she aspires to protect? As warrior and conqueror, as mother of the " wild beasts from the mountain " — their own general's description — who ravaged Nanking in token of their brotherly feelings; as home of the drug dealers who have peddled narcotics in China; of the bandit traders who stripped China of silver when the price of the metal went up; as paymaster of the Korean tools who made fortunes for their Japanese employers in the smuggling orgy of 1936. The Japanese at home closed their eyes to these things, hypnotizing themselves with incantations about the national mission and the Imperial Way. But as the fine maxims of the patriotic societies always finish in murder and terrorism, the new order that the Japanese state proclaims always comes to its victims in the form of conquest, rapine, and exploitation.

The practical question when the war is over will be: What can we do?

To clear our approach to peace let us ask a fair question. What responsibility or share of responsibility for the war do the Japanese, in their own minds, when they are speaking sincerely among themselves, lay upon our pre-war policy?

I had many Japanese friends whom I was constantly meeting in a private, informal, and personal way. They were for the most part engaged in the government services, or in business, or in the universities and the newspaper offices. Our way of life gave us a good deal in common. I think personal relations a more important thing in one's life than membership of a nation or a church or a race, and I have lived in so many countries that a difference in the color of a skin or in the shape of an eye aperture affects me but little.

These Japanese were men of my own stamp and their views were rather like my own. I do not pretend that they were representative or ruling views, but they were Japanese views and they were often met with among the intelligentsia. This class will be readily recognized by any foreigner who has lived in Japan. It was not a large class, relative to the body of the nation, but its influence had been great. It was the spiritual and intellectual successor of the class which had eagerly embraced world culture in the preceding generation.

These men would never dream of being " anti " in any dispute between their own country and another, but they were men of the world and could take a broader view than the masses who knew no country but their own. I shall try to pemmican their views in a brief dialogue. The date is any time between Chiang Kai-shek's withdrawal to Chungking and the attack on Pearl Harbor.

333

NIPPON: The war in China has been a great misfortune to Japan. We do not admit that we are alone to blame, for in the last twenty years the Chinese war lords have inflicted many injuries on us. If the Japanese army had not intervened in Manchuria that territory, which 100,000 Japanese had died to preserve from appropriation by Russia, would have been closed to us. If America and Britain had recognized the *fait accompli* in Manchuria, the history of our relations would have been entirely different.

BYAS: You could not expect us to recognize the seizure of Chinese territory. We had treaties obligating us to respect Chinese integrity and independence and you had signed those treaties with us and with China. But let us agree that Manchuria is water over the dam. You did what you wanted. We did not recognize, but we did not interfere. Could you not have been content with Manchuria?

NIPPON: Perhaps we ought to have been satisfied, but in politics what can be done is often different from what should be done. We are dealing with an actual situation. We are at war and our government cannot fight the army. What we need is peace. If peace is restored, the army will gradually be brought back under Cabinet control. Your interests in China will then be restored and respected. But peace without victory is unthinkable; it is at least utterly impossible for any Japanese government. So long as your press continues to attack us and proclaim its sympathy with China, while your governments send assistance to Chiang Kai-shek, our people will be inflamed against your countries and the army will become more obstinate. We need peace. Why will you not help us to obtain it? Your present policy is driving us into the arms of Germany.

334

BYAS: In what way do you suggest we could help you to regain peace?

NIPPON: If your governments withdrew support from China and brought pressure to bear in favor of peace, Chiang Kai-shek's supporters would leave him and he would make peace fast enough.

BYAS: That is asking us to help you defeat China, but that is your pidgin, not ours. I realize the difficulties of your statesmen. But you must understand the position of ours. They are subject to public opinion. We think the war in China wholly unnecessary, to say the least, and we have offered to mediate or do anything in our power to bring about a settlement. Instead of trying to prepare an approach to negotiations your army is continually stirring up the public with the fiction that Chinese resistance is only kept alive by British and American munitions. What about the oil and scrap iron we have been selling Japan?

NIPPON: Mediation is impossible. Japan and China are both Asiatic nations. They should settle their own differences. Our people believe that if you stopped assisting Chiang Kai-shek we could soon finish the war.

This was sometimes followed by the remark: " But China is a terribly big country." The Japanese were losing confidence not in the army's power to defeat any Chinese army brought against it, but in Japan's power to conquer China. The men with whom I spoke foresaw that war was leading Japan back to military government.

BYAS: I understand your internal difficulties. I have had to report a good many assassinations. But there is nothing we can do about that. The American and British governments would like peace in China. They would give a lot to separate

Japan from Hitler. But if you won't have mediation and won't make the kind of peace Chiang Kai-shek will accept, there's nothing we can do about that either.

That is a very foreshortened summary of the substance of many exchanges. They were not interviews, for no Japanese would have expressed such views for direct quotation. Often they were just short chats starting from some remark about the news of the day.

We understood each other well enough, and our thoughts were moving on converging lines. I wanted Japan to stay out of the Axis war, and I wanted to see her recover her friendships with countries whose influence had strengthened everything that was good in Japanese life. My Japanese friends feared the army fanatics and feared they would destroy the promising beginnings of a new national life that the previous generation had made. We both wanted civilian government restored and we knew that peace was the essential prerequisite.

But the Japanese army's face had to be saved; China had to accept defeat. Chiang Kai-shek had to come to the Japanese commander on bended knees. If he did that, everything would be made easy for him, but China's freedom would be gone. America and Britain could not connive at such a result.

So our conversations always led to the same dead end. The Japanese government could not control the army, or, for that matter, the jingo sentiments of the people; the army could not finish the war in China, and unless the war ended, the civilians could not recover the direction of policy. The vicious circle was complete.

When the time comes to make peace we cannot afford to forget the beginnings of the war. Aggression was unconcealed; Japan attacked China, America, Britain, and Holland so that she might extend her Empire. Those kindly people and sentimental thinkers who thought the " war guilt " clause of the Versailles Treaty excused Hitler can have clear minds as to the guilt of the present war.

In the matter of moral responsibility it is impossible to draw a practical distinction between the Japanese people and their rulers. Every diplomat, every correspondent, knew individual Japanese who disliked the whole policy leading up to war with America, but every recognized voice of public opinion supported it. Both Houses, the great and small newspapers, the political parties, the labor unions, the captains of industry, the educators, and the vast army of Grub Street all danced as the army piped. Those amiable and enlightened Japanese whose views I have depicted dutifully kept step with the majority. The political contortions that went on as one relatively moderate Cabinet after another fell showed that qualms were felt in high quarters, but not one word of warning or dissent was uttered. The nation had reached that state of " emotional attunement " or hive unanimity so much admired by patriotic philosophers.

It is not only the Japanese army's activities in the last dozen years nor Hitler's agitation in Germany that we have to understand, but the national mentality that sent the peoples of both countries cheering obediently into unnecessary wars.

They believed that war pays and their history shows why. The German Reich and the modern Japanese Empire both rose in the same period of time. Hirohito's grandfather was restored in 1868 and William I of Prussia proclaimed himself German Emperor in 1870. Long before Hitler appeared on the scene the German people had accepted the doctrine of blood and iron. By three wars — against Denmark in 1863, against Austria in 1865, and against France in 1870 — unprovoked and unnecessary except for his own policy, Bismarck created the German Empire. The German people were dazzled; in blood and iron they had found a magical short cut to greatness.

All of Germany's four wars and the fifth so far as it has gone (except for air raids) have been fought on her neighbors' lands. No German town has seen its citizens shot as hostages for crimes they did not commit and could not prevent; no German home has suffered the heartbreaking cruelties that Germans have inflicted on other homes. The German people have gone short, and German mothers have wept for lost sons, but for the German Reich it has been all gain and glory.

Modern Japan had made three wars and an " incident " in her short modern history before she embarked at Pearl Harbor on her fifth and greatest. In the 1914–18 war Japan's role was that of Autolycus rather than Achilles and it is not included in the list. In that war Japan did little fighting, but she gained the mandated islands — a fatal prize since without those outposts she might not have jumped into the present war. The first war against China in 1894 brought her Formosa, at once a rich tropical estate and a base for further aggressions. The second war, fought against Russia in 1904–5, enabled Japan to annex Korea and take control of South Manchuria. The " incident " of 1931 gave her Manchuria, a prize as large as Germany and France put together; its sequel, the present war on China, was first planned as a blitz which would give Japan North China and dominion over Mongolia. " As long as there is anything to divide there will be wars," has been the creed of the German and Japanese empire-makers. The Japanese of our day have been taught that huge armaments and successful wars raised them from a

" little " people to a great Empire. They do not share the conviction of our own people that peace pays better than war; they — the state that they set up and worship — have found that war paid well. Only complete defeat will teach the Japanese nation that war does not pay. There is no other way in which they can learn that their policy of progress by military force is a false one.

A stage will be reached in which Japan, her strength ebbing, but the will, the ambitions, and the subtlety of her military leaders unexhausted, will offer a speciously moderate peace in an effort to avert complete defeat.

Japan is not fighting this war for Hitler, though she is profiting by his war in Europe as he is profiting by her war in Asia. But the defeat of Hitler does not involve the defeat of Japan directly. He may be a prisoner or a fugitive, his German enemies trying to build a new Germany on the ruins he has left, and Japan still the mistress of East Asia and the South Seas. When that time comes Japan will be ready for either peace or war. She will plead the right of an Asiatic nation to hold the keys of Asia, and she will promise the open door and everything else, provided she keeps the key. It will be a plausible argument, cleverly calculated to appeal to peace-loving people, intent on recovering liberty to mind their own business. Americans will be asked if they want to continue the war in order to install Britain at Singapore instead of Japan. The Philippines will be restored and Japan will accept whatever future for the islands the American and Filipino people may decide; she will be co-guarantor with the United States of their independence, or, if her guarantee is contemptuously refused, she will humbly withhold it. The British and Dutch will be promised all the freedom for their enterprise they formerly extended to Japanese enterprise, and Americans will be told their interests in China and in Malaya will be safe if they accept Japan's wardenship.

It will be harder to disguise realities in China, but the attempt will be made. The Japanese will ask to be allowed to make their own peace with China. We shall be requested not to interfere in whatever arrangements those two Far Eastern nations make between themselves. If we agree, China will have to accept Japan's terms as Pétain had to accept Hitler's. The peace will be wrapped up in phrases about co-operation and a new order, but it will leave Japan the unquestioned master of China. After all that has happened in the last five years Japan cannot do less in her own interests than establish a regime that will prevent the Chinese people from growing strong enough to rise and seek revenge and freedom. We shall be told that what the Japanese and the Chinese settle among themselves is not our affair. The open door will be restored and Japan will be the doorkeeper.

Such an ending, or suspension, of the war, if the Japanese can get it, will be a Japanese victory. The Emperor will appear before the Imperial shrine and inform the ancestral gods that the valor of his soldiers and sailors has extended the power and glory of the Empire and laid the foundations of more power and glory to come. The totalitarian national-defense state — 20 per cent to the producer and 80 per cent to the government — will be solidly established. The military ruling class will be as broad as the nation. The feeble liberals will disappear as completely as the massacred Christians of the early seclusion era. The megalomania of the young officers and the gangster patriots will be confirmed.

The Japanese will be convinced that their superior qualities, their uniqueness, enabled them to succeed where Hitler failed. Their world mission will be no longer part dream, part gamble, but a solid proposition, proved by the acid test of war. We shall have to accept militant Japan, dominating one fourth of the world, as a permanent element in the life of the world; and since it is impossible for our own civilization to accept such conditions, we shall have to prepare to fight again for survival.

For our own future and not for that of Japan we must continue the war until the Japanese forces have been driven from the regions they have invaded. Yet in saving ourselves we are saving the Japanese people. The false philosophy they have taken to their heart will never be discredited until it comes back to them in defeat, humiliation, and loss. Peace without victory, if we accepted it, would be to them a mere cloak to save our face. They would readily join in the fraud for the benefits it would bring them, but the whole false morality which underlies their policy would be reinforced, and their gains would be the jumping-off place for fresh wars.

We are entitled to hope that the Japanese people will assert their right to representative government after their experience of military-bureaucratic government, but in the meantime we have to make peace with the same Japan that made the war, and we have to talk the language it understands. Our hopes of a better Japan will die unborn unless the present Japan is shown that war does not pay.

Chapter XXVI

SANCTIONS OF PEACE

The safeguards of peace, when it returns to the Far East, will be of two kinds: the sanctions that we devise and the moral and political consequences that will follow Japan's defeat. In the long run the latter may well be more important than the peace treaties.

The Japanese have never known defeat. They are brought up on an inflated tradition of success. No foreign potentate has ever tried to invade Japan except Kublai Khan in the thirteenth century (A.D. 1241). His failure is one of the first lessons taught to Japanese children; it has implanted in their minds a conviction of invincibility which vainglorious accounts of Japan's modern wars have strengthened. That illusion will be shattered as Japanese cities crackle under foreign bombs. Nothing in their history or their training has prepared the Japanese to stand up under defeat with the dour coolness of the British and the French, who have known many ups and downs in the course of their history.

The history of modern Japan is a story of studentship, of successful copying. In the palmy progressive days of the first half-century the favored exemplars were the United States and Britain. Many Japanese sincerely admired those models and enjoyed copying them. But the army's exemplar has always been Germany. In the last decade dedicated to war Hitler's Germany has been copied with slavish fidelity down to senseless imitative spasms of anti-Semitism — in a country where there are hardly fifty Jewish families, all of them foreign transients!

Upon minds so plastic the crash of defeat must have a tremendous effect. The Japanese people have invested their all in a " get rich quick " plan of military conquest. They will emerge from the war ruined gamblers. The collapse of the plan and the rout of their dictatorial fighting forces will set up in their minds a painful but educative train of thought. The reaction will take forms that we cannot clearly foresee, but some of the probabilities can be listed.

It is, to begin with, unlikely that there will be any effective demand for a return to the imitation of representative government that Japan had before the war. That system had all of the faults and few of the virtues of representative government in the West. It completely failed to prevent the army's encroachments on the political power. In the hour when their responsibility was put to the test, the elected parties were broken reeds, devoid of moral courage and political insight. They did not want war with America but they did nothing to prevent it, and when it came they supported it through thick and thin. Rehabilitation of such a system is of no importance to us since we have already found that it had no value as a safeguard of peace. The only safeguards of peace that will have any value for many years to come are those we can take care of ourselves.

Nor is revolution likely. Rioting and violence may follow defeat, but there are no elements among the Japanese people that could organize a revolutionary movement and formulate a revolutionary program. There is no communist party, no

socialist party, no labor movement worth the name. The political parties were never more than groups of partisans; they
stood for no principles; they represented no real division of
opinion; the only difference between Minseito and Seiyukai
was that they followed different leaders and dipped into different sugar bowls.

If we are foolish enough to demand a revolution in Japan
the results would be similar to those that followed the last
defeat of Germany. The new government would do the dirty
work of peacemaking and it would be the scapegoat to be
afterwards driven into the wilderness for all the miseries and
humiliations Japan will suffer. The lunatic patriot fringe
would make the welkin ring with cries that the nation had
been betrayed. The militarists would get out from under the
ruin they had caused and we should have provided them with
a springboard for another plunge.

It is our interest as well as their own that the Japanese
should get a system of government representing all classes of
the nation and equipped with the checks and balances needed
to prevent the military men from again dominating it. But
that is a problem the Japanese have to work out by their own
methods. Our business in making the peace is to protect ourselves from a recurrence of the evils inflicted upon us and
lay broad foundations of justice on which, as angry memories
fade, a stable and tolerant peace may rise.

In trying to forecast Japanese events it is constantly necessary to be on guard against expecting them to follow Western
patterns or even what to us would seem the logical course.
East and West often pursue similar aims, but there are surprising differences in the methods employed. The Japanese
will realize that responsibility for their calamity rests on the
fighting services and that changes are necessary to prevent the

failure from recurring. But where we would roughly oust
the generals from their privileged position the Japanese reaction may take the form of saying: " You got us into this mess;
now get us out of it."

When defeat is upon the Japanese in its grim reality the
Japanese code will require that all responsible tender their
resignations to the Emperor. General Tojo will be the first,
but he will not be alone. The Chiefs of the Army and Navy
General Staffs will also resign, and there may be dramatic
resignations from life. But the Emperor's government must
be carried on. The question of the next prime minister will
be settled as usual by confabs behind the scenes. Prince
Konoye, who will be one of the consultants, may be offered
the mandate and he may refuse with the full understanding
of his Imperial master and his advisers. The way having been
thus prepared, a general may succeed a general; but if it is
so it will not necessarily mean that Japan has returned to its
vomit. It may mean that the army is taking its medicine and
assuming responsibility for disaster. I do not suggest that this
is an inevitable reaction to defeat, but it is a possible one. It
is consistent with Japanese ideas of responsibility, and it has
some support in the fact that at almost every cabinet change
until the one that preceded Pearl Harbor Japanese liberals
could be heard lamenting that the army could not be made
to take open responsibility for its acts. We can be indifferent,
not allowing our plans to be affected in any way by the manner in which the Japanese choose to meet the post-war crisis.

It is desirable that the Japanese fighting forces should take
responsibility in the fullest way. It has been suggested that we
should insist on the Emperor signing the peace. The Emperor's signature (or rather seal) will be appended to the
peace treaty as a matter of course. The treaty would not be

valid without it, and it must be signed also by the Foreign Minister. All this is routine and the Emperor will have no more personal responsibility for that treaty than for any other act of administration. If we want some striking and unusual way of impressing the Japanese people with our opinion, we would do better to insist on the signatures of the Chiefs of the General Staffs. That would be one method of pinning responsibility on the proper quarter and it might provide Japanese moderates with a weapon against future military attempts to upset the treaty.

But the Japanese reaction might take the form of pity for the generals and admirals who were forced to do such violence to their feelings, and of readiness to applaud repudiation when the time came. Nor should we forget the possibility that a signer might commit hara-kiri next day and damn the treaty forever in the sentimental Japanese mind. We had better stick to realities. The real sanctions of peace will not be any Japanese signature, but the completeness of Japanese defeat.

Though there will be no revolution in the ordinary sense of that word, the shock of defeat and destruction will be so severe that ordinary political machinery will probably be unable to take the strain. Some exceptional means will have to be taken to quiet the minds of the people.

In times of crisis the Japanese have an innate tendency to fall back upon expedients they have tried before. The 1868 revolution was accomplished, almost bloodlessly, by drawing the Emperor from his seclusion and making him the figure-head of change. The Emperor is the only personage in the country whose prestige is untouched by the war, the only leader whose moral authority is so great that all the people will obey him. The immutable throne is a fixed point around which the state can rally its forces while inevitable changes are being made. If the Emperor's advisers find that no ordinary change will stave off a convulsion, they can decide that the Emperor himself must intervene. The people will be told that he has assumed the government to save the country. After all, he is no novice, but a man of over forty, with twenty years' experience of his duties behind him. It is conceivable that the wise and cautious statesmen who guided his early years as Regent and Emperor may see their labors rewarded by the emergence of a statesmanlike ruler able to rule. Under his ægis a family council of the nation would be formed to ensure internal tranquillity. There will be soldiers in that council, but they will be chastened and army dominance will be gone.

Some deferred effects of defeat may also be anticipated. Having no inherited political ideas suited to modern conditions, the Japanese must still copy and adapt those of others. Since it will be evident that the army took the wrong track and followed the wrong lead, there will be a swing back towards the institutions of the victors. They defeated Japan, therefore their methods must be better. A few years ago democracy seemed to be the rising power and many Japanese were following it; you could buy " Democracy " whisky on the Ginza. Taking up the threads they dropped, the Japanese will discard what has failed them and adapt what has proved stronger. They have always done so; they think it common sense. And it is.

We should not forget Japan's unfinished revolution. In 1868 the Japanese threw off the feudal skin that they had worn longer than any other civilized state. But the process was not completed and could not be completed so quickly or easily as the facile Japanese copyists imagined. A feudal government was abolished but a strong modern government

347

has not been found. Perhaps the Japanese will now carry their revolution a stage further and create a form of government responsible to the people. We cannot measure the moral change defeat will bring, nor can we forecast the political forms it will take, but, having regard to Japan's national character and past history, we can expect that the change will follow foreign models and that the models will be the systems of government which have proved the strongest.

Besides the internal changes which will originate in the minds of the Japanese people, there will be external changes in their circumstances. One of these will be a new balance of power in the Far East.

The greatest achievement of the Japanese militarists has been the awakening of a national spirit in China. It is impossible to guess how that spirit will grow. If the 400,000,000 Chinese were to be infected with the fanatical nationalism and the hive mind of Japan, the outlook would be grim. But such a development would require a radical change in national character. We need not say it is impossible, but its accomplishment would at least be a matter of scores of years and our peacemakers are not required to legislate so far ahead. The Chinese are fundamentally a pacific, trading, and producing people. They are strongly individualistic and apt to think that the prosperity of the individual and the family is more important than the welfare of the state.

The question of what a renascent and armed China may become is so speculative that it can be left in the clouds. The vision of 400,000,000 Chinese armed and regimented on the same scale as the 75,000,000 Japanese would indeed be one to stagger the prophets, but, like earthquakes in Manhattan, it is not an immediate danger. The Chinese government will not for a long time possess the authority and the resources which could convert the mighty man-power of China into a correspondingly strong military machine. If we allow ourselves to be bemused by such mirages we shall only lose sight of reality.

But it is reasonably certain that the new Chinese government will have the power and the will to establish forces at least as strong as those of Japan, and to maintain them at a strength which will make aggression an uninviting prospect to even the craziest Japanese officer. A changed balance of power is therefore one of the major items in the new Far Eastern future. Japan's sudden rise and the avidity with which the Japanese seized on modern armaments, destroyed the old balance in which Asia had slumbered for centuries. The present war is the outcome of a " disparity of power " which Japan was able to establish. This disparity will not return and policies based on it are dead. The Japanese have a phrase: " the opportunity of a thousand years," which they often used as the conclusive argument for an aggressive policy. In a sense they were right; the opportunity was one which, once lost, will not return.

While this disparity of power governed the Far Eastern situation, limitation of armaments had no interest for Japan. Limitation might stabilize her position vis-à-vis the United States and Britain but it could only weaken it vis-à-vis China. Now the shoe is on the other foot. The rise of China reduces Japan to a position not unlike that of England facing continental Europe. She will still be powerful, and in her homeland unconquerable, but she will have to bid good-by to her dreams of a continental empire as England said good-by to a similar ambition five centuries ago. With the disparity between China's potential and their own so great, the Japanese will in future see merits in arms limitation that they have not hitherto observed. Their interests will impel them to support reduction of armaments, and this change, which seems likely to be a lasting one, will be a buttress to whatever political supports of peace the post-war settlement may devise.

Chapter XXVII

GEOGRAPHICAL DISARMAMENT

This chapter offers some observations on the practical
questions that will come before the negotiators who will
eventually meet the representatives of Japan at a peace conference. They are concerned primarily with the question of
peace between Japan and the United States, but they are
written in the conviction that the war will have been fought
in vain if the victorious democracies do not lay the foundations of world peace. The suggestions that follow, though
they deal only with Japan, can be fitted into the " larger
framework " that Hoover and Gibson sketched in *Problems
of Lasting Peace.*

With the exception of Manchuria, where Japan's legitimate
and illegitimate interests now lie together on the bed that
was deliberately made for them by the Japanese army, the
changes proposed are drastic only when it is a question of
making it easy to keep the peace and difficult to break it. In
other respects they seek to provide an opportunity for change
to develop naturally rather than force it on the sick and exhausted peoples of the Far East before their convalescence
has well begun.

If I am accused of leniency towards Japan, the defense is
that I have not been lenient in respect to the means of war;

351

if my suggestions are carried out Japan will be delivered from the temptation to attack her neighbors and a vision of easy conquest will not again beckon headstrong Japanese soldiers down the bloody path of empire.

The first interest of the American people is their security. Japan's first act of war against the United States was the attack on Pearl Harbor. That attack was facilitated by Japanese possession of the mandated islands of the Pacific. The strategic importance of those islands in the eyes of the Japanese navy was the most potent of all the incentives to war which culminated at Pearl Harbor. Without those islands it is probable that Japan would not have embarked on the scheme of conquest which brought her into the World War as Hitler's ally. The possession of the islands made the scheme of conquest feasible and the attack on America hopeful.

Japan holds the islands by mandate of the League of Nations, granted under a decision of the Supreme Council of the Allied and Associated Nations at Paris in 1919. The use she found for them cannot be more clearly stated than in the words of Admiral Nobumasa Suetsugu, formerly commander-in-chief of the Japanese battle fleet. He called them " anchored aircraft carriers." They enabled Japan to extend by some 2,000 miles the range of her sea-air operations and they brought about a revolution in the ideas of the Japanese navy.

Until the islands were acquired from Germany, Japan's naval strategy was essentially defensive. The function of the Japanese fleet was to protect home territory and vital trade routes, to maintain communications between Japan and the mainland, and to provide a screen covering Japan's continental policies against interference by the Western powers.

The navy's revolt against the Washington limitation agreements had its roots in injured pride; but that feeling was controlled, as painful feelings can be controlled, by consciousness that the agreements carried countervailing advantages. The revolt did not become effective until air-consciousness had permeated the Naval General Staff. The old school was " blue-water "; it counted ships, guns, and miles; it made and kept the agreement because despite injured pride it gave Japan solid security.

With limitation came non-fortification. The United States left Guam untouched and Hongkong made no addition to its nineteenth-century defenses. Japan also agreed not to fortify the 2,400 islands and reefs she had taken from Germany. The latter was a worthless agreement; the islands did not need to be formally fortified to become of immense strategic importance in the air age. All that was required was a little dredging and excavation here and there for " commercial " harbors and a full survey showing where sheltered anchorages existed and where landing fields could be made.

The possibilities of sea-air power were gradually becoming visible. As the Naval General Staff in Tokyo studied the potentialities of their new bases Japan's strategy passed gradually and completely from the defensive to the offensive role. The change was clearly charted. The Washington and London naval treaties were abrogated. All efforts to retain Japan within the framework of any kind of arms-limitation agreement — by fixing the maximum size of ships, or the maximum caliber of guns, or simply by mutual publication of building programs — were firmly rejected by the navy. The civilian government was overruled and old statesmen were assassinated by young officers.

With the islands charted and surveyed the strategists of the Naval General Staff took their plans against the United States fleet out of the pigeonholes and redrew them. It was a far

more exciting exercise than ever before. Japan's defensive position had always been strong, and the Washington ratios
made it impregnable. As the strategists studied the possibilities of sea power plus island-based air power, they saw vast
opportunities opening for the offensive in the South Seas of
which they had long dreamed. The strategic problem was to
seize the Dutch East Indies and defy the rest of the world to
turn them out. The islands were at once a jumping-off place
from which Japan could invade and conquer the Dutch Indies and a bastion behind which she could defend her conquests from the American fleet. Singapore was a deadly obsta-
cle so long as the British were able to defend it against a major
attack, but Britain was fighting for its life in Europe and
Africa and on the Atlantic. To the naval strategists it was
clear that Japan's hour had come. She was standing at the
crossroads of destiny, as her leaders proclaimed, and the road
to glory and riches and power beckoned her.

Japan's " screen " strategy became a " pincer " strategy, the
sea-air arm clawing down over the mandated islands towards
Australia and Hawaii while the military arm thrust overland
towards Singapore. Engrossed in their own affairs, the democracies were completely taken by surprise and are today paying the terrible price of indolence and isolationism.

The economic value of the islands is paltry. They support
a few tribes of primitive people and supply the world with
a modest quantity of coconut shell and bird manure. They
are not a necessary part of Japan's defensive scheme. They
guard no canal like Panama or Suez, no ocean gateway like
Gibraltar. They are simply anchored aircraft carriers.

The islands were well enough when they were left to the
people who lived in them and navigated the sea in canoes.
A modern administration is a luxury for which those simple

people have little need. But as anchored aircraft carriers in the possession of an aggressive state the islands are a menace to the peace of the Pacific and to the security of the United States. The mandate now held by Japan should be summarily transferred to the United States.

Japan's other colonial possessions are Korea, Formosa, Southern Saghalien, and the Manchukuo Empire. The last has been given an elaborate shop-front intended to make believe that it is not a colony; it has an Emperor and a Prime Minister and a Cabinet, but all of these have been installed by Japan. Manchuria was seized in 1931 by the Japanese army. It is completely under Japanese control and the difference between "Manchukuo Empire" and "Japanese colony" is simply the difference between the "China incident" and the "China war." The regime conferred on the country by Japan has not been recognized by China or any of the United Nations. The population is almost entirely Chinese.

Formosa was ceded to Japan by treaty in 1895 after a war in which China had been defeated.

Korea was annexed in 1910, five years after the war with Russia. The Czarist Empire was then engaged in a policy of expansion in the Far East, and Korea, which had become derelict, was likely to fall under Russian influence. Its geographical situation, jutting out from the mainland to within a hundred miles of Nagasaki, would have made its occupation by an aggressive power a source of extreme danger to Japan. The administration of Theodore Roosevelt, and most other governments, considered the annexation of Korea a defensive move by Japan and they recognized the new regime.

Southern Saghalien was ceded by Russia in 1906 in lieu of an indemnity after the Russo-Japanese War.

A cross-fire of argument will develop at the peace conference over Manchuria. Japanese holdings there originally consisted of the South Manchuria Railway and the leased territory of Dairen, both taken over from Russia, which had acquired them by agreement with the Chinese government. Other railways were built by Japanese and Chinese capital and the northern section, formerly called the Chinese Eastern Railway, was purchased by Japan from the Soviet government. The South Manchuria Railway Company, a corporation which was rather more than semi-official, developed Japan's acquisitions with energy and efficiency. For thirty years its annual reports were a record of progress.

Up to 1931 Japan's interests in Manchuria rested on a legal basis. The ouster of those interests will seem to the Japanese a harsh action. The American peace commissioners will not be impressed by Japanese complaints; they will nevertheless wish to avoid decisions which would deprive the Japanese of the fruits of legitimate enterprise and exclude them from a field of opportunity they have themselves developed.

But the situation that the Japanese of today inherited from their predecessors no longer exists. It was abolished when the Japanese army cut through all agreements and created a puppet empire. The Japan-in-Manchuria with which the peace commissioners will have to deal is no longer a commercial corporation but a foreign usurping government. The forlorn Emperor, whose imperial dignity is about to die a second death, is an object of pity; but the puppet of the Japanese army cannot possibly be an acceptable figurehead to the Chinese inhabitants of Manchuria. He will regain his freedom, and his pension will be regular. But the whole façade must go with the Japanese soldiers who made it.

The transfer to the Chinese government of the railroads and harbors and public works constructed by the Japanese will be but a small indemnity for the cities wrecked, the colleges bombed, and the enterprises confiscated in China. There can be no more question of Japan retaining Manchuria than of her retaining Shanghai, or North China, or Hainan Island, or any other part of China.

But on broad grounds of policy looking to a peaceful future it would be unwise to deprive Japan of access to resources she needs and has developed in Manchuria. The Fushun coal mine and other enterprises of the same type might be the subject of new leases drawn as commercial contracts and not as the entering wedge of political domination. A precedent could be taken from the fishery grounds in Kamchatka which the Japanese have developed by agreement with Russia until they are a valuable part of Japan's food supply. The instruments of Japanese control must go, lock, stock, and barrel, but it is not beyond the resources of diplomacy to devise opportunities for peaceful Japanese enterprise and agricultural settlement in Manchuria's vast empty spaces while closing the door to political and military penetration.

The older colonies, Formosa, Korea, and Southern Saghalien, were ceded to Japan by their former owners, and Japan has been in uncontested occupation for forty years. She has developed their natural resources efficiently and her administration has been, on the whole, satisfactory.

The victors in the war can, if they choose, take them from Japan by exactly the same process as that by which Japan originally obtained them. But should we, or any of the democracies, be satisfied with that? We have to guard against such a revulsion of feeling as that which, after the last war, came to regard the Treaty of Versailles as harsh and oppressive and therefore impermanent. The settlement we desire must satisfy twentieth-century ideas rather than nineteenth-century stand-

357

ards. The new order we seek should be a universal one, not merely a United Nations order. Regions inhabited by primitive or backward races, unable to develop resources which the world needs, must somehow be administered and their riches made available to human society. If we are to escape from the vicious circle of nationalistic wars this can only be done by establishing and supporting, and when necessary reforming, a world trustee organization whose first duty it shall be to see that the riches of those colonial regions are freely open to all on equal terms.

The principle to guide us in dealing with Japan's older colonial possessions might be tentatively formulated thus: Japan to be deprived of all that she has used as instruments of war and confirmed in all that she has gained by peace. The formula is open to criticism, but it seems to me that it embodies a standard of fairness and tolerance which would endure after the heated emotions of war have faded.

Its application could be flexible. Japan would lose the mandated islands outright, but those islands have neither sentimental associations nor economic value to the Japanese people. They were instruments of aggression pure and simple. Another group of islands off the coast of Formosa, the Pescadores, were the bases from which the first air attacks on China were made. They would cease to be Japanese bases, but dismantlement and inspection might be as effective as forcible transfer. Japan's economic and in some cases her administrative rights would be respected, yet she would no longer have the instruments of attack. Under the disarmament plan, the same principle could be applied to outlying bases like the Bonin Islands, where there is no question of sovereignty involved.

In all the colonies Japan's economic interests would remain intact on the same no-monopoly principle that would be applied to other colonial regions. The question between Japan and the peace commissioners would be what mandatory or other rights Japan might look forward to retaining or eventually receiving in her older colonies, Formosa, Korea, and Southern Saghalien.

Formosa has been a Japanese colony for fifty years, and before then it was a Chinese colony. With its mixed population of Chinese immigrants and aboriginal headhunters, it must always be someone's colony. Geographically it is part of China, and the case for returning it to China is strong. But Japan's half-century of efficient administration should not be forgotten nor her economic needs. The Formosa question is whether the mandate (or whatever it may be called) should be continued in the hands of Japan, under supervision, or transferred to China, which, though the more legitimate holder, will have its hands full for many years.

Korea's case is different. Korea is definitely a separate country with a racially distinct people whose leaders naturally want independence. But to thrust self-government on Korea in its present stage of development would be a cruel gift. Administrators have to be trained, standards built up; an intelligent but wholly inexperienced people has to be protected from native exploitation while it learns how to use the machinery of representative government. Korea is separated from Japan by only one hundred miles of sea, and Japan cannot disinterest itself in Korea's future since Korea, either helpless, as she was before, or dominated by a hostile power, is a mortal danger to Japan. To expel Japan from Korea and shut her out from a share in its tutelage while tutelage continues might be a just punishment, but it would leave a rankling sense of insecurity. And Korea might shrink from the prospect of becoming a Far Eastern Alsace-Lorraine. My conclusion would be that, after an interval which should be distinctly stated in the treaty, Japan should, under supervision, be entrusted with the mandatory role in respect of Korea.

As there is almost no alien population in Southern Saghalien, administrative questions do not arise and the future of that territory might be settled on a commercial basis by Japan and Russia.

The new colonial order will require a system of impartial inspectorship. The defeated aggressors could not immediately expect to be entrusted with mandatory powers, but from the first it would be well to admit all, vanquished as well as victors, to the international inspectorate. This would give the defeated nations a pledge that our new order is one of justice in which they will eventually enjoy full equality.

Disarmament is the first safeguard of peace. Its basis must be equality of security. Equality of security is not by any means the same thing as equality in the number of warships or soldiers. The aggressor nations must be disarmed, and, if they remain disarmed, the victors will be able to allow their own arms budgets to sink gradually to a low level. There will have to be inspection and control. Inspection of their arsenals will be a bitter pill to the spy-mad Japanese, but it can be made a just pill by employing for the arms inspectorate the principle suggested for the supervision of colonial mandates. The inspection of Japanese arsenals, factories, and shipyards cannot be construed as an invidious national humiliation if Japanese officers exercise the same duties elsewhere. We, the common people, who want peace and low taxes and the elimination of incitements to war, will be wise if we demand independent, impartial examination of arms in all countries.

Chapter XXVIII

THE FUTURE

My original assignment in Japan was for two years. Interspersed with many " long leaves " it grew to twenty-three years. I liked the country and the life, gathered a library, and lived agreeably with my neighbors. I should not expect to be believed if I now said that all the people of Japan are like the people with whom this narrative has been mainly concerned. As the book closes I am teased by a feeling that it depicts only the scum on the surface of the stream. Yet though all of Japan is not in the picture — for it is still impossible to indict a nation — the Japan we are fighting is there. The young officers, the patriots and scoundrels, the bemused philosophers are the scum that reveals the force and direction of the boiling torrent. The creed of those men has been the policy of Japan since 1931.

Among the major causes of the war three stand out:

1. The delusion of a unique state with a special mission.

2. The constitutional vice which allows the fighting services to control the government.

3. The possession of jumping-off places for aggression and of the heaviest and best-organized armaments in Asia.

The peace we make will be directly concerned only with the third of these. The Japanese people must be their own liberators from a faked religion and a fraudulent Constitution. But our victory will start the process and help it along. It will cure them of the illusion that aggression pays and it will open wide a better way to their renascent national energies.

We are waging war, as President Roosevelt said, for our own survival. We consider it one of the most unnecessary wars in history. It was thrust upon us and our first business at the peace conference is to secure ourselves against such attacks in future. We can protect ourselves by physical means and we have the right to use those means to the fullest extent of their efficiency. We cannot silence the voices which will tell the Japanese people that they lost the war because their armaments were not great enough, but we can make it very difficult for the voices to convince the dupes that the opportunity will come again.

In the ruins of war we intend to lay the foundations of a new world order. That order will not arise in a day. Ingenious pens are drafting its statutes, but many a year of trial and error must pass before a federal world is built from that diverse and stubborn material, the nations of today. Meanwhile we need peace and we have had our lesson on the folly of supposing that a city which allows itself to be infested with armed gangs can have peace. The first measure of security is disarmament of the aggressors. In Chapter XXVII measures of geographical disarmament suited to the Pacific region were suggested. Those measures seek security not by pacts that can be broken or by elaborate schemes that can be circumvented but by depriving Japan of her geographical offensive armaments, the far-flung outposts and " anchored aircraft carriers " that enabled the two General Staffs in Tokyo to develop their plan of conquest in the South Seas.

Those forcible measures will protect ourselves; they are just and necessary. They will make it difficult for Japan to do wrong, but that is only half of a good peace. The makers of the peace treaty have to make it easy to do right. Bitterness and repentance cannot be a lasting mood. In a few years the mothers and widows of the farmers' sons who have died in China and Burma and the South Seas will also be dead and those commemorative visits to the shrines will no longer be pilgrimages of human sorrow but solemn tributes to heroes. We do not want them to become a false inspiration to another generation. We want the Japanese people to recognize the war for what it was — a bloody and useless sacrifice to false gods.

Along with physical war we wage a psychological war which looks to victory and beyond victory. We also consider a New Order necessary for East Asia and the world, a New Order intended to secure the best use of undeveloped resources everywhere for the benefit of all, and in that New Order there is a place for Japan.

Psychological warfare is not propaganda only; we cannot preach the Japanese into a belief that peace is better than war, our way of life better than theirs. But as the first step to conversion is conviction of sin, we can show them that war does not pay; and growth in grace will follow if the peace we make is so strongly guarded that the temptation to break it will not again seduce this generation.

The Japanese people today are drunk with victory. While that inflated mood prevails our propaganda is like a strayed bear in a bull market. But in due time Japanese headlines will carry less intoxicating news than the " victory " of Pearl Harbor, the fall of Singapore, the fall of Java, the fall of Burma, the fall of Bataan. The Japanese did not go to war to defend their homes. Not a peasant soldier is so stupid as to imagine that he is fighting because China attacked Japan. They know that they began the war for gain, and when the hope of easy gain is replaced by a dreadful fear that Japan may not enjoy but endure conquest their minds will be ready to let our message sink in. We can show them that only by peace can they redeem their country from the disaster to which its men of war have led them. The peace we shall make is one in which they can live and work and prosper and earn glory too, as some of their scientists earned it in the past when they left their stifling feudal atmosphere. They can be shown that the program of the United Nations promises their workers and farmers, their industrialists, and the thousands of young men who pour from their universities every year a better future than the program they are fighting for.

Japanese statesmen have tried to rationalize the army's scheme of conquest by relating it to a new order of regional empires. Mr. Hachiro Arita, when Foreign Minister, promulgated a plan for redistribution of sovereignty and resources by regions. He solved the problems of peace and materials simultaneously by making the strongest power in each region its overlord and exploiter. He claimed that the result would be an equitable distribution of resources and a stable equilibrium of forces.

His proposal assumed that the world can be divided into a number of great regional empires, each headed by the most powerful nation of the region, with the others grouped like satellites around it. The United States would have the American continent as its sphere; Germany would have Europe; Russia is big enough to be a world state by itself; the British Empire, outside of Asia, would be conceded its place in the sun; Japan would take East Asia and the South Seas.

Whatever possibilities there may be in regional plans, the Japanese have found that their scheme does not work in the

364

manner they expected. They have for five years been trying to make China the foundation stone in their regional empire. They have failed because the means employed do not aim at free co-operation but at subjugation. It is too late in the day to build new empires. The age of imperialism, as Mr. Sumner Welles said, is past. Even in Asia, where the dice were loaded in Japan's favor, the effort to establish a regional new order by conquest has been a failure. Some Japanese were beginning to see the marks of failure even before Japan staked her future on war with the United States and Britain. " Give us fifty years," said Foreign Secretary Matsuoka, " and the world will see what Japan can do." What does any business man think of a plan which will need fifty years to demonstrate its soundness?

What reason is there to suppose that those regional empires headed by military powers would be more peaceful than their military leaders are now? Why should we expect them to be satisfied with any distribution effected now? The " have lesses " would still see " have mores " around them. There would always be some materials that could not be divided up and some which even the most powerful states would have to get from others; there would be regions more desirable than others, and big military empires would still have their chronic craving for better strategic frontiers.

Economic inequalities cannot be abolished by any redistribution of territories. They can be made harmless by establishing equality of access to sources and markets. The modern world is an economic unit. The co-prosperity sphere that the Japanese need and that we all need is a free world. If the Japanese are seeking economic security and advancement, the principles outlined in the Atlantic Charter offer more than they could expect to gain from the new order in East Asia. They offer it in a better and safer way, for whereas Japan's efforts to construct a new order by violence have driven the Japanese people to lower standards of living than they have known for fifty years, the Atlantic Declaration offers them the opportunity of continuing on a larger scale the industrial expansion which brought them success in the past.

The old colonial order has crashed; if we set it up again on the old lines, it will crash again. The riches and raw materials of the tropics cannot be left to national capitalism for their development, nor their peoples left to the protection and administration of any single nation, however liberal. Colonial administrations will still be necessary for peoples in the adolescent stage — the Polynesians, the Malays, the Javanese, and the numberless tribes of Africa — who need guidance and help from their elders of the human family. In some cases the " masses " of these peoples could hardly have a worse government than that of native exploiters. Those tropical domains cannot be left to unrestricted national ownership. They must be given some form of international trusteeship which can protect the rights of the natives as well as those of the pioneers and discoverers and which can reward enterprise without permitting monopoly.

Japan abused her position as a colonial power in the old order. She undertook to administer the Pacific islands for peaceful commerce and she made them into bases of unprovoked attack on her neighbors. The islands will be taken from her, and the victorious powers will of necessity apply all political and military measures needed to protect themselves against renewed aggression. Not until the passions and fears that Japan by her policy has aroused have subsided can she expect to regain a place on whatever authority may take the place of the Council of the League of Nations.

But from the first we can and we should offer Japan guar-

366

antees of economic equality in the world's "co-prosperity sphere." Freedom must be the maxim of the new colonial order. The Japanese should be assured of free access to colonial markets as sellers of manufactured goods and not only as buyers of colonial products. In those markets the Japanese seller will have an advantage over ours so long as Japanese manufacturing costs are lower. But though Japanese standards are lower than ours they are the highest in Asia. It may be necessary to restrict Japanese goods in " white " markets where labor standards are higher, but in Asia, Africa, and the South Seas there are hundreds of millions of people living in primitive scarcity. Japan can supply them with necessities and petty luxuries — clothing, matches, rubber boots, bicycles, watches, cameras, beer, and what not — at prices they can afford to pay. If Japan can sell two shirts to a black man for the price our makers need for one we have no right to prevent the transaction.

The right to buy in colonial markets at world prices does not exhaust the Atlantic Charter's principle of equality of access. The Japanese should also have equality of opportunity to discover and develop natural resources in colonial domains. People who have seen their properties destroyed and plundered or consumed in the " scorched earth " policy (like the British rubber-growers who put the torch to half a billion dollars' worth of rubber as the Japanese were shelling Singapore) will not immediately be ready to welcome Japanese enterprise, and in any case the ruin of war will have to be made good first. But the Japanese should know that they will have the right of equal opportunity to cultivate rubber, mine tin, and prospect for oil in any undeveloped country on equal terms with all others. They cannot expect to begin exploitation immediately, but their commercial establishments, shipping offices, and banks might be allowed to reopen as soon as possible after the armistice. By so permitting them we should be giving tangibility to our promises and spreading the conviction among the Japanese people that our new order is equal and just.

We are laying the foundations of a new order which we conceive to be suited to the modern world in which we live. The riches of the earth will be freely and fairly open to all nations, and the primitive or backward or simply weak peoples will have the protection of an authority representing civilized humanity instead of being left to the chance that may give them a mild or a harsh taskmaster.

If we consider fifty years of modern Japan and not the gangster decade alone, we are entitled to believe that Japan has qualities that will again fit it to be a member of this new order. Japan is now possessed by the evil genius that it loves, but there is another Japan and it has a contribution to make to the world.

What is the idea that moves the world today? Surely it is the discovery that the industrial revolution has given humanity machines in place of helots. In every civilized country for a century the minds of men have been stirred by the new hope of fullness of life for all, for the humble workers and not merely for the talented few or the fortunate inheritors of wealth. Neither Americans nor Britons nor the citizens of Holland and Norway need to be preached at about peace; the wish for peace is in their bones. Their realization of the value and necessity of peace is surely due to their instinctive knowledge that at last they have the opportunity and the means to raise their standard of life to levels never before attained except by those we call the well-to-do. That motive is at work among the masses the world over.

We want to live in peace and devote our energies to our own well-being. We want to start on the tremendous task of adjusting our lives to a civilization of abundance. We want to raise the level of subsistence and to create economic security for all and on that foundation to erect a free universal culture such as the world has not seen.

In that order there can be a place for Japan.

INDEX

Index

ii

Index

Index

Index

Index

Index

viii

The text of this book was set on the Linotype in Baskerville. The punches for this face were cut under the supervision of George W. Jones, an eminent English printer. Linotype Baskerville is a facsimile cutting from type cast from the original matrices of a face designed by John Baskerville. The original face was one of the forerunners of the " modern " group of type faces.

Title page and binding designs by W. A. Dwiggins. The book was composed, printed, and bound by The Plimpton Press, Norwood, Massachusetts.

DATE DUE

GAYLORD			PRINTED IN U.S.A.